To my friend
Mike Baer

Great to be
working with
you again

Roger Dawson
April '95

Roger Dawson's
Secrets of Power Negotiating

Roger Dawson's
Secrets of Power Negotiating

By

Roger Dawson

Secrets of Power Negotiating®, Power Negotiation®, and Power Negotiators® are registered trademarks of Roger Dawson Productions.

Roger Dawson's Secrets of Power Negotiating
ISBN 1-56414-153-5, $21.99
Cover design by Dean Johnson Design, Inc.
Printed in the U.S.A. by Book-mart Press

Copies of this volume may be ordered by mail or phone directly from the publisher. To order by mail, please include price as noted above, $2.50 handling per order, and $1.00 for each book ordered. Send to: Career Press, Inc., 180 Fifth Ave., P.O. Box 34, Hawthorne, NJ 07507.

Or call toll-free 1-800-CAREER-1 (In Canada: 201-427-0229) to order using your VISA or MasterCard or for further information on all books published or distributed by Career Press.

Library of Congress Cataloging-in-Publication Data

Dawson, Roger.
    [Secrets of power negotiating]
    Roger Dawson's secrets of power negotiating / Roger Dawson.
      p. cm.
    Includes index.
    ISBN 1-56414-153-5
    1. Negotiation in business. I. Title.
HD58. 6. D39   1995
658.4--dc20
                                        94-46691
                                          CIP

Dedicated to:

My new family:

*Gisela, who very quickly became the
main event of my life*

*Julia, Dwight and John, the
three finest children anyone could hope for*

and Muffy

May we all live in harmony for the rest of our days.

Contents

Section Two
Why Money Isn't As Important As You Think

Section Three
Negotiating Pressure Points

Section Four
Negotiating With Foreigners

Section Five
Understanding The Players

Section Six
Developing Power Over the Other Side

About the Author

Roger Dawson was born in England, emigrated to California in 1962 and became a U.S. citizen 10 years later. Formerly the president of one of California's largest real estate companies, he became a full-time author and professional speaker in 1982.

His Nightingale-Conant cassette program *Secrets of Power Negotiating* is the largest-selling business cassette program ever published. Several of his books have been main selections of major book clubs.

Companies and associations throughout North America call on him for his expertise in negotiation, persuasion, and decision making; and for motivational keynote speeches. His seminar company, Roger Dawson Productions, P.O. Box 3326, La Habra, California 90631 (Tel 800 YDAWSON) conducts seminars throughout the country on Power Negotiating, Power Persuasion, Confident Decision Making and High Achievement.

Also by Roger Dawson

Books

You Can Get Anything You Want
Secrets of Power Persuasion
The Confident Decision Maker
The 13 Secrets of Power Performance

Audio Cassette Programs

Secrets of Power Negotiating
Secrets of Power Persuasion
Secrets of Power Performance
Confident Decision Making
The Personality Of Achievers
Secrets of Power Negotiating for Salespeople

Video Training Programs

Guide to Everyday Negotiating
Guide to Business Negotiating

What is Power Negotiating?

You have probably heard that the objective of a negotiation is to create a win-win solution. A creative way that both you and the other person can walk away from the negotiating table feeling that you've won. You may have had this demonstrated to you with the illustration of the two people who have only one orange but both want it. So they talk about it for a while and decide that the best they can do is split the orange down the middle and each settle for half of what they really need. To be sure that it's fair, they decide that one will cut and the other will choose. As they discuss their underlying needs in the negotiation, however, they find that one wants the orange to make juice, and the other needs it for the rind because he wants to bake a cake. They have magically found a way that both of them can win and neither has to lose.

Oh, sure!

That could happen in the real world, but it doesn't happen enough to make the concept meaningful. Let's face it, when you're sitting down in a negotiation, chances are that the other side is out for the same thing as you. There's not going to be a magical win-win solution. If they're buying, they want the lowest price and you want the highest price. If they're selling, they want the highest price and you want the lowest price. They want to take out of your pocket and put it right into theirs.

Power Negotiating takes a different position. Power Negotiating teaches you how to win at the negotiating table, but leave the other person feeling that he or she won. I'll teach you how to do this and do it in such a way that the other side permanently feels that they won. They don't wake up the next morning thinking, "Now I know what that person did to me. Wait until I see her again." No! They'll be thinking what a great time they had negotiating with you and how they can't wait to see you again.

The ability to make others feel that they won is so important that I'd almost give you that as a definition of a Power Negotiator. Two people might enter a negotiation in which the circumstances were exactly the same. Perhaps they're buying or selling real estate or equipment. Both might conclude the negotiation at exactly the same price and terms; but the Power Negotiator leaves the other person feeling that they won. The poor negotiator comes away with the other person feeling that he or she lost.

If you'll learn and apply the secrets of Power Negotiation that I'll teach you in this book, you'll never again feel that you lost to the other person. You'll always come away from the negotiating table knowing that you won and knowing that you have improved your relationship with the other person.

A special message to salespeople and sales managers

In the 10 years that I've been teaching Power Negotiating around the country, salespeople have taught me a great deal about the selling profession. They tell me that it's getting tougher out there. That buyers have more pressure on them than ever before to get your price down. And they've told me that buyers are much better negotiators than they were 5 or 10 years ago.

I hate to put it this bluntly, but here's what I think has happened: I think that the companies to which you sell have figured out that the best and quickest way for them to put money on their bottom line is to take it right off yours.

Think about it for a moment. The companies to which you sell have three ways to improve their profits. The first way is to sell more, which means going head to head with a competitor—to improve their market share by taking away some of their competitors' business. Or by creating new or different products and carving out a new market for themselves, something that is very expensive to do and filled with risk. The second way is to reduce their operating expenses by firing employees or buying expensive new equipment. The third way is to do a better job negotiating with their suppliers. To take money right off your bottom line and put it on theirs.

That's what General Motors decided to do when they put Ignacio Lopez in charge of its buying operations. In the first six months on the job, he saved General Motors 2 billion dollars by renegotiating contracts with suppliers. He took 2 billion from suppliers' bottom lines and put it right on General Motors bottom line. In six months!

So what's happening is that companies are upgrading the position of buyer. Whereas 10 years ago, you may have been selling to a buyer who moved up through the ranks, now you're dealing with someone who may have a master's degree in business. He or she may have just come back from a week-long negotiating course at Harvard University. Because doing a better job negotiating with you is a much easier way to improve their profits than increasing their market share or trying to shave a little more off their operating costs.

How do you as a salesperson respond to this assault on your company's profits and on your personal income? The answer is Power Negotiating. When you learn to become a Power Negotiator you'll know how to get anything you want from the buyers and still have them thinking that they won. Impossible? No, not to a Power Negotiator.

Section One

Playing the Power Negotiating Game

You play Power Negotiating by a set of rules, just like the game of chess. The big difference between negotiating and chess is that, in negotiating, the other person doesn't have to know the rules. The other person will respond predictably to the moves that you make. Not because of metaphysical magic, but because thousands of my students have told me their negotiating experience over the years, and from this feedback we know how the other person will react to any Power Negotiating move you make. Not every time of course, but the likelihood is so high that we now know that negotiating is more of a science than an art.

If you play chess, you know that the strategic moves of the game are called gambits (a word that also suggests an element of risk). There are Beginning Gambits to get the game started in your direction. There are Middle Gambits to keep the game moving in your direction. And there are Ending Gambits to use when you get ready to checkmate the other person or, in sales parlance, close the sale.

In the first section of this book, I'll teach you the Gambits of Power Negotiating. You'll learn the Beginning Gambits, the things that you do in the early stages of your contact with the other person, to be sure that you're setting the stage for a successful conclusion. As the negotiation progresses you'll find that every advance will depend on the atmosphere that you create in the early stages. You should determine the demands that you make and the attitude you present with a carefully made plan that encompasses all elements of the negotiation. Your Opening Gambits, based on a careful evaluation of the other person, the market, and the other side's company, will win or lose the game for you.

Then I'll teach you the Middle Gambits that keep the momentum going in your favor. During this phase, different things come into play. The moves made by each side create currents that swirl around the participants and push them in different directions. You'll learn how to respond to these pressures and continue to master the game.

Finally, I'll teach you the Ending Gambits that conclude the negotiation with you getting what you want and with the other person still feeling that he or she won. The last few moments can make all the difference. Just as in a horse race, there's only one point in the contest that counts and that's the finish line. As a Power Negotiator you'll learn how to smoothly control the process right down to the wire.

So let's get started learning the Gambits of Power Negotiating.

Chapter 1

Beginning Gambits: Ask for More than You Expect to Get

One of the cardinal rules of Power Negotiating is that you should ask the other side for more than you expect to get. Henry Kissinger went so far as to say, "Effectiveness at the conference table depends upon overstating one's demands." Think of some reasons why you should do this:

- Why should you ask the store for a bigger discount than you think you have a chance of getting?

- Why should you ask your boss for an executive suite even though you think you'll be lucky to get a private office?

- If you're applying for a job, why should you ask for more money and benefits than you think they'll give you?

- If you're dissatisfied with a meal in a restaurant, why should you ask the captain to cancel the entire bill, even though you think they will take off only the charge for the offending item?

If you're a salesperson:

- Why, if you are convinced that the buyer wants to spread the business around, should you still ask for it all?

- Why should you ask for full list price even if you know it's higher than the buyer is paying now?

- Why should you ask the other person to invest in the top of the line even when you're convinced they're so budget conscious that they'll never spend that much?

- Why should you assume that they'll want to buy your extended service warranty even though you know they've never done that in the past?

If you thought about this, you probably came up with a few good reasons to ask for more than you expect to get. The obvious answer is that it gives you some negotiating room. If you're selling, you can always come down, but you can never go up on price. If you're buying, you can always go up, but you can never come down. (When we get to Ending Gambits, I'll show you how to Nibble for more. Some things *are* easier to get at the end of the negotiation than they are at the beginning.) What you should be asking for is your MPP—your maximum plausible position. This is the most that you can ask for and still have the other side see some plausibility in your position.

The less you know about the other side, the higher your initial position should be, for two reasons:

1. You may be off in your assumptions. If you don't know the other person or his needs well, he may be willing to pay more than you think. If he's selling, he may be willing to take far less than you think.

2. If this is a new relationship you will appear much more cooperative if you're able to make larger concessions. The better you know the other person and his needs, the more you can modify your position. Conversely, if the other side doesn't know you, their initial demands may be more outrageous.

If you're asking for far more than your maximum plausible position, imply some flexibility. If your initial position seems outrageous to the other person and your attitude is "take it or leave it," you may not even get the negotiations started. The other person's response may simply be, "Then we don't have anything to talk about." You can get away with an outrageous opening position if you imply some flexibility.

If you're buying real estate directly from the seller, you might say, "I realize that you're asking $200,000 for the property and based on everything you know that may seem like a fair price to you. So perhaps you know something that I don't know, but based on all the research that I've done, it seems to me that we should be talking something closer to $160,000." At that the seller may be thinking, "That's ridiculous. I'll never sell it for that, but he does seem to be sincere, so what do I have to lose if I spend some time negotiating with him, just to see how high I can get him to go?"

If you're a salesperson you might say to the buyer, "We may be able to modify this position once we know your needs more precisely, but based on what we know so far about the quantities you'd be ordering, the quality of the packaging, and not needing just-in-time inventory, our best price would be in the region of $2.25 per widget." At that the other person will probably be thinking, "That's outrageous, but there does seem to be some flexibility there, so I think I'll invest some time negotiating with her and see how low I can get her to go."

Unless you're already an experienced negotiator, here's the problem you will have with this. Your real MPP is probably much higher than you think it is. We all fear being ridiculed by the other person (something that I'll talk more about later when we discuss Coercive Power). So we're all reluctant to take a position that will cause the other person to laugh at us or put us down. Because of this intimidation, you will probably feel like modifying your MPP to the point where you're asking for less than the maximum amount that the other person would think is plausible.

Another reason for asking for more than you expect to get will be obvious to you if you're a positive thinker: You might just get it. You don't know how the universe is aligned that day. Perhaps your patron saint is leaning over a cloud looking down at you and thinking, "Wow, look at that nice person. She's been working so hard for so long now, let's just give her a break." So you might just get what you ask for and the only way you'll find out is to ask for it.

In addition, asking for more than you expect to get increases the perceived value of what you are offering. If you're applying for a job and asking for more money than you expect to get, you implant in the personnel director's mind the thought that you are worth that much. If you're selling a car and asking for more than you expect to get, it positions the buyer into believing that the car is worth more.

Another advantage in asking for more than you expect to get is that it prevents the negotiation from deadlocking. Take a look at the Persian Gulf War. What were we asking Saddam Hussein to do? (Perhaps asking is not exactly the right word.) President George Bush, in his State of the Union address, used a beautiful piece of alliteration, probably written by Peggy Noonan, to describe our opening negotiating position. He said, "I'm not bragging, I'm not bluffing, and I'm not bullying. There are three things this man has to do. He has to get out of Kuwait. He has to restore the legitimate government of Kuwait (not do what the Soviets did in Afghanistan and install a puppet government). And he has to make reparations for the damage that he's done." That was a very clear and precise opening negotiating position. The problem was that this was also our bottom line. It was also the least for which we were prepared to settle. No wonder the situation deadlocked. It had to deadlock because we didn't give Saddam Hussein room to have a win.

If we'd have said, "Okay. We want you and all your cronies exiled. We want a non-Arab neutral government installed in Baghdad. We want United Nations supervision of the removal of all military equipment. In addition, we want you out of Kuwait, the legitimate Kuwaiti government restored, and reparation for the damages that you did." Then we could have gotten what we wanted and still given Saddam Hussein a win.

I know what you're thinking. You're thinking, "Roger, Saddam Hussein was not on my Christmas card list last year. He's not the kind of guy I want to give a win to." I agree with that. However, it creates a problem in negotiation. It creates deadlocks.

From the Persian Gulf scenario, you could draw one of two conclusions. The first (and this is what Ross Perot might say) is that our State Department negotiators are complete, blithering idiots. What's the second possibility? Right. That this was a situation where we wanted to create a deadlock, because it served our purpose. We had absolutely no intention of settling for just the three things that George Bush demanded in his State of the Union address. General Schwarzkopf in his biography *It Doesn't Take a Hero* said, "The minute we got there, we understood that anything less than a military victory was a defeat for the United States." We couldn't let Saddam Hussein pull 600,000 troops back across the border, leaving us wondering when he would choose to do it again. We had to have a reason to go in and take care of him militarily.

So that was a situation where it served our purpose to create a deadlock. What concerns me is that when you're involved in a negotiation, you inadvertently create deadlocks because you don't have the courage to ask for more than you expect to get.

A final reason—and the reason Power Negotiators say that you should ask for more than you expect to get—is that it's the only way that you can create a climate where the other person feels that he or she won. If you go in with your best offer up front, there's no way that you can negotiate with the other side and leave them feeling that they won.

- These are the inexperienced negotiators always wanting to start with their best offer.

- This is the job applicant who is thinking, "This is a tight job market and if I ask for too much money, they won't even consider me."

- This is the person who's selling a house or a car and thinking, "If I ask too much, they'll just laugh at me."

- This is the salesperson who is saying to her sales manager, "I'm going out on this big proposal today, and I know that it's going to be competitive.

I know that they're getting bids from people all over town. Let me cut the price up front or we won't stand a chance of getting the order."

Power Negotiators know the value of asking for more than you expect to get. It's the only way that you can create a climate in which the other side feels that he or she won.

Let's recap the five reasons for asking for more than you expect to get:

1. You might just get it.

2. It gives you some negotiating room.

3. It raises the perceived value of what you're offering.

4. It prevents the negotiation from deadlocking.

5. It creates a climate in which the other person feels that he or she won.

In highly publicized negotiations, such as when the football players or airline pilots go on strike, the initial demands that both sides make are absolutely outlandish. I remember being involved in a union negotiation in which the initial demands were unbelievably outrageous. The union's demand was to triple the employees' wages. The company's opening demand was to make it an open shop—in other words, a voluntary union that would effectively destroy the union's power at that location. Power Negotiators know that the initial demands in these types of negotiations are always extreme, however, so they don't let it bother them.

Power Negotiators know that as the negotiations progress, they will work their way toward the middle where they will find a solution that both sides can accept. Then they can both call a press conference and announce that they won in the negotiations.

An attorney friend of mine, John Broadfoot from Amarillo, Texas, tested this theory for me. He was representing a buyer of a piece of real estate, and even though he had a good deal worked out, he thought, "I'll see how Roger's rule of 'Asking for More than You Expect to Get' works." So he dreamt up 23 paragraphs of requests to make of the seller. Some of them were absolutely ridiculous. He felt sure that at least half of them would get thrown out right away. To his amazement he found that the seller of the property took strong objection to only one of the sentences in one of the paragraphs.

Even then John, as I had taught him, didn't give in right away. He held out for a couple of days before he finally and reluctantly conceded. Although he had given away only one sentence in 23 paragraphs of requests, the seller still felt that he had won in the negotiation. So always leave some room to let the other person have a win. Power Negotiators always ask for more than they expect to get.

Bracketing

The next question has to be: If you're asking for more than you expect to get, for how much more than you expect to get should you ask? The answer is that you should bracket your objective. Your initial proposal should be an equal distance on the other side of your objective as their proposal.

Let me give you some simple examples:

- The car dealer is asking $15,000 for the car. You want to buy it for $13,000. You should make an opening offer of $11,000.

- One of your employees is asking if she can spend $400 on a new desk. You think that $325 is reasonable. You should tell her that you don't want her to exceed $250.

- You're a salesperson, and the buyer is offering you $1.60 for your widgets. You can live with $1.70. Bracketing tells you that you should start at $1.80. Then if you end up in the middle, you'll still make your objective.

Of course it's not always true that you'll end up in the middle, but that is a good assumption to make if you don't have anything else on which to base your opening position. Assume that you'll end up in the middle, mid-way between the two opening negotiating positions. If you track that, I think that how often it happens will amaze you. In little things and in big things.

In little things. Your son comes to you and says he needs $20 for a fishing trip he's going to take this weekend. You say, "No way. I'm not going to give you $20. Do you realize that when I was your age I got 50 cents a week allowance, and I had to work for that. I'll give you $10 and not a penny more."

Your son says, "I can't do it for $10, Dad."

Now you have established the negotiating range. He's asking for $20. You're willing to pay $10. See how often you end up at $15. In our culture, splitting the difference seems fair.

In big things. In 1982, we were negotiating the payoff of a huge international loan with the government of Mexico. They were about to default on an $82 billion loan. Their chief negotiator was Jesus Herzog, their finance minister. Treasury Secretary Donald Regan and Federal Reserve Board Chairman Paul Volcker represented our side. In a creative solution, we asked Mexico to contribute huge amounts of petroleum to our strategic petroleum reserve, which Herzog agreed to do. That didn't settle it all, however. We proposed to the Mexicans that they pay us a $100 million dollar negotiating fee, which was a politically acceptable way for them to pay us accrued interest. When President Lopez Portillo heard what we were asking for, he went ballistic. He said the equivalent of: You tell Ronald Reagan to drop dead. We're not paying the United States a negotiating fee. Not one peso.

So now we had the negotiating range established. We asked for $100 million. They offered zero. Guess what they ended up paying us? That's right. $50 million.

So often, in little things and in big things, we end up splitting the difference. With bracketing, Power Negotiators are assured that if that happens, they still get what they want.

To bracket, you must get the other person to state his position first. If the other person can get you to state your position first, then he can bracket you so that, if you end up splitting the difference as so often happens, he ends up getting what he wanted. That's an underlying principle of negotiating that I'll get back to later: Get the other person to state his position first. It may not be as bad as you fear, and it's the only way you can bracket his proposal.

Conversely, don't let the other person trick you into committing first. If the status quo is fine with you, and there is no pressure on you to make a move, be bold enough to say to the other person, "You're the one who approached me. The way things are satisfies me. If you want to do this, you'll have to make a proposal to me."

Another benefit of bracketing is that it tells you how big your concessions can be as the negotiation progresses. Let's take a look at how this would work with the three situations I described earlier:

- The car dealer is asking $15,000 for the car. You want to buy it for $13,000. You made an opening offer of $11,000. Then if the dealer comes down to $14,500, you can go up to $11,500 and you will still have your objective bracketed. If the dealer's next move is to $14,200, you can also shift your position by $300 and go to $11,800.

- One of your employees is asking if she can spend $400 on a new desk. You think that $325 is reasonable. You suggested $250. If the employee responds by saying that she may be able to get what she needs for $350, you can respond by telling her that you might be able to find $300 in the budget. Because you've both moved $50, your objective will still be in the middle.

- Remember the buyer offering you $1.60 for your widgets? You told the buyer that your company would be losing money at a penny less than $1.80. Your goal is to get $1.70. The buyer comes up to $1.63. You can now move down to $1.77 and your goal will still be in the middle of the two proposals that are on the negotiating table. In that way you can move in on your target and know that if the other side offers to split the difference you can still make your goal.

There's a danger here, however. You should not become so predictable with your responses that the other side can detect your pattern of concessions. I illustrated this with mathematically computed concessions to make my point clear, but you should vary your moves slightly so your reason for making a move cannot easily be determined. Later, in Chapter 16, I'll go into more detail on patterns of concessions.

A politically correct fable about asking for more than you expect to get

There was once a very old couple who lived in a dilapidated thatched hut on a remote Pacific island. One day a hurricane blew through the village and demolished their home. Because they were much too old and poor to rebuild the hut, the couple moved in with their daughter and her husband. This arrangement precipitated an unpleasant domestic situation, as the daughter's hut was barely big enough for herself, her husband, and their four children, let alone the in-laws.

The daughter went to the wise person of the village, explained the problem and asked, "Whatever will we do?"

The wise person puffed slowly on a pipe and then responded, "You have chickens, don't you?"

"Yes," she replied, "we have 10 chickens."

"Then bring the chickens into the hut with you."

This seemed ludicrous to the daughter, but she followed the wise person's advice. The move naturally exacerbated the problem, and the situation was soon unbearable, as feathers as well as hostile words flew around the hut. The daughter returned to the wise person, pleading again for advice.

"You have pigs, do you not?"

"Yes, we have three pigs."

"Then you must bring the pigs into your hut with you."

That seemed to be ridiculous advice, but to question the wise person was unthinkable, so she brought the pigs into the hut. Life was now truly unlivable, with 8 people, 10 chickens, and 3 pigs sharing one tiny, noisy hut. Her husband complained that he couldn't hear CNN over the racket.

The next day the daughter, fearing for her family's sanity, approached the wise person with a final desperate plea. "Please," she cried, "we can't live like this. Tell me what to do and I'll do it, but please help us."

This time the wise person's response was puzzling, but easier to follow. "Now remove the chickens and the pigs from your hut."

She quickly evicted the animals, and the entire family lived happily together for the rest of their days.

The moral of the story is that a deal always looks better after you have thrown something out.

Ask for more than you expect to get. It seems like such an obvious principle, but it's something that you can count on in a negotiation. In thousands of workshop situations and in tens of thousands of traceable real life situations, this is something participants have proved repeatedly. The more you ask for, the more you're going to get.

Key points to remember:

- Ask for more than you expect to get. For five reasons:

    1. You might just get it.

    2. It gives you some negotiating room.

    3. It raises the perceived value of what you're offering.

    4. It prevents the negotiation from deadlocking.

    5. It creates a climate in which the other side feels that they won.

- Your objective should be to advance your MPP—your maximum plausible position.

- If your initial proposal is extreme, imply some flexibility. This encourages the other side to negotiate with you.

- The less you know about the other side, the more you should ask for. A stranger is more likely to surprise you, and you can build goodwill by making bigger concessions.

- Bracket the other side's proposal so that if you end up splitting the difference, you still get what you want.

- You can bracket only if you get the other person to state his or her position first.

- Continue bracketing as you zero in on your objective with concessions.

Chapter 2

Beginning Gambits: Never Say Yes to the First Offer

The reason that you should never say Yes to the first offer (or counter-offer) is that it automatically triggers two thoughts in the person's mind.

Let's say that you're thinking of buying a second car. The people down the street have one for sale, and they're asking $10,000. That is such a terrific price on the perfect car for you that you can't wait to get down there and snap it up before somebody else beats you to it. On the way there you start thinking that it would be a mistake to offer them what they're asking, so you decide to make a super low offer of $8,000 just to see what their reaction is. You show up at their house, look the car over, take it for a short test drive, and then say to the owners, "It's not what I'm looking for, but I'll give you $8,000."

You're waiting for them to explode with rage at such a low offer, but what actually happens is that the husband looks at the wife and says, "What do you think, dear?"

The wife says, "Let's go ahead and get rid of it."

Does this exchange make you jump for joy? Does it leave you thinking, "Wow, I can't believe what a deal I got. I couldn't have gotten it for a penny less"?

I don't think so. I think you're probably thinking:

1. I could have done better.

2. Something must be wrong.

Now let's consider a more sophisticated example and also put yourself in the other person's shoes for a moment. Let's say that you're a buyer for a maker of aircraft engines, and you're about to meet with a salesperson who represents the manufacturer of engine bearings, something that's a vital component for you. Your regular supplier has let you down, and you need to make an emergency purchase from this new company. This is the only company that can supply, within 30 days, the bearings that you need to prevent a shut down of your assembly line. If you can't supply the engines on time, it will invalidate your contract with the aircraft manufacturer who gives you 85 percent of your business. Under these circumstances, the price of the bearings you need is definitely not a high priority. As your secretary announces the arrival of the salesperson, however, you think to yourself, "I'll be a good negotiator. Just to see what happens I'll make him a super low offer."

The salesperson makes his presentation and assures you that he can ship on time to your specifications. He quotes you a price of $250 each for the bearings. This surprises you because you have been paying $275 for them. You manage to mask your surprise and respond with, "We've been paying only $175." (In business we call this a lie, and it is done all the time.) To which the salesperson responds, "Okay, we can match that."

At this point you almost certainly have two responses:

1. I could have done better.

2. Something must be wrong.

In the thousands of seminars that I've conducted over the years, I've posed a situation like this to audiences and can't recall getting anything other than these two responses. Sometimes people reverse them, but usually the response is automatic, "I could have done better," and "Something must be wrong."

Let's look at each of these responses separately:

First Reaction: I could have done better. The interesting thing about this is that it doesn't have a thing to do with the price. It has to do only with the way the other person reacts to the proposal. What if you'd offered $7,000 for the car, or $6,000, and they told you right away they'd take it? Wouldn't you still think you could have done better? What if that bearing salesperson had agreed to $150 or $125? Wouldn't you still think you could have done better?

Several years ago I bought 100 acres of land in Eatonville, Washington— a beautiful little town just west of Mount Rainier. The seller was asking $185,000 for the land. I analyzed the property and decided that if I could get it for $150,000, it would be a terrific buy. So I bracketed that price and asked the real estate agent to present an offer to the seller at $115,050. (Specific numbers build credibility, so you're more likely to get them to accept an offer like this than to counter it. More about this later.)

I went back to my home in La Habra Heights, California, leaving the agent to present the offer to the seller. Frankly, I thought I'd be lucky if they came back with any kind of counter-offer on a proposal this low. To my amazement I got the offer back in the mail a few days later, accepted at the price and terms that I had proposed. I'm sure that I got a terrific buy on the land. Within a year I'd sold 60 of the acres for more than I paid for the whole hundred. Later I sold another 20 acres for more than I paid for the whole hundred. So when they accepted my offer, I should have been thinking, "Wow. That's terrific, I couldn't have gotten a lower price." That's what I should have been thinking, but I wasn't. I was thinking, "I could have done better." So it doesn't have anything to do with the price—it has to do only with the way the other person reacts to the proposal.

Second Reaction: Something must be wrong. My second reaction when I received the accepted offer on the land was, "Something must be wrong. I'm going to take a really thorough look at the preliminary title report when it comes in. Something must be going on that I don't understand, if they're willing to accept an offer that I didn't think they would.

The second thought you'd have when the seller of that car said Yes to your first offer is that something must be wrong. The second thought that the buyer of the bearings will have is, "Something must be wrong. Maybe something's changed in the market since I last negotiated a bearing contract. Instead of going ahead, I think I'll tell this salesperson that I've got to check with a committee and then talk to some other suppliers."

These two reactions will go through anybody's mind if you say Yes to the first offer. Let's say your son came to you and said, "Could I borrow the car tonight?" and you said, "Sure, son, take it. Have a wonderful time." Wouldn't he automatically think, "I could have done better. I could have gotten $10 for the movie out of this"? And wouldn't he automatically think, "What's going on here? How come they want me out of the house? What's going on that I don't understand?"

This is a very easy negotiating principle to understand, but it's very hard to remember when you're in the thick of a negotiation. You may have formed a mental picture of how you expect the other side to respond and that's a dangerous thing to do. Napoleon Bonaparte once said, "The unforgivable sin of a commander is to 'form a picture'—to assume that the enemy will act a certain way in a given situation, when in fact his response may be altogether different." So you're expecting them to counter at a ridiculously low figure and to your surprise the other person's proposal is much more reasonable than you expected it to be. For example:

- You've finally plucked up the courage to ask your boss for an increase in pay. You've asked for a 15 percent increase in pay, but you think you'll be lucky to get 10 percent. To your astonishment your boss tells you that he or she thinks you're doing a terrific job, and they'd love to give you the increase in pay. Do you find yourself thinking what a wonderfully generous company this is that you work for? I don't think so. You're probably wishing you'd asked for a 25 percent increase.

- Your son asks you for $100 to take a weekend hiking trip. You say, "No way. I'll give you $50 and not a penny more." In reality you have bracketed his proposal (see Chapter one) and expect to settle for $75. To your surprise your son says, "That would be tight, Dad, but okay, $50 would be great." Are you thinking how clever you were to get him down to $50? I don't think so. You're probably wondering how much less he would have settled for.

- You're selling a piece of real estate that you own. You're asking $100,000. A buyer makes an offer at $80,000, and you counter at $90,000. You're thinking that you'll end up at $85,000, but to your surprise the buyer immediately accepts the $90,000 offer. Admit it—aren't you thinking that if they jumped at $90,000, you could have gotten them up more?

Here are some situations that you might run into if you're a salesperson:

- You sell vacuum cleaners to department store chains. You know that the buyer expects you to contribute advertising money to their Labor Day Weekend mailer, and you're expecting her to ask for $25,000. You have only $20,000 left in your advertising fund. To your surprise she asks for only $10,000. There's a real danger that you'll say Yes too quickly.

- You sell MRI (magnetic resonance imaging) equipment to hospitals. Your list price is $1.2 million, but you typically end up selling it for $900,000. City Hospital has been getting bids from every supplier in the business, and you have every reason to believe that you're going to have to sell at rock-bottom price to get the order. So you're expecting them to counter at $800,000, if you're lucky. To your amazement they come back at $950,000. There's a real danger that you'll say Yes too quickly.

- You lease fleets of cars, and you've been trying to get the business of a huge engineering company. Finally they make a proposal to you. They want to lease 300 cars and 400 light trucks. You're expecting them to propose 6 percent under invoice. To your surprise they come back at only 4.5 percent under invoice, well within your negotiating range. There's a real danger that you'll say Yes too quickly.

So Power Negotiators are careful that they don't fall into the trap of saying Yes too quickly, which automatically triggers in the other person's mind:

1. I could have done better. (And next time I will. A sophisticated person won't tell you that he felt that he lost in the negotiation; but he will tuck it away in the back of his mind, thinking "The next time I deal with this person I'll be a tougher negotiator. I won't leave any money on the table next time.")

2. Something must be wrong.

Turning down the first offer may be tough to do, particularly if you've been calling on the person for months and just as you're about to give up, she comes through with a proposal. It will tempt you to grab what you can. When this happens, be a Power Negotiator—remember not to say Yes too quickly.

Many years ago I was president of a real estate company in southern California that had 28 offices and 540 sales associates.

One day a magazine salesman came in, trying to sell me advertising space in his magazine. I was familiar with the magazine and knew it to be an excellent opportunity, so I wanted my company to be in it. He made me a very reasonable proposal that required a modest $2,000 investment. Because I love to negotiate, I started using some Gambits on him and got him down to the incredibly low price of $800. You can imagine what I was thinking at that point. Right. I was thinking, "Holy cow. If I got him down from $2,000 to $800 in just a few minutes, I wonder how low I can get him to go if I keep on negotiating?" So I used a Middle Gambit on him called Higher Authority (see Chapter 7). I said, "This looks fine. I do just have to run it by my board of directors. Fortunately they're meeting tonight. Let me run it by them and get back to you with the final okay."

A couple of days later I called him back and said, "You'll never know how embarrassed I am about this. You know, I really felt that I wouldn't have any problem at all selling the board of directors on that $800 price you quoted me, but they're so difficult to deal with right now. The budget has been giving everyone headaches lately. They did come back with a counteroffer, but it's so low that it embarrasses me to tell you what it is."

There was a long pause, and he finally said, "How much did they agree to?"
"$500."

"That's okay. I'll take it," he said. And I felt cheated. Even though I'd negotiated him down from $2,000 to $500, I still felt that I could have done better.

There's a postscript to this story. I'm always reluctant to tell stories such as this at my seminars for fear that it may get back to the person with whom

I was negotiating. However, several years later I was speaking at the huge California Association of Realtors convention being held that year in San Diego. I told this story in my talk, never imagining that the magazine sales-man was standing in the back of the room. As I finished my presentation, I saw him pushing his way through the crowd. I braced myself for what I expected to be a verbal assault. However, he shook my hand and said with a smile, "I can't thank you enough for explaining that to me. I had no idea the impact that my tendency to jump at a quick deal was having on people. I'll never do that again."

I used to think that it was a 100 percent rule that you should never say Yes to the first offer. Until I heard from a man in Los Angeles who told me, "I was driving down Hollywood Boulevard last night, listening to your cassette tapes in my car. I stopped at a gas station to use the rest room. When I came back to my car, somebody stuck a gun in my ribs and said, 'Okay buddy. Give me your wallet.' Well, I'd just been listening to your tapes, so I said, 'I'll give you the cash, but let me keep the wallet and the credit cards, fair enough?' And he said, 'Buddy, you didn't listen to me, did you? *Give me the wallet!*'" So sometimes you *should* say Yes to the first offer, but it's almost a 100 percent rule that you should Never Jump at the First Offer.

Key points to remember:

- Never say Yes to the first offer or counter-offer from the other side. It automatically triggers two thoughts: I could have done better (and next time I will) and Something must be wrong.

- The big danger is when you have formed a mental picture of how the other person will respond to your proposal, and he comes back much higher than you expected. Prepare for this possibility so it won't catch you off guard.

Chapter 3

Beginning Gambits: Flinch at Proposals

Power Negotiators know that you should always Flinch—react with shock and surprise at the other side's proposals.

Let's say that you are in a resort area and stop to watch one of those charcoal sketch artists. He doesn't have the price posted, and he has the shill sitting on the stool. You ask him how much he charges, and he tells you $15. If that doesn't appear to shock you, his next words will be, "And $5 extra for color." If you still don't appear shocked, he will say, "And we have these shipping cartons here, you'll need one of these too."

Perhaps you are married to someone, who would never Flinch like that because it's beneath his or her dignity. My first wife was like that. We would walk into a store, and she would say to the clerk, "How much is the coat?"

The clerk would respond, "$2,000."

My wife would say, "That's not bad!" I would be having a heart attack in the background.

I know it sounds dumb and I know it sounds ridiculous, but the truth of the matter is that when people make a proposal to you, they are watching for your reaction. They may not think for a moment that you'll go along with their request. They've just thrown it out to see what your reaction will be. For example:

- You sell computers and the buyer asks you to include an extended warranty.

- You're buying a car and the dealer offers you only a few hundred dollars for your trade-in.

- You sell contractor supplies and the buyer asks you to deliver to the job site at no extra charge.

- You're selling your house and the buyer wants to move in two weeks before the transaction closes.

In each of these situations, the other side may not have thought for a moment that you would go along with the request, but if you don't Flinch, he or she will automatically think, "Maybe I will get them to go along with that. I didn't think they would, but I think I'll be a tough negotiator and see how far I can get them to go."

It's very interesting to observe a negotiation when you know what both sides are thinking. Wouldn't that be fascinating for you? Wouldn't you love to know what's going on in the other person's mind when you're negotiating with her? When I conduct the one- or two-day Secrets of Power Negotiating seminars, we break up into groups and do some negotiating to practice the principles that I teach. I create a workshop and customize it to the industry in which the participants are involved. If they are medical equipment salespeople, they may find themselves negotiating the sale of laser surgery equipment to a hospital. If they are owners of print shops, the workshop may involve the acquisition of a smaller printing company in an outlying town.

I break the audience up into buyers, sellers, and referees. The referees are in a very interesting position because they have been in on the planning sessions of both the buyers and the sellers. They know each side's negotiating range. They know what the opening offer is going to be, and they know how far each side will go. So the sellers of the printing company would go as low as $700,000, but they may start as high as $2 million. The buyers may start at $400,000, but they're prepared to go to $1.5 million if they have to. So the negotiating range is $400,000 to $2 million, but the acceptance range is $700,000 to $1.5 million. The acceptance range embraces the price levels at which the buyers' and the sellers' negotiating ranges overlap. If they do overlap and there is an acceptance range, it's almost certain that the final price to which they agree will fall within this range. If the top of the buyers' negotiating range is lower than the bottom of the sellers' negotiating range, then one or both sides will have to compromise their objectives.

The negotiation starts with each side trying to get the other side to put their offer on the table first. After a while someone has to break the ice, so the sellers may suggest the $2 million (which is the top of their negotiating range). They believe $2 million is ridiculously high, and they barely have the nerve to propose it. They think they're going to get laughed out of the room the minute they do. However, to their surprise, the buyers don't appear to be that shocked. The sellers expect the buyers to say, "You want us to do what? You must be out of your minds." What they actually respond with is much milder, perhaps, "We don't think we'd be prepared to go that high." In an instant the negotiation changes. A moment ago the $2 million had seemed to be an impossible goal. Now the sellers are thinking that perhaps they're not as far apart as they thought they were. Now they're thinking, "Let's hang in. Let's be tough negotiators. Maybe we will get this much."

Flinching is critical because most people believe more what they see than what they hear. The visual overrides the auditory in most people. It's safe for you to assume that at least 70 percent of the people with whom you negotiate will be visuals. What they see is more important than what they hear. I'm sure you've been exposed to some neuro-linguistic programming. You know that people are either visual, auditory, or kinesthetic (what they feel is paramount). There are a few gustatory (taste) and olfactory (smell) people around, but not many and they're usually chefs or perfume blenders.

If you'd like to know what you are, close your eyes for ten seconds and think of the house in which you lived when you were ten years old. You probably saw the house in your mind, so you're a visual. Perhaps you didn't get a good visual picture, but you heard what was going on, perhaps trains passing by or children playing. That means you're auditory. Auditories tend to be very auditory. Neil Berman is a psychotherapist friend of mine in Santa Fe, New Mexico. He can remember every conversation he's ever had with a patient, but if he meets them in the supermarket he doesn't remember them. The minute they say good morning to him, he thinks, "Oh yes, that's the bi-polar personality with anti-social tendencies." The third possibility is that you didn't so much see the house or hear what was going on, but you just got a feeling for what it was like when you were ten. That makes you a kinesthetic.

Assume that people are visual unless you have something else to go on. Assume that what they see has more impact than what they hear. That's why it's so important to respond with a Flinch to a proposal from the other side.

Don't dismiss Flinching as childish or too theatrical until you've had a chance to see how effective it can be. It's so effective that it usually surprises my students when they first use it. A woman told me that she Flinched when selecting a bottle of wine in one of Boston's finest restaurants and the wine steward immediately dropped the price by five dollars. A man told me that a simple Flinch caused the salesperson to take $2,000 of the price of a Corvette.

A speaker friend of mine attended my seminar in Orange County, California, and decided to see if he could use it to get his speaking fees up. At the time he was just getting started and was charging $1,500. He went to a company and proposed that they hire him to do some in-house training. The training director said, "We might be interested in having you work for us, but the most we can pay you is $1,500."

In the past he would have said, "That's what I charge." But now he gasped in surprise and said, "$1,500? I couldn't afford to do it for just $1,500."

The training director frowned thoughtfully. "Well," he said, "the most we've ever offered any speaker is $2,500, so that's the very best we can do." That meant $1,000 in additional bottom-line profit dollars per speech to my friend and it took him only 15 seconds to do. Not bad pay.

Key points to remember:

- Flinch in reaction to a proposal from the other side. They may not expect to get what they're asking for, but if you don't show surprise, you're communicating that it's a possibility.

- A concession often follows a Flinch. If you don't Flinch, it makes the other person a tougher negotiator.

- Assume that the other person is a visual unless you have something else on which to go.

- Even if you're not face to face with the other person, you should still gasp in shock and surprise. Phone Flinches can be very effective also.

Chapter 4

Beginning Gambits: Avoid Confrontational Negotiation

What you say in the first few moments of a negotiation often sets the climate of the negotiation. The other person quickly gets a feel for whether you are working for a win-win solution, or whether you're a tough negotiator who's out for everything they can get.

That's one problem that I have with the way that attorneys negotiate—they're very confrontational negotiators. You get that white envelope in the mail with black, raised lettering in the top left-hand corner and you think, "Oh no. What is it this time?" You open up the letter and what's the first communication from them? It's a threat. What they're going to do to you, if you don't give them what they want.

I remember conducting a seminar for 50 attorneys who litigated medical malpractice lawsuits, or, as they prefer to call them, physician liability lawsuits. I've never met an attorney who was eager to go to a negotiating seminar even though that's what they do, and these people were no exception to the rule. However, the organization that was giving the attorneys business told them that they were expected to attend my seminar if they wanted to get any more cases from the organization. So the attorneys weren't too happy about having to spend Saturday with me in the first place, but once we got started, they became involved and were having a good time. I got them absorbed in a workshop involving a surgeon being sued over an unfortunate incident involving a nun and walked around the room to see how they were doing. I couldn't believe how confrontational they were being. Most of them started with a vicious threat and then became more abusive from that point on. I had to stop the exercise and tell them that if they wanted to settle the case without expensive litigation (and I doubted their motives on that score) that they should never be confrontational in the early stages of the negotiation.

So be careful what you say at the beginning. If the other person takes a position with which you totally disagree, don't argue. Arguing always intensifies the other person's desire to prove him- or herself right. You're much better off to agree with the other person initially and then turn it around using the Feel, Felt, Found formula. Respond with, "I understand exactly how you *feel* about that. Many other people have *felt* exactly the same way as you do right now. (Now you have diffused that competitive spirit. You're not arguing with them, you're agreeing with them.) But you know what we have always *found*? When we take a closer look, we have always found that ... "

Let's look at some examples:

- You're selling something, and the other person says, "Your price is way too high." If you argue with him, he has a vested interest in proving you wrong and himself right. Instead you say, "I understand exactly how you feel about that. Many other people have felt exactly the same way as you do when they first hear the price. When they take a closer look at what we offer, however, they have always found that we offer the best value in the marketplace."

- You're applying for a job, and the human resources director says, "I don't think you have enough experience in this field." If you respond with, "I've handled much tougher jobs than this in the past," it may come across as, "I'm right and you're wrong." It's just going to force her to defend the position she's taken. Instead say, "I understand exactly how you feel about that. Many other people would feel exactly the same way as you do right now. However, there are some remarkable similarities between the work I've been doing and what you're looking for that are not immediately apparent. Let me tell you what they are."

- If you're a salesperson and the buyer says, "I hear that you people have problems in your shipping department," arguing with him will make him doubt your objectivity. Instead say, "I understand how you could have heard that because I've heard it too. I think that rumor may have started a few years ago when we relocated our warehouse; but now major companies such as General Motors and General Electric trust us with their just-in-time inventories, and we never have a problem."

- If the other person says, "I don't believe in buying from off-shore suppliers. I think we should keep the jobs in this country," the more you argue, the more you'll force him into defending his position. Instead say, "I understand exactly how you feel about that because these days many other people feel exactly the same way as you do. But do you know what we have found? Since we have been having the initial assembly done in Thailand, we have actually been able to increase our American work force by more than 42 percent and this is why..."

So instead of arguing up front, which creates confrontational negotiation, get in the habit of agreeing and then turning it around. Remember Winston Churchill, from my old country? He was a grand old man, but he had one big weakness—he loved to drink. He was always battling with Lady Astor, who favored prohibition. One day she came up to him and said, "Winston, you are disgusting. You are drunk." He was a good enough negotiator to know that you shouldn't argue. You should agree and then turn it around. He said, "Lady Astor, you're absolutely right, I am drunk. But you're ugly, and in the morning, *I* shall be sober."

At my seminars I sometimes ask a person in the front row to stand. As I hold my two hands out, with my palms facing toward the person I've asked to stand, I ask him to place his hands against mine. Having done that and without saying another word, I gently start to push against him. Automatically, without any instruction, he always begins to push back. People shove when you shove them. Similarly, when you argue with someone, it automatically makes him or her want to argue back.

The other great thing about Feel, Felt, Found is that it gives you time to think. Perhaps you're in a bar and this woman is saying to you, "I wouldn't let you buy me a drink if you were the last man in the world." You haven't heard anything like this before. It shocks you. You don't know what to say; but if you have Feel, Felt, Found in the back of your mind, you can say, "I understand exactly how you feel about that. Many other people have felt exactly the same way. However, I have always found..." By the time you get there, you'll have thought of something to say. Similarly, you sometimes catch other people at a bad moment. You may be a salesperson who is calling to get an appointment, and the person says to you, "I don't have any more time to waste talking to some lying scum-sucking salesperson." You calmly say, "I understand exactly how you feel about that. Many other people have felt exactly the same way. However..." By the time you get there you will have recovered your composure and will know exactly what to say.

Key points to remember:

- Don't argue with people in the early stages of the negotiation because it creates confrontation.
- Use the Feel, Felt, Found formula to turn the hostility around.
- Having Feel, Felt, Found in the back of your mind gives you time to think when the other side throws some unexpected hostility your way.

Chapter 5

Beginning Gambits: Play the Reluctant Seller and Look Out for the Reluctant Buyer

Imagine for a moment that you own a sailboat, and you're desperate to sell it. It was fun when you first got it, but now you hardly ever use it, and the maintenance and slip fees are eating you alive. It's early Sunday morning, and you've given up a chance to play golf with your buddies because you need to be down at the marina cleaning your boat. You're scrubbing away and cursing your stupidity for ever having bought the boat. Just as you're thinking, "I'm going to give this turkey away to the next person who comes along," you look up and see an expensively dressed man with a young woman on his arm coming down the dock. He's wearing Gucci loafers, white slacks, and a blue Burberry's blazer topped off with a silk cravat. His young girlfriend is wearing high heels, a silk sheath dress, big sunglasses, and huge diamond earrings.

They stop at your boat, and the man says, "That's a fine looking boat, young man. By any chance is it for sale?"

His girlfriend snuggles up to him and says, "Oh, let's buy it, Poopsy. We'll have so much fun."

You feel your heart start to burst with joy, and your mind is singing, "Thank you, Lord! Thank you, Lord!"

Expressing that sentiment is not going to get you the best price for your boat, is it? How are you going to get the best price? By playing Reluctant Seller. You keep on scrubbing and say, "You're welcome to come aboard, although I hadn't thought of selling the boat." You give them a tour of the boat, and at every step of the way you tell them how much you love the boat and how much fun you have sailing her. Finally you tell them, "I can see how perfect this boat would be for you and how much fun you'd have with it, but I really don't think I could ever bear to part with it. However, just to be fair to you, what is the very best price you would give me?"

Power Negotiators know that this Reluctant Seller technique squeezes the negotiating range before the negotiating even starts. If you've done a good job of building the other person's desire to own the boat, he will have formed a negotiating range in his mind. He may be thinking, "I'd be willing to go to $30,000, $25,000 would be a fair deal, and $20,000 would be a bargain." So his negotiating range is from $20,000 to $30,000. Just by playing Reluctant Seller, you will have moved him up through that range. If you had appeared eager to sell, he may have offered you only $20,000. By playing Reluctant Seller you may move him to the mid-point or even the high point of his negotiating range—before the negotiations even start.

One of my Power Negotiators is an extremely rich and powerful investor, a man who owns real estate all over town. He probably owns real estate worth $50 million, owes $35 million in loans, and therefore has a net worth of about $15 million. Very successful—what you could justifiably call a heavy hitter. He likes wheeling and dealing.

Like many investors, his strategy is simple: Buy a property at the right price and on the right terms, hold onto it and let it appreciate, then sell at a higher price. Many smaller investors bring him purchase offers for one of his holdings, eager to acquire one of his better-known properties. That's when this well-seasoned investor knows how to use the Reluctant Seller Gambit.

He reads the offer quietly, and when he's finished he slides it thoughtfully back across the table, scratches above one ear, saying something like, "I don't know. Of all my properties, I have very special feelings for this one. I was thinking of keeping it and giving it to my daughter for her college graduation present, and I really don't think that I would part with it for anything less than the full asking price. You understand; this particular property is worth a great deal to me. But look, it was good of you to bring in an offer for me and in all fairness, so that you won't have wasted your time, what is the very best price that you feel you could give me?" Many times I saw him make thousands of dollars in just a few seconds using the Reluctant Seller philosophy.

Power Negotiators always try to edge up the other side's negotiating range before the real negotiating ever begins.

I remember an ocean-front condominium that I bought as an investment. The owner was asking $59,000 for it. It was a hot real estate market at the time, and I wasn't sure how eager the owner was to sell or if they had any other offers on it. So I wrote up three offers, one at $49,000, another at $54,000 and a third at $59,000. I made an appointment to meet with the seller, who had moved out of the condo in Long Beach and was now living in Pasadena. After talking to her for a while, I determined that she hadn't had any other offers and that she was eager to sell. So I reached into my brief-case, where I had the three offers carefully filed and pulled out the lowest of them. She accepted it, and when I sold the condo a few years later, it fetched $129,000. (Be aware that you can do this only with a "For Sale by Owner." If a real estate agent has listed the property, that agent is working for the seller and is obligated to tell the seller if he's aware that the other side would pay more. Another reason why you should always list property with an agent when you're selling.)

So Power Negotiators always play Reluctant Seller when they're selling. Even before the negotiation starts, it squeezes the other side's negotiating range.

Now let's turn this around and consider the Reluctant Buyer. Put yourself on the other side of the desk for a moment. Let's say that you're in charge of buying new computer equipment for your company. How would you get a salesperson to give you the lowest possible price? I would let the other person come in and have her go through her entire presentation. I would ask all the questions I could possibly think of, and when I finally couldn't think of another thing to ask, I would say, "I really appreciate all the time you've taken. You've obviously put a lot of work into this presentation, but unfortu-nately it's just not the way we want to go; however I sure wish you the best of luck." I would pause to examine the crestfallen expression on the salesper-son's face. I would watch her slowly package her presentation materials "with a heavy heart," as Lyndon Johnson used to say. Then at the very last moment, just as her hand hit the door knob on the way out, I would come back with this magic expression. There are some magic expressions in nego-tiating. If you use them at exactly the right moment, the predictability of the other person's response is amazing. I would say, "You know, I really do ap-preciate the time you took with me. Just to be fair to you, what is the very lowest price that you would take?"

Would you agree with me that it's a good bet that the first price the sales-person quoted is not the real bottom line? Sure, it's a good bet. The first price a salesperson quotes is what I call the "wish number." This is what she is wishing the other person would do. If the other person said okay to that, she would probably burn rubber all the way back to her sales office and run in screaming, "You can't believe what just happened to me. I was over at XYZ

Company to make a bid on the computer equipment they need for their new headquarters. I went over the proposal and they said, 'What's your absolute bottom-line price?' I was feeling good so I said, 'We never budge off list price less a quantity discount, so the bottom line is $225,000,' and held my breath. The president said, 'It sounds high, but if that's the best you can do, go ahead and ship it.' I can't believe it. Let's close the office and go celebrate." So the first price quoted is what I call the wish price.

Somewhere out there, as the song says, there's a "walk-away" price. A price at which the salesperson will not or cannot sell. The other person doesn't know what the walk-away price is, so he or she has to do some probing, some seeking of information. He or she has to try some negotiating Gambits to see if they can figure out the salesperson's walk-away price.

When you play Reluctant Buyer, the salesperson is not going to come all the way from the wish price to the walk-away price. Here's what will typically happen. When you play Reluctant Buyer, the salesperson will typically give away half of his or her negotiating range. If that computer salesperson knows that the bottom line is $175,000, $50,000 below the list price, he will typically respond to the Reluctant Buyer Gambit with, "Well, I tell you what. It's the end of our quarter, and we're in a sales contest. If you'll place the order today, I'll give it to you for the unbelievably low price of $200,000." He'll give away half their negotiating range, just because you played Reluctant Buyer.

Remember that when people do this kind of thing to you, it's just a game that's being played. Power Negotiators don't get upset about it. They just learn to play the negotiating game better than the other side. When the other person does it to you, the correct response to this Gambit is to go through the following sequence of Gambits:

"I don't think that there is any flexibility in the price, but if you'll tell me what it would take to get your business (getting the other side to commit first), I'll take it to my people (Higher Authority—a middle negotiating Gambit that I'll cover later), and I'll see what I can do for you with them (Good Guy/Bad Guy—an ending negotiating Gambit.)"

Key points to remember:

- Always play Reluctant Seller.
- Look out for the Reluctant Buyer.
- Playing this Gambit is a great way to squeeze the other side's negotiating range before the negotiation even starts.
- The other person will typically give away half his or her negotiating range just because you use this.
- When it's used on you: (1) Get the other person to commit. (2) Go to a Higher Authority. (3) Close with Good Guy/Bad Guy.

Chapter 6

Beginning Gambits: Use the Vise Technique

The Vise is another very effective negotiating Gambit, and what it will do will amaze you. The Vise Gambit is the simple little expression: "You'll have to do better than that." Here's how Power Negotiators use it: Let's say that you own a small steel company that sells steel products in bulk. You are calling on a fabricating plant where the buyer has listened to your proposal and your pricing structure. You ignored his insistence that he's happy with his present supplier and did a good job of building desire for your product. Finally the other person says to you, "I'm really happy with our present vendor, but I guess it wouldn't do any harm to have a backup supplier to keep them on their toes. I'll take one carload if you can get the price down to $1.22 per pound."

You respond with the Vise Gambit by calmly saying, "I'm sorry you'll have to do better than that."

An experienced negotiator will automatically respond with the Counter-Gambit, which is, "Exactly how much better than that do I have to do?" trying to pin you down to a specific. However, it will amaze you how often inexperienced negotiators will concede a big chunk of their negotiating range simply because you did that.

What's the next thing that you should do, once you've said, "You'll have to do better than that"?

You have it. *Shut Up!* Don't say another word. The other side may just make a concession to you. Salespeople call this the silent close, and they all learn it during the first week that they are in the business. You make your proposal and then shut up. The other person may just say Yes, so it's foolish to say a word until you find out if he or she will or won't.

I once watched two salespeople do the silent close on each other. There were three of us sitting at a circular conference table. The salesman on my right wanted to buy a piece of real estate from the salesman on my left. He made his proposal and then shut up, just as they taught him in sales training school. The more experienced salesperson on my left must have thought, "Son of a gun. I can't believe this. He's going to try the silent close on *moi*? I'll teach him a thing or two. I won't talk either."

So then I was sitting between two strong-willed people who were both silently daring the other to be the next one to talk. I didn't know how this was ever going to get resolved. There was dead silence in the room, except for the grandfather clock ticking away in the background. I looked at each of them and obviously they both knew what was going on. Neither one was willing to give in to the other. I didn't know how this was ever going to get resolved. It seemed as though half an hour went by, although it was probably more like five minutes, because silence seems like such a long time. Finally the more experienced salesperson broke the impasse by scrawling the word "DE-CIZION?" on a pad of paper and sliding it across to the other. He had deliberately misspelled the word decision. The younger salesperson looked at it and without thinking said, "You misspelled decision." And once he started talking, he couldn't stop. (Do you know a salesperson like that? Once they start talking they can't stop?) He went on to say, "If you're not willing to accept what I offered you, I might be willing to come up another $2,000; but not a penny more." He re-negotiated his own proposal before he found out if the other person would accept it or not.

So to use the Vise technique, Power Negotiators simply respond to the other side's proposal or counter-proposal with, "I'm sorry, you'll have to do better than that." And then shut up.

During the Vietnam War, Secretary of State Henry Kissinger asked an undersecretary of state to prepare a report on the political situation in South East Asia. The undersecretary worked hard on the paper and was proud of what he had done. It was extremely comprehensive and bound in leather with gold engraving. However, Kissinger quickly returned it to him with the notation, "You'll have to do better than this. H.K." The undersecretary went to work and dug out more information, added more charts, and sent it back to Kissinger. This time he knew that he'd given birth to a true work of bureaucratic art. Again it came back with the notation, "You'll have to do better than this. H.K." Now it became a major challenge for him. He put his staff to work on the report around the clock, determined that it would be the best position paper that Kissinger had ever seen. When finally he had put the finishing touches on it, he was reluctant merely to send it to Kissinger, so he made an appointment and took it in himself. As he presented it, he said, "Mr. Kissinger, you've sent this back to me twice. My entire staff has dedicated the last two weeks to this report. Please don't send it back again. It's not going to get any better than this. This is the best I can do." Kissinger calmly placed it on his desk and said, "In that case, I will read it."

A client called me up after a Secrets of Power Negotiating seminar that I had conducted for their managers and told me, "Roger, I thought you might like to know that we just made $14,000 using one of the Gambits that you taught us. We are having new equipment put into our Miami office. Our standard procedure has been to get bids from three qualified vendors and then take the lowest bid. So I was sitting here going over the bids and was just about to okay the one I'd decided to accept. Then I remembered what you taught me about the Vise technique. So I thought, 'What have I got to lose?' and scrawled across it, 'You'll have to do better than this,' and mailed it back to them. Their counter-proposal came back $14,000 less than the proposal that I was prepared to accept."

You may be thinking, "Roger, you didn't tell me whether that was a $50,000 proposal, in which case it would have been a huge concession, or a multi-million dollar proposal, in which case it wouldn't have been that big a deal." Don't fall into the trap of negotiating percentages when you should be negotiating dollars. The point was that he made $14,000 in the two minutes that it took him to scrawl that counter-proposal across the bid. Which meant that while he was doing it, he was generating $420,000 per hour of bottom-line profits. That's pretty good money, isn't it?

This is another trap into which attorneys fall. When I work with attorneys, it's clear that if they're negotiating a $50,000 lawsuit, they might send a letter back and forth over $5,000. If it's a million dollar lawsuit, they'll kick $50,000 around as though it doesn't mean a thing, because they're mentally negotiating percentages, not dollars.

If you make a $2,000 concession to a buyer, it doesn't matter if it got you a $10,000 sale or a million dollar sale. It's still $2,000 that you gave away. So it doesn't make any sense for you to come back to your sales manager and say, "I had to make a $2,000 concession, but it's a $100,000 sale." What you should have been thinking was, "$2,000 is sitting in the middle of the negotiating table. How long should I be willing to spend negotiating further to see how much of it I could get?"

Have a feel for what your time's worth. Don't spend half an hour negotiating a $10 item (unless you're doing it just for the practice). Even if you got the other side to concede all of the $10, you'd be making money only at the rate of $20 an hour for the half hour you invested in the negotiation. To put this in perspective for you, if you make $100,000 a year, you're making about $50 an hour. So you should be thinking to yourself, "Is what I'm doing right now, generating more than $50 per hour?" If so, it's part of the solution. If you're aimlessly chatting with someone at the water cooler, or talking about last night's television movie, or anything else that is not generating $50 an hour, it's part of the problem.

Here's the point. When you're negotiating with someone—when you have a deal in front of you that you could live with—but you're wondering if you could hang in a little bit longer and do a little bit better, you're not making $50 an hour. No, sir. No, ma'am. You're making $50 a minute and probably $50 a second.

And if that's not enough, remember that a negotiated dollar is a bottom-line dollar. It's not a gross-income dollar. So the $2,000 that you may have conceded in seconds because you thought it was the only way you could have gotten the sale is worth many times that in gross sales dollars. I've trained executives at discount retailers and health maintenance organizations (HMOs) where the profit margin is only 2 percent. They do a billion dollars' worth of business a year, but they bring in only 2 percent in bottom-line profits. So at their company, a $2,000 concession at the negotiating table has the same impact on the bottom-line as getting a $100,000 sale.

You're probably in an industry that does better than that. I have trained people at some companies where the bottom line is an incredible 25 percent of the gross sales, but that's the exception. In this country, the average profit margin is about 5 percent of gross sales. So probably that $2,000 concession you made is the equivalent of making a $40,000 sale. So let me ask you something. How long would you be willing to work to get a $40,000 sale? An hour? Two hours? All day? I've had many sales managers tell me, "For a $40,000 sale, I expect my sales people to work as long as it takes." However fast-paced your business, you're probably willing to spend several hours to make a $40,000 sale. So why are you so willing to make a $2,000 concession at the negotiating table? It has the same impact on the bottom line as a $40,000 sale if you're in a business that generates the typical 5 percent bottom-line profit.

A negotiated dollar is a bottom-line dollar. *You'll never make money faster than you will when you're negotiating!*

So Power Negotiators always respond to a proposal with, "You'll have to do better than that." And when the other person uses it on them, they automatically respond with the Counter Gambit, "Exactly how much better than that do I have to do?"

Key points to remember:

- Respond to a proposal or counter-proposal with the Vise technique: "You'll have to do better than that."

- If it's used on you, respond with the Counter Gambit, "Exactly how much better than that do I have to do?" This will pin the other person down to a specific.

- Concentrate on the dollar amount that's being negotiated. Don't be distracted by the gross amount of the sale and start thinking percentages.

- A negotiated dollar is a bottom-line dollar. Be aware of what your time's worth on an hourly basis.

- You'll never make money faster than you will when you're Power Negotiating.

Chapter 7

Middle Gambits: Handling the Person Who Has No Authority to Decide

One of the most frustrating situations you can run into is trying to negotiate with the person who claims that he or she doesn't have the authority to make a final decision. Unless you realize that this is simply a negotiating tactic that's being used on you, you have the feeling that you'll never get to talk to the real decision maker.

When I was president of the real estate company in California, I used to have salespeople coming in to sell me things all the time: advertising, photocopy machines, computer equipment, and so on. I would always negotiate the very lowest price that I could, using all of these Gambits. Then I would say to them, "This looks fine. I do just have to run it by my board of directors, but I'll get back to you tomorrow with the final okay."

The next day I could get back to them and say, "Boy, are they tough to deal with right now. I felt sure I could sell it to them, but they just won't go along with it unless you can shave another couple of hundred dollars off the price." And I would get it. There was no approval needed by the board of directors, and it never occurred to me that this deception was underhanded. I, and the people with whom you deal see it as well within the rules by which one plays the game of negotiating.

So when the other person says to you that they have to take it to the committee, or the legal department, it's probably not true, but it is a very effective negotiating tactic that they're using on you.

Let's first look at why this is such an effective tactic, and then I'll tell you how to handle it when the other side uses it on you.

Why the other side loves to use Higher Authority

You would think that if you were going out to negotiate something you would want to have the authority to make a decision. At first glance it would seem that you would have more power if you were able to say to the other person, "I have the power to make a deal with you."

So you have a tendency to say to your manager, "Let me handle this. Give me the authority to cut the best possible deal." Power Negotiators know that you put yourself in a weakened negotiating position when you do that. You should always have a higher authority with whom you have to check before you can change your proposal or make a decision. Any negotiator who presents himself as the decision maker has put himself at a severe bargaining disadvantage. You have to put your ego on the back burner to do this, but you'll find it very effective.

The reason that this is so effective is simple. When the other person knows that you have the final authority to make a deal, he knows that he has only to convince you. He doesn't have to work quite as hard to give you the benefits of his proposal if you're the final authority. Once you've given your approval, he knows that he has consummated the deal.

Not so if you are telling him that you have to answer to a higher authority. Whether you have to get approval from region, head office, management, partners, or board of directors, the other person has to do more to convince you. He must make an offer that you can take to your higher authority and get approved. He knows that he must completely win you to his side so that you will want to persuade your higher authority to agree to his proposal.

Higher Authority works much better when the higher authority is a vague entity such as a committee or a board of directors. For example: Have you ever actually met a loan committee at a bank? I never have. Bankers at my seminars have consistently told me that for loans of $500,000 or less, somebody at that bank can make a decision without having to go to the loan committee. However, the loan officer knows that if she said to you, "Your package is on the president's desk," you would say, "Well, let's go talk to the president right now. Let's get it resolved." You can't do that with the vague entity.

So if you use the Higher Authority Gambit, be sure that your higher authority is a vague entity, such as a pricing committee, the people back at corporate, or the marketing committee. If you tell the other person that your manager would have to approve it, what's the first thought that they are going to have? Right. "Then why am I wasting time talking to you? If your manager is the only one who can make a decision, get your manager down here." However, when your higher authority is a vague entity, it appears to be unapproachable. In all the years that I told salespeople that I had to run it by my board of directors, I only once had a salesperson say to me, "When does your board of directors meet? When can I make a presentation to them?"

The use of Higher Authority is a way of putting pressure on people without confrontation. For example, when I used to have the time for it, I invested in apartment buildings and houses. When I first bought the buildings, it felt great to tell the tenants that I owned the property. It was an ego trip for me. But when my portfolio became substantial I realized that it wasn't that much fun anymore, because the tenants assumed that the owner of the property was made of money. So why would it be a problem to replace the carpeting in their unit because of a small cigarette burn, or to replace the drapes because of a small tear? Why would it be a problem if the rent's going to be late this month? In their eyes I was rich. I must be because I had all that property. Why was this upsetting me?

The moment I learned the power of the Higher Authority Gambit and started a company that I called Plaza Properties, many of these problems went away. I became the president of that company that was, to the tenants, a property management company handling their building for a vague group of investors out there somewhere.

Then when they'd say, "We've got this cigarette burn in the carpet, and it needs to be replaced," I'd say, "I don't think I can get the owners to do that for you just yet. I'll tell you what though, you keep the rent coming in on the first of the month, and in about six months I'll go to bat for you with the owners. Let me see what I can do for you with them at that time." That's Good Guy/Bad Guy, an Ending Gambit that I'll teach you later.

If they would say, "Roger, we're not going to have the rent until the 15th of the month," I would say, "Wow, I know exactly how it goes. Sometimes it can get difficult, but unfortunately on this property I just don't have any leeway. The owners of this property told me that if the rent's not in by the fifth of the month I just have to file an eviction notice. So what can we do to get the rent in on time?"

It's a very effective way of pressuring people without confrontation. So I'm sure you can see why the other person loves using it on you. Look at the benefits to the other side when they tell you that they have to get your proposal approved by a committee:

- They can put pressure on you without confrontation: "We'd be wasting our time taking a proposal that high to the committee."

- It unbalances you as a negotiator because it's so frustrating to feel that you're not able to present to the real decision maker.

- By inventing a higher authority, they can set aside the pressure of making a decision. When I was a real estate broker I would teach our agents that before they put buyers in their cars to show them property, they should say to them, "Just to be sure I understand, if we find exactly the right home for you today, is there any reason why you wouldn't make a decision today?" The buyer may have interpreted this as putting pressure on them to decide quickly. What it really accomplished was that it eliminated their right, under the pressure of the closing situation, to delay by inventing a higher authority. If the agent didn't do this, they would very often defer the decision by saying, "We can't decide today because Uncle Harry is helping us with the down payment, and we have to run it by him."

- It sets them up for using the Vise technique: "You'll have to do better than that if you want to get it past the committee."

- It puts you in the position of needing the other person to be on your side if it's to be approved by the committee.

- They can make suggestions to you without implying that it's something to which they'd agree: "If you can come down another 10 percent, you may have a chance of the committee approving it."

- It can be used to force you into a bidding war: "The committee has asked me to get five bids, and it looks as though they're going to take the lowest one."

- The other person can squeeze your price without revealing what you're up against: "The committee is meeting tomorrow to make a final decision. I know they've already gotten some really low bids, so there may not be any point in you submitting, but there's always a chance if you can come in with a super low proposal."

- It sets the other person up to use Good Guy/Bad Guy: "If it were up to me, I'd love to keep on doing business with you, but the bean counters on the committee care only about the lowest price."

At this point you may be thinking, "Roger, I can't use this. I own a small company that manufactures patio furniture, and everybody knows that I own it. They know that I don't have anybody above me with whom I have to check."

Sure you can use it. I own my own company too, but there are decisions that I won't make unless I've checked with the people to whom I've delegated that area of responsibility. If somebody asks me about doing a seminar for their company, I'll say, "Sounds good to me, but I have to check with my marketing people first, fair enough?" So if you own your own company, your higher authority becomes the people in your organization to whom you've delegated authority.

In international negotiations the President is always careful to protect himself by maintaining the position that he cannot make a decision until he has gotten the approval of his negotiators and ultimately the Senate. During the Cold War, the Soviets would go to great lengths to trick our Presidents into waiving their resort to higher authority. Soviet leader Leonid Brezhnev knew that Richard Nixon had a powerful ego and appealing to it could cause him to waive aside his previously stated need to get the approval of his negotiating team. During the 1976 summit meetings, Brezhnev suggested that they stop the meetings early one day because he was tired and wanted to get some sleep. At 10 o'clock that night he called the White House and insisted on meeting with Nixon to discuss something urgent that had come up. Henry Kissinger wrote about it in his book *Years of Upheaval,* saying, "It was gross breach of protocol. It was also a transparent attempt to catch Nixon off guard and with luck separate him from his advisors."

At the Reagan/Gorbachev summit in Reykjavik, Iceland, the balance of world power teetered on the brink of an abyss when the two leaders met alone in the ancient city meeting hall down by the bay. With our State Department officials anxiously gnashing their teeth outside, Ronald Reagan came within a hair's width of agreeing to dismantle all of our nuclear weapons. It was something that would have played right into Soviet hands and would have given them the economic relief that they needed. It may even have been enough to avoid the eventual break up of the Soviet Union. Fortunately, Reagan felt obligated to refer to his advisors and thus averted disaster. So don't worry about the people knowing that you own the company. Even the President of the United States uses the Higher Authority Gambit.

The Counter-Gambits to Higher Authority

So you can see why people love to use the Higher Authority Gambit on you. Fortunately Power Negotiators know how to handle this challenge smoothly and effectively.

Your first approach should be trying to remove the other person's resort to higher authority before the negotiations even start, by getting him to admit that he could make a decision if the proposal was irresistible. This is exactly the same thing that I taught the real estate agents to say to the buyers before putting them in the car, "Let me be sure I understand, if we find exactly the right property for you today, is there any reason why you wouldn't make a decision today?" It's exactly the same thing that the car dealer will do to you when, before he lets you take it for a test drive, he says, "Let me be sure I understand, if you like this car as much as I know you're going to like it, is there any reason why you wouldn't make a decision today?" Because they know that if they don't remove the resort to higher authority up front, then there's a danger that under the pressure of asking for a decision, the other person will invent a higher authority as a delaying tactic. Such as, "Look, I'd love to give you a decision today, but I can't because my father-in-law has to look at the property (or the car)" or, "Uncle Joe is helping us with the down payment and we need to talk to him first."

One of the most frustrating things that you encounter is taking your proposal to the other person and having her say to you, "Well, that's fine. Thanks for bringing me the proposal. I'll talk to our committee (or our attorney or the owners) about it and if it interests us we'll get back to you." Where do you go from there? If you're smart enough to counter the Higher Authority Gambit before you start, you can remove yourself from that dangerous situation.

So before you present your proposal to the other person, before you even get it out of your briefcase, you should casually say, "Let me be sure I understand. If this proposal meets all of your needs (now that's as broad as any statement can be, isn't it?), is there any reason why you wouldn't give me a decision today?"

It's a fairly harmless thing for the other person to agree to because the other person is thinking, "If it meets all of my needs? No problem, there's loads of wriggle room there." However, look at what you've accomplished if you can get them to respond with, "Well, sure if it meets *all* of my needs, I'll give you an okay right now." Look at what you've accomplished:

1. You've eliminated their right to tell you that they want to think it over. If they say that, you say, "Well, let me go over it one more time. There must be something I didn't cover clearly enough because you did indicate to me earlier that you were willing to make a decision today."

2. You've eliminated their right to refer it to a higher authority. You've eliminated their right to say, "I want our legal department to see it, or the purchasing committee to take a look at it."

What if you're not able to remove their resort to higher authority? I'm sure that many times you'll say, "If this proposal meets all of your needs, is there any reason why you wouldn't give me a decision today?" and the other person will reply, "I'm sorry, but on a project of this size, everything has to get approved by the specifications committee. I'll have to refer it to them for a final decision."

Here are the three steps that Power Negotiators take when they're not able to remove the other side's resort to higher authority:

Step number one—appeal to their ego. With a smile on your face you say, "But they always follow your recommendations, don't they?" With some personality styles that's enough of an appeal to his ego that he'll say, "Well, I guess you're right. If I like it, then you can count on it." But often he'll still say, "Yes, they usually follow my recommendations, but I can't give you a decision until I've taken it to the committee."

If you realize that you're dealing with egotistical people, try pre-empting their resort to higher authority early in your presentation, by saying, "Do you think that if you took this to your supervisor, she'd approve it?" Often an ego-driven person will make the mistake of proudly telling you that he doesn't have to get anybody's approval.

The second step is to get their commitment that they'll take it to the committee with a positive recommendation. So you say, "But you will recommend it to them—won't you?" Hopefully, you'll get a response similar to, "Yes, it looks good to me, I'll go to bat for you with them."

Getting the other side's commitment that they're going to recommend it to the higher authority is very important because it's at this point that they may reveal that there really isn't a committee. I remember when I first came to this country in 1962, I went to work for a bank in California, and after nine months I found that I couldn't stand the excitement of working in the banking industry, so I looked around for something else. I applied for a position as a management trainee at Montgomery Ward, the department store chain. Before I could go to work for them, the manager to whom they would assign me for training had to approve. So they sent me up to Napa, California, to interview with the local store manager, Lou Johnson. For whatever reason, the interview didn't go well. I knew that I wasn't going to get the job—probably because I was so new in the country that Lou didn't believe that I was here to stay. I had absolutely no intention of going back to England, but I could understand his concern. Finally he said to me, "Roger, thank you for coming in for the interview. I'll report back to the committee at head office, and you'll be hearing from them."

I said to him, "You will recommend me to them, won't you?" That's step number two, asking for a commitment that they'll go in with a positive recommendation. I saw his mind swinging from one side to the other. He apparently didn't want to recommend me to his committee. On the other hand, he didn't want the confrontation of telling me that he wasn't going to recommend me. His mind went from one side to the other for a few minutes, and finally he said, "Well, yes, I guess I'm willing to give you a try." With this he immediately revealed that there was no higher authority. There was no committee. He was the one making the decision.

So in stage two, Power Negotiators get the other person's commitment that she will go to the higher authority with a positive recommendation. There are only two things that can happen at this point. Either she'll say, yes, she will recommend it to them, or she'll say, no she won't—because ... Either way you've won. Her endorsement would be preferable, of course, but any time you can draw out an objection you should say, "Hallelujah" because objections are buying signals. People are not going to object to your price unless buying from you interests them. If buying from you doesn't interest them, they don't care how high you price your product or service.

For a while I dated a woman who was really into interior decorating. One day she excitedly dragged me down to the Orange County Design Center to show me a couch covered in kidskin. The leather was as soft and as supple as anything I'd ever felt. As I sat there, she said, "Isn't that a wonderful couch?"

I said, "No question about it, this is a wonderful couch."

She said, "And it's only $12,000."

I said, "Isn't that amazing? How can they do it for only $12,000?"

She said, "You don't have a problem with the price?"

"I don't have a problem with the price at all." Why didn't I have a problem with the price? Right. Because I had absolutely no intention of paying $12,000 for a couch, regardless of what they covered it with. Let me ask you this: If buying the couch interested me, would I have a problem with the price? Oh, you better believe I'd have a problem with the price!

Objections are buying signals. We knew in real estate that if we were showing property, and the people were "Ooooing and aaahing" all over the place, if they loved everything about the property, they weren't going to buy. The serious buyers were the ones who were saying, "Well the kitchen's not as big as we like. Hate that wallpaper. We'd probably end up knocking out that wall." Those were the ones who would buy.

If you're in sales, think about it. Have you ever in your life made a big sale where the person loved your price up front? Of course not. All serious buyers complain about the price.

Your biggest problem is not an objection, it's indifference. I would rather they said to you, "I wouldn't buy widgets from your company if you were the last widget vendor in the world, because..." than have them say to you, "I've been using the same source of widgets for 10 years, and he does fine. I'm just not interested in taking the time to talk about making a change." Indifference is your problem, not objections.

Let me prove this to you. Give me the opposite of the word love. If you said hate, think again. As long as they're throwing plates at you, you have something there you can work with. It's indifference that's the opposite of love. When they're saying to you, like Rhett Butler in *Gone With the Wind*, "Quite frankly, my dear, I don't give a damn"— that's when you know the movie is about over. Indifference is your problem, not objections. Objections are buying signals.

So when you say to them, "You will recommend it to them, won't you?" they can either say, yes they will, or no they won't. Either way you've won. Then you can move to step three:

Step Three: The qualified subject-to close. The subject-to close is the same one that your life insurance agent uses on you when he or she says, "Quite frankly, I don't know if we can get this much insurance on someone your age. It would be 'subject to' you passing the physical anyway, so why don't we just write up the paper work 'subject to' you passing the physical?" The life insurance agent knows that if you can fog a mirror during that physical, he or she can get you that insurance. But it doesn't sound as though you're making as important a decision as you really are.

The qualified subject-to close in this instance would be: "Let's just write up the paper work 'subject to' the right of your specifications committee to reject the proposal within a 24-hour period for any specifications reason." Or, "Let's just write up the paper work 'subject to' the right of your legal department to reject the proposal within a 24-hour period for any legal reason."

Notice that you're not saying subject to their acceptance. You're saying subject to their right to decline it for a specific reason. If they're going to refer it to an attorney, it would be a legal reason. If they're going to refer it to their CPA, it would be a tax reason and so on. But try to get it nailed down to a specific reason.

So the three steps to take if you're not able to get the other person to waive his resort to higher authority, are:

1. Appeal to the other person's ego.

2. Get the other person's commitment that he'll recommend it to the higher authority.

3. Use the qualified subject-to close.

What's the counter to the Counter-Gambit? What if someone was trying to remove your resort to higher authority like that? If the other person says to you, "You do have the authority to make a decision, don't you?" you should say, in so many words, "It depends on what you're asking. There's a point at which I have to go to my marketing committee."

Let's say that you're selling aluminum garden sheds to a chain of warehouse hardware centers, and they're asking you to participate in their holiday weekend mailer. Your sales manager has set aside $30,000 for this, but the buyer at the chain is asking you to commit to $35,000. You should shake your head and say, "Wow. That's a lot more than I expected. I'd have to take that to the advertising committee. I'd feel comfortable giving you the go ahead at $25,000, but anything above that and I'd have to hold off until I find out what the committee has to say." Without creating a confrontation, you've put the other person in a position in which he might prefer to go with the $25,000, rather than have the entire mailer on hold until you can get back to him. Note that you've also bracketed his proposal. Assuming that you end up splitting the difference, then you'll still be within budget.

One more thing about the Higher Authority Gambit. What if you've got somebody trying to force you to a decision before you're ready to make it?

Let's say that you're an electrical sub-contractor, and you're negotiating a shopping center bid. The general contractor is pressuring you to commit to price and start date and wants a decision right now. He's saying, "Harry, I love you like a brother, but I'm running a business, not a religion. Give me what I need on this one right now, or I'll have to go with your competitor." (I'll show you later how a person under time pressure tends to become much more flexible.)

How do you handle it? Very simple. You say, "Joe, I'm happy to give you a decision. In fact, I'll give you an answer right now if you want it. But I have to tell you—if you force me to a decision now, the answer has to be no. Tomorrow, after I've had a chance to talk to my estimating people, the answer might be yes. So why don't you wait until tomorrow and see what happens, fair enough?"

You may find yourself in a situation in which escalating authority is being used on you. You think that you have cut a deal, only to find that the head buyer has to approve it and won't. So you sweeten the deal only to find that the vice-president won't give approval. Escalating authority is in my mind outrageously unethical, but you do run into it. I'm sure that you've experienced it when trying to buy a car. After some preliminary negotiation, the salesperson surprises you by immediately accepting your low offer. After getting you to commit to a price (which sets you up psychologically to accept the idea that you will buy that car) the salesperson will say something like, "Well, this looks good. All I have to do is run this by my manager and the car is yours."

You can feel the car keys and ownership certificate in your hands already, and you are sitting there in the closing room congratulating yourself on getting such a good deal, when the salesperson returns with the sales manager. The manager sits down and reviews the price with you. He says, "You know, Fred was a little out of line here." Fred looks properly embarrassed. "This price is almost $500 under our factory invoice cost." He produces an official-looking factory invoice. "Of course, you can't possibly ask us to take a loss on the sale, can you?"

Now you feel embarrassed yourself. You're not sure how to respond. You thought you had a deal, and Fred's higher authority just shot it down. Unaware that the dealer could sell you the car for 5 percent under invoice and still make money because of factory incentives, you fall for the sales manager's appeal to your being a reasonable person and nudge your offer up by $200. Again you think you've bought the car, until the sales manager explains that at this incredibly low price, he needs to get his manager's approval. And so it goes. You find yourself working your way through a battalion of managers, each one able to get you to raise your offer by a small amount.

If you find the other side using escalating authority on you, remember these Counter-Gambits:

- You can play this game also, by bringing in your escalating levels of authority. The other person will quickly catch on to what you're doing and call a truce.

- At each escalating level of authority you should go back to your opening negotiating position. Don't let them salami close you by letting each level of authority cut off another slice of your markup.

- Don't think of it as a firm deal until you have final approval, and the ink is dry on the contract. If you start mentally spending the profits or driving the car, you'll be too emotionally involved in the sale to walk away.

- Above all, don't get so frustrated that you lose your temper with them and walk away from what could be a profitable transaction for everybody. Sure the tactic is unfair and unethical, but this is a business and not a religion, right? You're there to grease the wheels of commerce, not to convert the sinners.

Being able to use and handle the resort to higher authority is critical to you when you're Power Negotiating. Always maintain your own resort to higher authority. Always try to remove the other person's resort to a higher authority.

Key points to remember:

- Don't let the other side know that you have the authority to make a decision.
- Your higher authority should be a vague entity, not an individual.
- Even if you own your company you can still use this by referring down through your organization.
- Leave your ego at home when you're negotiating. Don't let the other person trick you into admitting that you have authority.
- Attempt to get the other person to admit that he could approve your proposal if it meets all of his needs. If that fails, go through the three counter gambits:
  - Appeal to his ego.
  - Get his commitment that he'll recommend to his higher authority.
  - Go to a qualified subject-to close.
- If they are forcing you to make a decision before you're ready to do so, offer to decide but let them know that the answer will be no, unless they give you time to check with your people.
- If they're using escalating authority on you, revert to your opening position at each level and introduce your own levels of escalating authority.

Chapter 8

Middle Gambits: The Declining Value of Services

Here's something that you can count on when dealing with another person: Any concession you make to that person will quickly lose its value. The value of any material object you buy may go up in value over the years, but the value of services always appears to decline rapidly after you have performed those services.

Power Negotiators know that any time you make a concession to the other side in a negotiation you should ask for a reciprocal concession right away. The favor that you did the other side loses value very quickly. Two hours from now the value of it will have diminished rapidly.

Real estate salespeople are very familiar with the principle of the declining value of services. When a seller has a problem getting rid of a property, and the real estate salesperson offers to solve that problem for a 6 percent listing fee, it doesn't sound as though it's an enormous amount of money. However, the minute the realtor has performed the service by finding the buyer, then suddenly that 6 percent starts to sound like a tremendous amount of money. "Six percent. That's $12,000," the seller is saying. "For what? What did she do? All she did was put it in a multiple listing service." A realtor did much more than that to market the property and negotiate the contract, but remember the principle: The value of a service always appears to diminish rapidly after you have performed that service.

I'm sure you've experienced that, haven't you? A person with whom you do a small amount of business has called you. He's in a state of panic because the supplier from whom they get the bulk of their business has let them down on a shipment. Now their entire assembly line has to shut down tomorrow unless you can work miracles and get a shipment to them first thing in the morning. Sound familiar? So you work all day and through the night, rescheduling shipments all over the place. Against all odds, you're able to get a shipment there just in time for the assembly line to keep operating. You even show up at their plant and personally supervise the unloading of the shipment and the buyer loves you for it. He comes down to the dock, where you are triumphantly wiping the dirt off your hands, and says, "I can't believe you were able to do that for me. That is unbelievable service. You are absolutely incredible. Love you, love you, love you."

So you say, "Happy to do it for you, Joe. That's the kind of service we can give when we have to. Don't you think it's time we looked at my company being your main supplier?"

He replies, "That does sound good, but I don't have time to talk about it now because I've got to get over to the assembly line and be sure that it's running smoothly. Come to my office Monday morning at 10 o'clock and we'll go over it. Better yet, come by at noon and I'll buy you lunch. I really appreciate what you did for me. You are fantastic. Love you, love you, love you."

So all weekend long, you think to yourself, "Boy. Have I got this one made. Does he owe me." Monday rolls around, however, and negotiating with him is just as hard as ever. What went wrong? The declining value of services came into play. The value of a service always appears to decline rapidly after you have performed the service.

If you make a concession during a negotiation, get a reciprocal concession right away. Don't wait. Don't be sitting there thinking that because you did them a favor, they owe you and that they will make it up to you later. With all the goodwill in the world, the value of what you did goes down rapidly in their mind.

For the same reason, consultants know that you should always negotiate your fee up front, not afterward.

Plumbers know this, don't they? They know that the time to negotiate with you is before they do the work, not after. I had a plumber out to the house. After looking at the problem he slowly shook his head and said, "Mr. Dawson, I have identified the problem, and I can fix it for you. It will cost you $150."

I said, "Fine, go ahead."

You know how long it took him to do the work? Five minutes. I said, "Now wait a minute. You're going to charge me $150 for five minutes' work? I'm a nationally known speaker, and I don't make that kind of money."

He replied, "I didn't make that kind of money either—when I was a nationally known speaker."

Key points to remember:

- The value of a material object may go up, but the value of services always appears to go down.
- Don't make a concession and trust that the other side will make it up to you later.
- Negotiate your fee before you do the work.

Chapter 9

Middle Gambits: Never Offer to Split the Difference

In this country we have a tremendous sense of fair play. Our sense of fair play dictates to us that if both sides give equally, then that's fair. If Fred puts his home up for sale at $200,000, Susan makes an offer at $190,000, and both Fred and Susan are eager to compromise, both of them tend to be thinking, "If we settled at $195,000 that would be fair, because we both gave equally." Maybe it's fair and maybe it isn't. It depends on the opening negotiating positions that Fred and Susan took. If the house is really worth $190,000 and Fred was holding to his over-inflated price only to take advantage of Susan having fallen in love with his house, then it's not fair. If the house is worth $200,000 and Susan is willing to pay that, but is taking advantage of Fred's financial problems, then it isn't fair. So don't fall into the trap of thinking that splitting the difference is the fair thing to do when you can't resolve a difference in price with the other side.

With that misconception out of the way, let me point out that Power Negotiators know that splitting the difference does not mean splitting it down the middle. Just split the difference twice and the split becomes 75 percent/ 25 percent; furthermore you may be able to get the other side to split the difference three or more times. I once negotiated with a bank that had a blanket encumbrance over several properties that I owned. I had sold one property out from under the blanket, and our contract entitled them to a $32,000 paydown of the loan. I offered them $28,000. I got them to offer to split the difference at $30,000. Over a period of weeks until this four-unit building closed, I was able to get them to offer to split the difference again at $29,000; and at $28,500 and finally they agreed to $28,250.

Here's how this Gambit works:

The first thing to remember is that you should never offer to split the difference yourself, but always encourage the other person to offer to split the difference.

Let's say that you're a building contractor. You have been working on getting a remodeling job that you bid at $86,000 and for which they offered $75,000. You've been negotiating for a while, during which time you've been able to get the owners of the property up to $80,000 and you've come down to $84,000 with your proposal. Where do you go from there? You have a strong feeling that if you offered to split the difference they would agree to do so, which would mean agreeing at $82,000.

Instead of offering to split the difference, here's what you should do. You should say, "Well, I guess this is just not going to fly. It seems like such a shame though, when we've both spent so much time working on this proposal." (I'll teach you later about how people become more flexible in relationship to how long they've been negotiating.) "We've spent so much time on this proposal, and we've come so close to a price with which we could both live. It seems like a shame that it's all going to collapse, when we're only $4,000 apart."

If you keep stressing the time that you've spent on it and the small amount of money that you're apart on the price, eventually the other people will say, "Look, why don't we split the difference."

You act a little dumb and say, "Let's see, splitting the difference, what would that mean? I'm at $84,000 and you're at $80,000. What you're telling me is you'd come up to $82,000? Is that what I hear you saying?"

"Well, yes," they say. "If you'll come down to $82,000, then we'll settle for that." In doing this you have immediately shifted the negotiating range from $80,000 to $84,000. The negotiating range is now $82,000–$84,000, and you have yet to concede a dime.

So you say, "$82,000 sounds a lot better than $80,000. Tell you what, let me talk to my partners," (or whatever other higher authority you've set up) "and see how they feel about it. I'll tell them you came up to $82,000, and we'll see if we can't put it together now. I'll get back to you tomorrow."

The next day you get back to them and you say, "Wow, are my partners tough to deal with right now. I felt sure that I could get them to go along with $82,000, but we spent two hours last night going over the figures again, and they insist that we'll lose money if we go a penny below $84,000. But good golly. We're only $2,000 apart on this job now. Surely, we're not going to let it all fall apart when we're only $2,000 apart?"

If you keep that up long enough, eventually they'll offer to split the difference again.

If you are able to get them to split the difference again, this Gambit has made you an extra $1,000 of bottom-line profit. However, even if you can't get them to split the difference again and you end up at the same $82,000 that you would have done if *you* had offered to split the difference, something very significant happened here. What was the significant thing that happened?

Right. They think they won because you got them to propose splitting the difference at $82,000. Then you got your partners to reluctantly agree to a proposal that the other side made. If you had suggested splitting the difference, then you would have been putting a proposal on the table and forcing them to agree to a proposal that you had made.

That may seem like a very subtle thing to you, but it's very significant in terms of who felt they won and who felt they lost. Remember, the essence of Power Negotiating is to always leave the other side thinking that he or she won.

So the rule is never offer to split the difference, but always encourage the other person to offer to split the difference.

Key points to remember:

- Don't fall into the trap of thinking that splitting the difference is the fair thing to do.
- Splitting the difference doesn't mean down the middle because you can do it more than once.
- Never offer to split the difference yourself; instead encourage the other person to offer to split the difference.
- By getting them to offer to split the difference, you put them in a position of suggesting the compromise. Then you can reluctantly agree to their proposal, making them feel that they won.

Chapter 10

Middle Gambits: Handling Impasses

In extended negotiations you will frequently encounter impasses, stalemates, and deadlocks in your negotiations with people. Here's how I define the three terms:

- Impasse. You are in complete disagreement on one issue, and it threatens the negotiations.
- Stalemate. Both sides are still talking, but seem unable to make any progress toward a solution.
- Deadlock. The lack of progress has frustrated both sides so much that they see no point in talking to each other any more.

It's easy for an inexperienced negotiator to confuse an impasse with a deadlock:

- You manufacture auto parts, and the purchasing agent at the automobile manufacturer in Detroit says, "You'll have to cut your price by 2 percent a year for the next 5 years, or we'll have to re-source." You know it's impossible to do that and still make a profit, so it's easy to think you've deadlocked when you've really reached only an impasse.
- You're a contractor, and a building owner says to you, "I'd love to do business with you, but you charge too much. I have three other bids that are way below what you're asking." Your firm policy is that you won't participate in bid shopping, so it's easy to think you've deadlocked when you've really reached only an impasse.

- You own a retail store, and a customer is yelling at you, "I don't want to talk about it. Take it back and give us credit, or the next person you hear from will be my attorney!" You know that the item would work properly if the customer would permit you to teach them how to use it. However, they're so upset that you think you've reached a deadlock, when you've really reached only an impasse.

- You manufacture bath fixtures, and the president of a plumbing supply company in New Jersey pokes his cigar in your face and growls, "Let me tell you the facts of life, buddy boy. Your competition will give me 90 days credit, so if you won't do that, we don't have anything to talk about." You know that your company hasn't made an exception to their 30 days net rule in the 72 years they've been in business, so it's easy to think you've deadlocked, when you've really reached only an impasse.

All of these may sound like deadlocks to the inexperienced negotiator, but to the Power Negotiator they're only impasses. There's a very easy Gambit that you can use whenever you reach an impasse. It's called the Set Aside Gambit.

We used it very effectively with the Israelis right after the 1973 Arab-Israeli War. We went to them and said, "Please at least sit down and talk to the Egyptians. Because if you don't, somebody's going to start World War III around here." They threw us what we could easily have perceived to be a deadlock—the killer in the negotiations. They said, "Well, we might be willing to talk to them, but we want you to understand up front—there's one thing that is absolutely non-negotiable. We will never, ever withdraw from the Sinai Desert. We took it during the 1967 war, that's where our oil wells are. We'll never, ever withdraw from the Sinai."

Haven't you had someone present something that forcefully with you? "We might talk about doing business with you, but we would absolutely never, ever go along with these payment terms. If that's what you want, forget it. You get paid in 90 days just like all of our other suppliers. If you can live with that, we'll talk. If you can't, we don't have anything to talk about."

With the Israelis, we were smart enough to use the Set Aside Gambit. It's very, very effective. It will amaze you how this Gambit will resolve what appears to be a major issue when you're negotiating with people. We said, "That's fine. We understand exactly how you feel about the Sinai. That's where your oil fields are. You took it during the 1967 war. However, let's just set that issue aside for a moment. Let's talk about some of the other issues that are important to you."

Although we didn't reveal it to the Israelis, we also knew that the Egyptians were just as adamant about getting the Sinai back as the Israelis were about not relinquishing it. By using the Set Aside Gambit, however, we were able to gain momentum as we settled minor issues. Then when we returned to the issue of withdrawing from the Sinai, it was much more resolvable than it appeared to be at first. As you know, we eventually did see the Israelis withdrawing from the Sinai—although they assured us initially that it was the last thing in the world they would ever do.

In 1991, Secretary of State James Baker was again faced with an intransigent Israel as he tried to get Israel to the peace table with the PLO. The Israelis initial position was that any settlement that came out of the talks would require them to give up some territory so the Israelis didn't want to give credence to that idea by attending any talks with their enemy. James Baker was a good enough negotiator to know that he should set aside the impasse issue and create momentum on minor issues. So he said in effect, "Fine, we realize that you're not ready for peace talks yet, but let's just set that issue aside for a moment. If we did have peace talks, where should we have them? Would it make more sense to do it in Washington, or the Middle East, or perhaps a neutral city such as Madrid?" We inched the negotiations forward by talking about that for a while. Then we raised the issue of PLO representation at the talks. If the PLO were represented at the talks, who would be acceptable representatives from the PLO? After we had created momentum on these minor issues, we found it much easier to get the Israelis to agree to meet with, and finally recognize, the Palestine Liberation Organization.

The Set Aside Gambit is what you should use when you're talking to a buyer and she says to you, "We might be interested in talking to you, but we have to have a prototype from you by the first of the month for our annual sales meeting in New Orleans. If you can't move that quickly, let's not waste time even talking about it."

Even if it's virtually impossible for you to move that quickly, you still use the Set Aside Gambit, "I understand exactly how important that is to you, but let's just set that aside for a minute and talk about the other issues. Tell me about the specs on the job. Do you require us to use union labor? What kind of payment terms are we talking about?"

When you use the Set Aside Gambit, you resolve many of the little issues first to establish some momentum in the negotiation before leading up to the big issues. As I'll teach you in Chapter 73 on win-win negotiating, don't narrow it down to just one issue (with only one issue on the table, there has to be a winner and there has to be loser). By resolving the little issues first, you create momentum that will make the big issues much easier to resolve. Inexperienced negotiators always seem to think that you need to resolve the big issues first. "If we can't get together on the major things like price and terms why waste much time talking to them about the little issues?" Power Negotiators understand the other side will become much more flexible after you've reached agreement on the small issues.

Key points to remember:

- Don't confuse an impasse with a deadlock. True deadlocks are very rare, so you've probably reached only an impasse.
- Handle an impasse with the Set Aside Gambit: "Let's just set that aside for a moment and talk about some of the other issues, may we?"
- Create momentum by resolving minor issues first, but don't narrow the negotiation down to only one issue. For more on this see Chapter 73 on win-win negotiating.

Chapter 11

Middle Gambits: Handling Stalemates

Somewhere between an impasse and a deadlock you will sometimes encounter a stalemate. That's when both sides are still talking, but seem unable to make any progress toward a solution.

Being in a stalemate is similar to being "in irons," which is a sailing expression meaning that the boat has stalled with its head into the wind. A boat will not sail directly into the wind. It will sail almost into the wind, but it won't sail directly into it. To sail into the wind you must sail about 25 degrees off course to starboard and then tack across the wind 25 degrees to port. It's hard work to keep resetting the sails that way, but eventually you'll get where you want to go. To tack across the wind you must keep the bow of the boat moving smoothly through the wind. If you hesistate you can get stuck with your bow into the wind. If you lose momentum as you tack, there is not enough wind to move the bow of the boat around. When a skipper is "in irons" he or she has to do something to correct the problem. Perhaps reset the sails or waggle the tiller or wheel or do anything that will regain momentum. Similarly, when negotiations stall you must change the dynamics to reestablish momentum. Here are some things that you can do, other than changing the monetary amount involved:

- Change the people in the negotiating team. A favorite expression that attorneys use is, "I have to be in court this afternoon, so my partner Charlie will be taking my place." The court may be a tennis court, but it's a tactful way of changing the team.

- Remove a member who may have irritated the other side. A sophisticated negotiator won't take offense at being asked to leave because he or she may have played a valuable role as a Bad Guy. Now it's time to alternate the pressure on the other side by making the concession of removing them from your team.

- Change the venue by suggesting that you continue the discussion over lunch or dinner.

- Ease the tension by talking about their hobbies or a piece of gossip that's in the news or by telling a funny story.

- Explore the possibility of a change in finances, such as extended credit, a reduced deposit with the order, or restructured payments. Any of these may be enough to change the dynamics and move you out of the stalemate. Remember that the other side may be reluctant to raise these issues for fear of appearing to be in poor financial condition.

- Discuss methods of sharing the risk with the other side. Taking on a commitment that may turn sour might concern them. Try suggesting that one year from now you'll take back any unused inventory that is in good condition for a 20% restocking fee. Perhaps a weasel clause in the contract that applies should the market change will assuage their fears.

- Try changing the ambiance in the negotiating room. If the negotiations have been low key with an emphasis on win-win, try becoming more competitive. If the negotiations have been hard driving, try switching to more of a win-win mode.

- Suggest a change in specifications, packaging, or delivery method to see if this shift will make the people think more positively.

- It may be possible to get them to overlook any difference of opinion provided you agree to a method of arbitrating any dispute should it become a problem in the future.

When a sailboat is "in irons" the skipper may know exactly how to reset the sails, but sometimes he simply has to try different things to see what works. If negotiations stalemate, you have to try different things to see what will regain momentum for you. It reminds me of something I was told many years ago about a road construction crew in India busily digging a tunnel through the side of a hill. It seemed like a very primitive operation; there were thousands of workers armed with picks and shovels, and it was amazing that they would even attempt such an undertaking with nothing but laborers.

A tourist walked up to the foreman and asked him, "How in the world do you go about this?"

"It's very simple, really," he answered. "I blow a whistle and all the workers on this side start digging through the hill. On the other side of the hill we have another crew of workers and we tell them to start digging through the hill toward us. If the two crews meet in the middle, then we have a tunnel. If they don't meet, then we have two tunnels."

Handling a stalemate is like that. Something will happen when you change the dynamics in an attempt to create momentum, but you're never sure what it will be.

Key points to remember:

- Be aware of the difference between an impasse, a stalemate, and a deadlock. In a stalemate both sides still want to find a solution, but neither can see a way to move forward.

- The response to a stalemate should be to change the dynamics of the negotiation by altering one of the elements.

Chapter 12

Middle Gambits: Handling Deadlocks

In the previous two chapters, I've shown you how to handle the first two levels of problems that can occur, the impasse and the stalemate. If things get any worse, you may reach a deadlock, something that I define as, "Both sides are so frustrated with the lack of progress that they see no point in talking to each other any more."

Deadlocks are rare, but if you do reach one, the *only* way to resolve it is to bring in a third party—someone who will act as a mediator or arbitrator. There is a major difference between an arbitrator and a mediator. In the case of an arbitrator, both sides agree before the process starts that they will abide by the decision of the arbitrator. If a union critical to the public's welfare goes on strike, such as the union of transportation or sanitation workers, the federal government will eventually insist that an arbitrator be appointed, and both sides will have to settle for the solution that the arbitrator thinks is fair. A mediator doesn't have that kind of power. A mediator is simply someone brought in to facilitate a solution. He or she simply acts as a catalyst, using his or her skills to seek a solution that both sides will accept as reasonable.

Inexperienced negotiators are reluctant to bring in a mediator because they see their inability to resolve a problem as being a failure on their part. "I don't want to ask my sales manager for help because he'll think of me as a poor negotiator," is what is running through their minds. Power Negotiators know that there are many reasons why a third party can resolve a problem, other than that they are better negotiators. Here are some of the reasons:

- A mediator can go to both sides separately and suggest to each that they take a more reasonable position. An arbitrator can even force this by telling both sides to bring in a final solution within 24 hours, telling them that he will pick the more reasonable of the two proposals. This forces each side to be more reasonable because they each fear that the other will present a more attractive plan. It becomes in effect, a closed-bid auction of ideas.

* A mediator listens better to each side because she's not having to filter the information through a prejudiced position. Because she has less at stake, she may well hear something to which an opponent would be deaf.

* A mediator can persuade better because both sides perceive him as having less to gain. As I pointed out in my book *Secrets of Power Persuasion*, you lose much of your ability to persuade if the listener sees you as having something to gain. For example, a buyer will believe a salesperson much more readily if he knows that the salesperson is not on commission.

* When negotiating directly, you tend to assume that if the other side floats a trial balloon, they would be willing to agree to what they're suggesting. A mediator can go to each side and propose a solution without implying that the other side is willing to comply.

* An arbitrator can get both sides back to the negotiating table without having to promise concessions.

An arbitrator or a mediator can be effective only if both sides see them as reasonably neutral. Sometimes you must go to great lengths to assure this perception. Each side may insist on a team of three arbitrators, so each side selects one and those two must agree on a third. They should all be members of the American Arbitration Association to assure that they adhere to the highest ethical standards. The association has strict rules for the way their members can arbitrate and still stay within the law.

You probably won't be going to that much trouble. You'll be using a mediator, not an arbitrator, and chances are that your mediator will be your manager or someone else from your organization. If you bring in your manager to resolve a dispute with a customer, what is the chance that your customer will perceive him or her as neutral? Somewhere between nil and zero, right? So your manager must do something to create a feeling of neutrality in the other person's mind. The way to do this is for your manager to make a small concession to the other person early in the mediation process.

Your manager comes in and, even if he's fully aware of the problem, says, "I haven't really had a chance to get into this yet. Why don't you both explain your position and let me see if I can come up with a solution that you can both live with?" The terminology is important here. By asking both sides to explain their positions, he is projecting that he comes to the process without prejudice. Also note that he's avoiding the use of "we" when he refers to you.

Having patiently heard both sides out, he should then turn to you and say, "Are you being fair pushing that? Perhaps you could give a little on the terms (or some other detail)? Could you live with 60 days?" Don't feel that your manager is failing to support you. What's he's trying to do is position himself as neutral in your customer's eyes.

I once took part in a negotiation for the sale of one company to another. We had two teams of attorneys that were working trying to resolve the many differences. After weeks of negotiating we appeared to reach an absolute deadlock. One of the attorneys resolved the deadlock when he was smart enough to say, "This is obviously going to take more time than I thought. I have to be in court this afternoon, but I'll tell you what: My partner Joe will be in after lunch to take my place."

So Joe came in after lunch. He was completely new to the situation. Each side had to explain where they were in the negotiations. Joe took great pains to position himself as neutral. He did this by saying to his side, "Are we being fair to them, by pushing that point? Maybe we could give a little bit there."

That caused the other person to think, "Well, he seems much more reasonable than the last person. Maybe we can find a way past this after all." Having positioned himself as neutral, Joe was able to find common ground in the negotiations that got us past the deadlock.

So, anytime you reach a deadlock in the negotiations, bring in a third party who's perceived as reasonably neutral by the other parties.

That's what President Carter was able to do at Camp David. It took years and years for the United States to position itself as neutral with Egypt. They always saw us as the enemy and the Soviet Union as their friends. Henry Kissinger saw a remarkable opportunity to change all that, and he jumped at it. He was in Anwar El Sadat's office at a time when Sadat was desperately trying to get the Soviets to clear the Suez Canal, which was shut down by wrecks of ships sunk during the war.

The Soviets were probably willing to do that, but their bureaucracy was so great that they couldn't move fast enough. Kissinger said, "Would you like us to help you?" An astonished Sadat said, "You would do that?" Kissinger picked up the phone in Sadat's office and called President Nixon in the White House. Within days, the sixth fleet was on its way to the Suez. With this one act, Kissinger and Nixon started the process of positioning us as reasonably neutral between the Israelis and the Egyptians—an act that eventually led to President Carter's success at Camp David.

Don't assume that you must avoid impasses, stalemates, and deadlocks at all cost. An experienced negotiator can use them as tools to pressure the other side. Once your mindset is that a deadlock is unthinkable, it means that you're no longer willing to walk away and you have surrendered your most powerful pressure point, as you'll see in Chapter 17.

Key points to remember:

- The only way to resolve a true deadlock is by bringing in a third party.

- The third party can act as a mediator or an arbitrator. Mediators can only facilitate a solution, but both sides agree up front that they will abide by an arbitrator's final decision.

- Don't see having to bring in a third person as a failure on your part. There are many reasons why third parties can reach a solution that the parties to the negotiation couldn't reach alone.

- The third party must be seen as neutral by both sides.

- If she is not seen as neutral, she should position herself as such by making a small concession to the other side early in the negotiation.

- Keep an open mind about the possibility of a deadlock. You can only develop your full power as a Power Negotiator if you're willing to walk away. By refusing to consider a deadlock, you're giving away a valuable pressure point.

Chapter 13

Middle Gambits:
Always Ask for a Trade-Off

The Trade-Off Gambit tells you that anytime the other side asks you for a concession in the negotiations, you should automatically ask for something in return. The first time you use this Gambit, you'll get back the money you invested in this book many times over. From then on using it will earn you thousands of dollars every year. Let's take a look at a couple of ways of using the Trade-Off Gambit:

- Let's say that you have sold your house, and the buyers ask you if they could move some of their furniture into the garage three days before closing. Although you wouldn't want to let them move into the house before closing, you see an advantage in letting them use the garage. It will get them emotionally involved and far less likely to create problems for you at closing. So you're almost eager to make the concession, but I want you to remember the rule: However small the concession they're asking you for, always ask for something in return. Say to them, "Let me check with my family (vague higher authority) and see how they feel about that; but let me ask you this: If we do that for you, what will you do for us?"

- Perhaps you sell fork lifts and you've sold a large order to a warehouse-style hardware store. They've requested delivery on August 15th—30 days ahead of their grand opening. Then the operations manager for the chain calls you and says, "We're running ahead of schedule on the store construction. We're thinking of moving up the store opening to take in the Labor Day weekend. Is there any way you could move up delivery of those fork lifts to next Wednesday?" You may be thinking, "That's great. They're sitting in our local warehouse ready to go, so I'd much rather move up the shipment and get paid sooner. We'll deliver them tomorrow if you want them." Even though your initial inclination is to say, "That's fine," I still want you to use the Trade-Off Gambit. I want you to say, "Quite frankly I don't know whether we can get them there that soon. I'll have to check with my scheduling people," (note the use of a vague higher authority) "and see what they say about it. But let me ask you this, if we can do that for you, what can you do for us?"

One of three things is going to happen when you ask for something in return:

1. *You might just get something.* The buyers of your house may be willing to increase the deposit, buy your patio furniture, or give your dog a good home. The hardware store owners may just have been thinking, "Boy, have we got a problem here. What can we give them as an incentive to get them to move this shipment up?" So they may just concede something to you. They may just say, "I'll tell accounting to cut the check for you today." Or "Take care of this for me, and I'll use you again for the store that we're opening in Chicago in December."

2. *By asking for something in return, you elevate the value of the concession.* When you're negotiating, why give anything away? Always make a big deal out of it. You may need that later on. Later you may be doing the walk through with the buyers of the house, and they've found a light switch that doesn't work. You're able to say, "Do you know how it inconvenienced us to let you move your furniture into the garage? We did that for you, and now I want you to overlook this small problem." Later on you may need to be able to go to the people at the hardware store and say, "Do you remember last August when you needed me to move that shipment up for you? You know how hard I had to talk to my people to get them to re-schedule all our shipments? We did that for you, so don't make me wait for our money. Cut me the check today, won't you?" When you elevate the value of the concession, you set it up for a trade-off later on.

3. *It stops the grinding away process.* This is the key reason why you should always use the Trade-Off Gambit. If they know that every time they ask you for something, you're going to ask for something in return, then it stops them constantly coming back for more. I can't tell you how many times a student of mine has come up to me at seminar, or called my office and said to me, "Roger, can you help me

with this? I thought I had a sweetheart of a deal put together. I didn't think that I would have any problems at all with this one. But in the very early stages they asked me for a small concession. I was so happy to have their business that I told them, 'Sure, we can do that.' A week later they called me for another small concession and I said: 'All right, I guess I can do that too.' Ever since then, it's been one darn thing after another. Now it looks as though the whole thing is going to fall apart on me." He should have known up front that when the other person asked him for that first small concession, he should have asked for something in return. "If we can do that for you, what can you do for us?"

I trained the top 50 salespeople at a Fortune 500 company that manufactures office equipment. They have what they call a Key Account Division that negotiates their largest accounts with their biggest customers. These people are heavy hitters. A salesperson at the seminar had just made a $43 million sale to an aircraft manufacturer. (That's not a record. When I trained people at a huge computer manufacturer's training headquarters, a salesperson in the audience had just closed a $3 billion sale—and he was in my seminar taking notes!) This Key Account Division had its own vice-president, and he came up to me afterward to tell me, "Roger, that thing you told us about trading-off was the most valuable lesson I've ever learned in any seminar. I've been coming to seminars like this for years and thought that I'd heard it all, but I'd never been taught what a mistake it is to make a concession without asking for something in return. That's going to save us hundreds of thousands of dollars in the future."

Jack Wilson, who produced my video training tapes, told me that soon after I taught him this Gambit, he used it to save several thousand dollars. A television studio called him and told him that one of their camera operators was sick. Would Jack mind if they called one of the camera operators that Jack had under contract and ask him if he could fill in? It was really just a courtesy call. Something that Jack would have said, "No problem," to in the past. However, this time he said, "If I do that for you, what will you do for me?" To his surprise, they said, "Tell you what. The next time you use our studio, if you run overtime, we'll waive the overtime charge." They had just conceded several thousand dollars to Jack, on something that he never would have asked for in the past.

Please use these Gambits word for word the way that I'm teaching them to you. If you change even a word, it can dramatically change the effect. If, for example, you change this from, "If we can do that for you, what can you do for us?" to "If we do that for you, you will have to do this for us," you have become confrontational. You've become confrontational at a very sensitive point in the negotiations—when the other side is under pressure and is asking you for a favor. Of course, you're tempted to take advantage of this situation and ask for something specific in return. Don't do it. It could cause the negotiation to blow up in your face.

When you ask what they will give you in return, they may say, "Not a darn thing," or "You get to keep our business, that's what you get." That's fine, because you had everything to gain by asking and you haven't lost anything. If necessary, you can always revert to a position of insisting on a trade-off by saying, "I don't think I can get my people to agree to that unless you're prepared to accept a charge for expedited shipping" or "unless you're willing to move up the payment date."

Key points to remember:

- When asked for a small concession by the other side, always ask for something in return.
- Use this expression: "If we can do that for you, what can you do for us?"
- You may just get something in return.
- It elevates the value of the concession so that you can use it as a trade-off later on.
- Most important, it stops the grinding away process.
- Don't change the wording and ask for something specific in return because it's too confrontational.

Chapter 14

Ending Gambits: Good Guy/Bad Guy

Good Guy/Bad Guy is one of the best known negotiating gambits. Charles Dickens first wrote about it in his book *Great Expectations*. In the opening scene of the story, the young hero Pip is in the graveyard when out of the sinister mist comes a large, very frightening man. This man is a convict, and he has chains around his legs. He asks Pip to go into the village and bring back food and a file, so he can remove the chains. The convict has a dilemma, however. He wants to scare the child into doing as he's asked, yet he mustn't put so much pressure on Pip that he'll be frozen in place or bolt into town to tell the policeman.

The solution to the convict's problem is to use the Good Guy/Bad Guy Gambit. Taking some liberty with the original work, what the convict says in effect, is: "You know, Pip, I like you and I would never do anything to hurt you. But I have to tell you that waiting out here in the mist is a friend of mine and he can be violent and I'm the only one who can control him. If I don't get these chains off—if you don't help me get them off—then my friend might come after you. So you have to help me. Do you understand?" Good Guy/Bad Guy is a very effective way of putting pressure on people, without confrontation.

I'm sure you've seen Good Guy/Bad Guy used in the old police movies. Officers bring a suspect into the police station for questioning, and the first detective to interrogate him is a rough, tough, mean-looking guy. He threatens the suspect with all kinds of things that they're going to do to him. Then he's mysteriously called away to take a phone call, and the second detective, who's brought in to look after the prisoner while the first detective is away, is the warmest, nicest guy in the entire world. He sits down and makes friends with the prisoner. He gives him a cigarette and says, "Listen kid, it's really not as bad as all that. I've kind of taken a liking to you. I know the ropes around here. Why don't you let me see what I can do for you?" It's a real temptation to think that the Good Guy's on your side when, of course, he really isn't.

Then the Good Guy would go ahead and close on what salespeople would recognize as a minor point close. "All I think the detectives really need to know," he tells the prisoner, "is where did you buy the gun?" What he really wants to know is, "Where did you hide the body?"

Starting out with a minor point like that and then working up from there works very well, doesn't it? The car salesperson says to you, "If you did invest in this car would you get the blue or the gray?" "Would you want the vinyl upholstery or the leather?" Little decisions lead to big ones. The real estate salesperson who says, "If you did invest in this home, how would you arrange the furniture in the living room?" Or, "Which of these bedrooms would be the nursery for your new baby?" Little decisions grow to big decisions.

People use Good Guy/Bad Guy on you much more than you might believe. Look out for it anytime you find yourself dealing with two people. Chances are you'll see it being used on you, in one form or another.

For example, you may sell corporate health insurance plans for an HMO and have made an appointment to meet with the Vice-President of Human Resources at a company that manufactures lawn mowers. When the secretary leads you in to meet with the vice president, you find to your surprise that the president of the company wants to sit in and listen in on your presentation.

That's negotiating two on one, which is not good, but you go ahead and everything appears to be going along fine. You feel that you have a good chance of closing the sale until the president suddenly starts getting irritated. Eventually he says to his vice president, "Look, I don't think these people are interested in making a serious proposal to us. I'm sorry, but I've got things to do." Then he storms out of the room.

This really shakes you up if you're not used to negotiating. Then the vice-president says, "Wow. Sometimes he gets that way, but I really like the plan that you presented, and I think we can still work this out. If you could be a little more flexible on your price, then I think we can still put it together. Tell you what—why don't you let me see what I can do for you with him?"

If you don't realize what they're doing to you, you'll hear yourself say something like, "What do you think the president would agree to?" Then it won't be long before you'll have the vice-president negotiating for you—and he or she is not even on your side.

If you think I'm exaggerating on this one, consider this: Haven't you, at one time or another, said to a car salesperson, "What do you think you could get your sales manager to agree to?" As if the salesperson is on your side, not on theirs? Haven't we all at one time been buying real estate and have found the property we want to buy, so we say to the agent that has been helping us find the property, "What do you think the sellers would take?" Let me ask you something. Who is your agent working for? Who is paying her? It's not you, is it? She is working for the seller, yet she has effectively played Good Guy/Bad Guy with you. So look out for it, because you run into it a lot.

When I was the president of a large real estate company in California, we had one branch that consistently lost money. The branch had been open about a year, but we had signed a three-year lease on the premises, which committed us to try to make it work for two more years. No matter how hard I tried, however, I couldn't find a way to either increase the income or decrease the expenses of the office. The biggest problem was the lease. We were paying $1,700 a month, and that one expense was killing our profit.

I called the landlord and explained my problem to him and tried to get him to reduce the rent to $1,400 a month, a figure at which we could have eked out a profit. He said, "You have two more years on that lease, and you're just going to have to live with it." I used every other Gambit I knew, but nothing would budge him. It looked as though I would just have to accept the situation.

Finally, I tried the Good Guy/Bad Guy Gambit combined with a great deal of time pressure. Several weeks later I called him up at 5:50 in the evening. "About that lease," I said. "A problem has come up here. I want you to know that I really agree with your position. I signed a three-year lease, there are more than two years left on it, and there isn't any question that we should live with it. But here's the problem. I have to go in to my board of directors meeting in half an hour, and they're going to ask me if you've been willing to reduce the lease to $1,400. If I have to tell them no, they'll tell me to close the office."

The landlord protested, "But I'll sue."

"I know. I agree with you entirely," I said. "I'm squarely on your side, but the problem is the board of directors with whom I have to deal. If you threaten to sue, they'll just say, 'Okay, let him sue. This is Los Angeles County, and it will take him two years to get into court.'"

His response demonstrates how effective the Good Guy/Bad Guy Gambit can be. He said, "Would you go into that board meeting and see what you can do for me? I'd be willing to split the difference and reduce the lease to $1,550, but if they won't settle for that, I could drop it as low as $1,500." The

Gambit had worked so well that he actually asked me to negotiate for him with my own board of directors.

See how effective it can be in putting pressure on the other person without confrontation? What would have happened if I had said to him, "Go ahead and sue me. It'll take you two years to get into court"? It would have upset him so much that we would have spent the next two years talking to each other through attorneys. By using a vague higher authority as my bad guy, I was able to put incredible pressure on him without having him get upset with me.

Power Negotiators use several Counter-Gambits to Good Guy/Bad Guy:

- The first Counter-Gambit is simply to identify the Gambit. Although there are many other ways to handle the problem, this one is so effective that it's probably the only one you need to know. Good Guy/Bad Guy is so well known that it embarrasses people when they get caught using it. When you notice the other person using it you should smile and say, "Oh, come on—you aren't going to play Good Guy/Bad Guy with me are you? Come on, sit down, let's work this thing out." Usually their embarrassment will cause them to retreat from the position.

- You could respond by creating a bad guy of your own. Tell them that you'd love to do what they want, but you have people back in the head office who are obsessed with sticking to the program. You can always make a fictitious bad guy appear more unyielding than a bad guy who is present at the negotiation.

- You could go over their heads to their supervisor. For example, if you're dealing with a buyer and head buyer at a distributorship, you might call the owner of the distributorship and say, "Your people were playing Good Guy/Bad Guy with me. You don't approve of that kind of thing, do you?" (Always be cautious about going over someone's head. The strategy can easily backfire because of the bad feelings it can cause.)

- Sometimes just letting the bad guy talk resolves the problem, especially if he's being obnoxious. Eventually his own people will get tired of hearing it and tell him to knock it off.

- You can counter Good Guy/Bad Guy by saying to the Good Guy, "Look, I understand what you two are doing to me. From now on anything that he says, I'm going to attribute to you also." Now you have two bad guys to deal with, so it diffuses the Gambit. Sometimes just identifying them both in your own mind as bad guys will handle it, without you having to come out and accuse them.

- If the other side shows up with an attorney or controller who is clearly there to play bad guy, jump right in and forestall their role. Say to them, "I'm sure you're here to play bad guy, but let's not take that approach. I'm as eager to find a solution to this situation as you are, so why don't we all take a win-win approach. Fair enough?" This really takes the wind out of their sails.

This Gambit is very, very effective even when everybody knows what's going on. It was how Presidents Carter and Reagan got the hostages out of Iran, wasn't it? You remember that? Carter had lost the election. He was very eager to do something about the Iranian hostage situation before he left the White House and Reagan could take credit for their release. So he started playing Good Guy/Bad Guy with the Ayatollah. He said to him, "If I were you, I'd settle this thing with me. Don't take a chance on this new team coming into office in January. My goodness, have you taken a look at these guys? The President's a former cowboy actor. The Vice President is the former head of the C.I.A. The Secretary of State is Alexander Haig. These guys are crazier than Englishmen. There's no telling what they might do."

Reagan, playing along with it, said, "Hey, if I were you, I'd settle with Carter. He's a nice guy. You're definitely not going to like what I'll have to say about it, when I get into the White House." And sure enough, we saw the hostages being released on the morning of Reagan's inauguration. Of course the Iranians were aware of Good Guy/Bad Guy, but they didn't want to take a chance that Reagan would follow through with his threats. It demonstrated that these Gambits work even when the other side knows what you're doing.

In 1994, Jimmy Carter was again called upon to play the Good Guy when he and Colin Powell went to Haiti to see if they could get General Cedras to give up power without a fight. Powell was there to impress the might of the armed forces upon Cedras. Carter was there to cozy up the dictator, even suggesting he come to Plains, Georgia, and teach a class in Sunday School when the crisis was over.

Key points to remember:

- People use Good Guy/Bad Guy on you much more than you might believe. Look out for it whenever you're negotiating with two or more people.

- It is a very effective way of putting pressure on the other person without creating confrontation.

- Counter it by identifying it. It's such a well-known tactic that when you catch them using it, they get embarrassed and back off.

- Don't be concerned that the other side knows what you're doing. Even if they do, it can still be a powerful tactic. In fact, when you're Power Negotiating with someone who understands all of these Gambits, it becomes more fun. It's like playing chess with a person of equal skill rather than someone whom you can easily outsmart.

Chapter 15

Ending Gambits: Nibbling

Power Negotiators know that by using the Nibbling Gambit, you can get a little bit more even after you have agreed on everything. You can also get the other person to do things that she had refused to do earlier.

Car salespeople understand this, don't they? They know that when they get you on the lot, a kind of psychological resistance has built up to the purchase. They know to first get you to the point where you're thinking, "Yes, I'm going to buy a car. Yes, I'm going to buy it here." Even if it means closing you on any make and model of car, even a stripped down model that carries little profit for them. Then they can get you into the closing room and start adding all the other little extras that really build the profit into the car.

So the principle of Nibbling tells you that you can accomplish some things more easily with a Nibble later on in the negotiations.

Children are brilliant Nibblers, aren't they? If you have teenage children living at home, you know that they don't have to take any courses on negotiating. But you have to—just to stand a chance of surviving the whole process of bringing them up—because they're naturally brilliant negotiators. Not because they learn it in school, but because when they're little everything they get, they get with negotiating skills. When my daughter Julia graduated from high school, she wanted to get a really great high school graduation gift from me. She had three things on her hidden agenda. Number one, she wanted a five-week trip to Europe. Number two, she wanted $1,200 in spending money. And number three, she wanted a new set of luggage.

She was smart enough not to ask for everything up front. She was a good enough negotiator to first close me on the trip, then come back a few weeks later and show me in writing that the recommended spending money was $1,200, and got me to commit to that. (I'll stress the importance of the "in writing" part in Chapter 31.) Then right at the last minute she came to me and she said, "Dad, you wouldn't want me going to Europe with that ratty old set of luggage would you? All the kids will be there with new luggage." And she got that too. Had she asked for everything up front, I would have negotiated out the luggage and negotiated down the spending money.

What's happening here is that a person's mind always works to reinforce decisions that it has just made. Power Negotiators know how this works and use it to get the other side to agree to something that he or she wouldn't have agreed to earlier in the negotiation.

Why is Nibbling such an effective technique? To find out why this works so well, a couple of psychologists did a study at a race track in Canada. They studied the attitude of people immediately before they placed the bet and again immediately after they placed the bet. They found out that before the people placed the bet, they were very uptight, unsure, and anxious about what they were about to do. Compare this to almost anyone with whom you negotiate: They may not know you, they may not know your company, and they certainly don't know what's going to come out of this relationship. Chances are they're uptight, unsure, and anxious.

At the race track, the researchers found out that once people had made the decision to go ahead and place the bet, suddenly they felt very good about what they had just done and even had a tendency to want to double the bet before the race started. In essence their minds did a flip-flop once they had made the decision. Before they decided, they were fighting it; once they'd made the decision, they supported it.

If you're a gambler, you've had that sensation, haven't you? Watch them at the roulette tables in Atlantic City or Vegas. The gamblers place their bets. The croupier spins the ball. At the very last moment people are pushing out additional bets. The mind always works to reinforce decisions that it has made earlier.

I spoke at a Philadelphia convention when the Pennsylvania lottery prize was fifty million dollars, and many of the people in the audience were holding tickets. To illustrate how people's minds work to reinforce the decisions that they have made, I tried to buy a lottery ticket from somebody in the audience. Do you think he would sell me one? No, he wouldn't, even for fifty times the purchase price. I'm sure that, before he bought that ticket, he was uptight and anxious about betting money on a 100 million to one shot. However, having made the decision, he refused to change his mind. The mind works to reinforce decisions that it has made earlier.

So one rule for Power Negotiators is that you don't necessarily ask for everything up front. You wait for a moment of agreement in the negotiations and then go back and Nibble for a little extra.

You might think of the Power Negotiating process as pushing a ball up-hill, a large rubber ball that's much bigger than you. You're straining to force it up to the top of the hill. The top of the hill is the moment of first agreement in the negotiations. Once you reach that point, then the ball moves easily down the other side of the hill. This is because people feel good after they have made the initial agreement. They feel a sense of relief that the tension and stress is over. Their minds are working to reinforce the decision that they've just made, and they're more receptive to any additional suggestions you may have.

So after the other side has agreed to make any kind of purchase from you, it's time for the "Second Effort." Vince Lombardi always used to talk about the second effort. He'd show football clips of receivers who almost caught the ball, but it just slipped through their fingers. But instead of giving up, they made the second effort. They dove and caught the ball before it hit the ground. He was also proud of film clips of the running back that the defense almost brought down, but who still wriggled free and made the touchdown. Lombardi used to say that everyone makes the first effort. You wouldn't be on the team if you didn't know how to play the game well and were doing everything the coach expects you to do when you're on the field. Every-body's doing that. The players on the other team are doing that. The players who would like to replace you on the team are capable of doing that. Lombardi was fond of pointing out that the difference between good players and great players is that the great ones always make the second effort. Just doing everything their coach expects them to do isn't good enough for the great ones. Let's translate that philosophy into workplace situations:

- If you're a receptionist you need to realize that it isn't enough to know how to do your job and do everything that your boss asks you to do. Your boss expects anyone in your position to do that. You have to look for opportunities to make the extra effort. Perhaps you learn how to hang in with a complaining customer a little longer until you can satisfy her without having to turn her over to your boss.

- If you're an architect you must realize that it isn't enough to create a design that will please your clients. Clients expect any architect in the country to do that. You have to learn a little more about the customer than anyone else would, so that you can come up with a design that will blow their socks off.

- If you're a salesperson you must understand that you wouldn't be selling for your company unless you knew how to play the selling game well and were out there doing everything that your company expects you to do. However, everybody's doing that. The people who sell for your competition are doing that. The people who apply for your job every day are capable of doing that. The difference between a good salesperson and a great salesperson is that the great ones always make another effort. Even when they know their sales manager would pat them on the back and tell them not to feel bad because they did everything they could to get the sale, that's not good enough for the superstar salespeople. They always make another effort.

So always go back at the end for that second effort. Perhaps as a receptionist, one of your duties is to sell extended warranty contracts on equipment that customers bring in for repair. You explain the program, but the customer resists. Have the courage before the customer leaves to make that second effort. You might say, "Mr. Jones, could we take one more look at that extended warranty? What you may be overlooking is the preventative maintenance factor. If you know that repair work won't cost you a penny, you'll call us much sooner than you would if you had to pay for it. The sooner you have repairs made, the longer the equipment will last. Yes, it's a good deal for us, but it's an even better deal for you." You have a good chance of Mr. Jones saying, "Well, all right, if you think it's that important, I'll go ahead."

As an architect you may have trouble convincing your client that he should put the highest quality carpet in the lobby of his new hotel, and you have to back off it. After you have reached agreement on the other issues, have the courage to say, "Could we take another look at upgrading the carpet in the lobby? I realize that it's a huge investment, but nothing projects the quality image better than having your guests sink into plush carpeting the moment they get into the door. I don't recommend it for everybody, but with this type of project I really think it's very, very important." And you have a good chance of your client saying, "Well, all right, if you think it's that important, let's go ahead."

Perhaps you sell packaging equipment, and you're trying to convince your customer that she should go with the top of the line model, but she's balking at that kind of expense. You back off, but come back and Nibble for it before you leave. After you've reached agreement on all the other points, you say, "Could we take another look at the top-of-the-line model? I don't recommend it for everyone, but with your volume and growth potential, I really think it's the way for you to go and all it means is an additional investment of $500 a month." And you have a good chance of her saying, "Well, all right, if you think it's that important, let's go ahead."

Always go back at the end to make a second effort on something that you couldn't get them to agree to earlier.

Look out for people Nibbling on you

There's a point in the negotiation when you are very vulnerable, and that point is when you *think* the negotiations are all over.

I bet you've been the victim of a Nibble at one time or another. You've been selling a car or a truck to someone. You're finally feeling good because you've found the buyer. The pressure and the tension of the negotiations has drained away. He's sitting in your office writing out the check. But just as he's about to sign his name he looks up and says, "That does include a full tank of gas, doesn't it?"

You're at your most vulnerable point in the negotiations for these two reasons:

1. You've just made a sale, and you're feeling good. When you feel good, you tend to give things away that you otherwise wouldn't.

2. You're thinking, "Oh, no. I thought we had resolved everything. I don't want to take a chance on going back to the beginning and re-negotiating the whole thing. If I do that I might lose the entire sale. Perhaps I'm better off just giving in on this little point."

So you're at your most vulnerable just after the other person has made the decision to go ahead. Look out for people Nibbling on you. Making a huge sale has excited you so much that you can't wait to call your sales manager and tell her what you've done. The other person tells you that he needs to call purchasing and get a purchase order number for you. While he's on the phone, he puts his hand over the mouthpiece and says, "By the way, you can give us 60 days on this, can't you? All of your competitors will." Look out for people Nibbling on you. Because you've just made a big sale, and you're afraid to reopen the negotiations for fear of losing it, you'll have to fight to avoid the tendency to make the concession.

(*An aside to sales managers:* When your salespeople have this happen to them, they're not going to come back to you and say, "Boy, was that person a good negotiator. He slid that Nibble in on me and before I even knew what he'd done, I'd agreed to 60-day terms." Nooooh. Your salesperson's going to come back to you and say, "I got the order, but I had to give them 60-day terms to get it.")

Preventing the other side from Nibbling on you

Try to prevent the possibility of a Nibble by these techniques:

- Show them in writing what any additional concessions will cost them. List extended terms if you ever make them available, but show what it costs them to do that. List the cost of training, installation, extended warranties, and anything else for which they might Nibble.

- Don't give yourself the authority to make any concessions. Protect yourself with Higher Authority (see Chapter 7) and Good Guy/Bad Guy (see Chapter 14).

Countering the Nibble when the other person does it to you

The Counter Gambit to the Nibble is to gently make the other person feel—cheap. You have to be very careful about the way you do this because obviously you're at a sensitive point in the negotiation. You smile sweetly and say: "Oh, come on, you negotiated a fantastic price with me. Don't make us wait for our money, too. Fair enough?" So that's the Counter Gambit to the Nibble when it's used against you. Be sure that you do it with a big grin on your face, so that they don't take it too seriously.

So consider these points when you go into negotiations:

- Are there some elements that you are better off to bring up as a Nibble, after you have reached initial agreement?

- Do you have a plan to make a second effort on anything to which you can't get them to agree the first time around?

- Are you prepared for the possibility of them Nibbling on you at the last moment?

Preventing post-negotiation Nibbles

Sometimes the other person wishes he Nibbled on you during the negotiation, so he decides to Nibble on you afterward. This could include the following:

- The other person agrees to 30-day terms, but deliberately takes 60 days or more to pay.

- He pays in 30 days but still deducts the Net 15 discount.

- He requests free additional accounting breakdowns, sometimes just to delay payment.

- He protests a charge for installation, claiming that you didn't cover this with him.

- He rejects a charge for training, saying that your competition doesn't charge.

- He contracts for carload shipments, but calls at the last moment to cut the shipment and insist on the carload price.

- He refuses to pay, or slashes the billing, for engineering charges although during the negotiation he waived this aside as unimportant.

- He requests extra certifications and is unwilling to pay for them.

You can avoid most of this unpleasantness by:

- Negotiating all the details up front and getting them in writing. Don't leave anything to "We can work that out later." Don't be lazy and feel that if you avoid an issue you are closer to making the sale.

- Use the Gambits to create a climate in which the other person feels that he or she won. If they felt they won, then they are much less likely to Nibble—either during the negotiation or afterward.

So Power Negotiators always take into account the possibility of being able to Nibble. Timing is very critical—catching the other parties when the tension is off and they're feeling good because they think the negotiations are all over.

On the other hand, look out for the other side Nibbling on you at the last moment, when you're feeling good. At that point you're the most vulnerable and liable to make a concession that half an hour later you'll be thinking— why on Earth did I do that? I didn't have to do that. We'd agreed on everything already.

Key points to remember:

• With a well-timed Nibble, you can get things at the end of a negotiation that you couldn't have gotten the other side to agree to earlier.

• It works because the other person's mind reverses itself after it has made a decision. He may have been fighting the thought of buying from you at the start of the negotiation. After he has made a decision to buy from you, however, you can Nibble for a bigger order, upgraded product, or additional services.

• Being willing to make that additional effort is what separates great salespeople from merely good salespeople.

• Stop the other person from Nibbling on you by showing her in writing the cost of any additional features, services, or extended terms, and by not revealing that you have the authority to make any concessions.

• When the other person Nibbles on you, respond by making him feel cheap, in a good-natured way.

• Avoid post-negotiation Nibbling by addressing and tying up all the details and using Gambits that cause them to feel that they won.

Chapter 16

Ending Gambits: How to Taper off Concessions

In extended negotiations over price, be careful that you don't set up a pattern in the way that you make concessions. Let's say that you're selling a used car and you've gone into the negotiation with a price of $15,000, but you would go as low as $14,000. So you have a negotiating range of $1,000.

The way in which you give away that $1,000 is very critical. There are several mistakes that you should avoid:

- *Equal-sized concessions.* This means giving away your $1,000 negotiating range in four increments of $250. Imagine what the other person's thinking if you do that. She doesn't know how far she can push you, all she knows is that every time she pushes she gets another $250. So she's going to keep on pushing. In fact, it's a mistake to make any two concessions of equal size. If you were buying the car, and the owner made a $250 concession and when pushed made another $250 concession, wouldn't you bet that the next concession will be $250 also?

- *Making the final concession a big one.* Let's say that you made a $600 concession followed by a $400 concession. Then you tell the other person, "That's absolutely our bottom line. I can't give you a penny more." The problem is that $400 is too big a concession to be your final concession. The other person is probably thinking that you made a $600 concession, followed by a $400 concession, so he's sure that he can get at least another $100 out of you. He says, "We're getting close. If you can come down another $100, we can talk." You refuse, telling him that you can't even come down another $10, because you've given him your bottom line already. By now the other person is really upset, because he's thinking, "You just made a $400 concession and now you won't give me another lousy $10. Why are you being so difficult?" So avoid making the last concession a big one because it creates hostility.

- *Never give it all away up front.* Another variation of the pattern is to give the entire $1,000 negotiating range away in one concession. When I set this up as a workshop at my seminars, it's amazing to me how many participants will turn to the person with whom they're to negotiate and say, "Well, I'll tell you what he told me." Such naiveté is a disastrous way to negotiate. I call it "Unilateral Disarmament." It's what some pacifists would have us do about nuclear arms: Dismantle all our nuclear weapons and hope that the Russians and the Ukrainians would reciprocate. I don't think that's very smart.

  So you're thinking, "How on Earth would a person be able to get me to do a stupid thing like that?" It's easy. Someone who looked at your car yesterday calls you up and says, "We've located three cars that we like equally well, so now we're just down to price. We thought the fairest thing to do would be to let all three of you give us your very lowest price, so that we can decide." Unless you're a skilled negotiator, you'll panic and cut your price to the bone, even though they haven't given you any assurance that there won't be another round of bidding later.

  Another way that the other side can get you to give away your entire negotiating range up front is with the "we don't like to negotiate" ploy. Let say you're a salesperson trying to get a new account with a company. With a look of pained sincerity on his face, their buyer says, "Let me tell you about the way we do business here. Back in 1926, when he first started the company, our founder said, 'Let's treat our vendors well. Let's not negotiate prices with them. Have them quote their lowest price and then tell them whether we'll accept it or not.' So that's the way we've always done it. So just give me your lowest price, and I'll give you a yes or a no. Because we don't like to negotiate here." The buyer is lying to you. He loves to negotiate. That is negotiating—seeing if you can get the other side to make all of their concessions to you before the negotiating even starts.

- *Giving a small concession to test the waters.* Giving a small concession first to see what happens tempts us all. You initially tell the other person, "Well, I might be able to squeeze another $100 off the price, but that's about our limit." If they reject that, you might think, "This isn't going to be as easy as I thought." So you offer another $200. That still doesn't get them to buy the car so in the next round you give away another $300 and then you have $400 left in your negotiating range, so you give them the whole thing.

You see what you've done there? You started with a small concession and you built up to a larger concession. You'll never reach agreement doing that, because every time they ask you for a concession, it just gets better and better for them.

So all of these are wrong because they create a pattern of expectations in the other person's mind. The best way to make concessions is first to offer a reasonable concession that might just cinch the deal. Maybe a $400 concession wouldn't be out of line. Then be sure that if you have to make any future concessions, they're smaller and smaller. Your next concession might be $300 and then $200 and then $100. By reducing the size of the concessions that you're making you convince the other person that he has pushed you about as far as you will go.

If you want to test how effective this can be, try it on your children. Wait until the next time they come to you for money for a school outing. They ask you for $100. You say, "No way. Do you realize that when I was your age my weekly allowance was 50 cents. Out of that I had to buy my own shoes and walk ten miles to school in the snow, uphill both ways. So I would take my shoes off and walk barefoot to save money (and other stories that parents the world over tell their children). No way am I going to give you $100. I'll give you $50 and that's it."

"I can't do it on $50," your children protest in horror.

Now you have established the negotiating range. They are asking for $100. You're offering $50. The negotiations progress at a frenzied pace and you move up to $60. Then $65 and finally $67.50." By the time you've reached $67.50, you don't have to tell them that they're not going to do any better. By tapering your concessions, you have subliminally communicated that they're not going to do any better.

However, Power Negotiators know how to do ever better than that. Power Negotiators know how to take away a concession that they have already offered the other side, and I'll tell you how to do that in the next chapter.

Key points to remember:

- The way that you make concessions can create a pattern of expectations in the other person's mind.

- Don't make equal size concessions because the other side will keep on pushing.

- Don't make your last concession a big one because it creates hostility.

- Never concede your entire negotiating range just because the other person calls for your "last and final" proposal or claims that he or she "doesn't like to negotiate."

- Taper the concessions to communicate that the other side is getting the best possible deal.

Chapter 17

Ending Gambits: The Withdrawing an Offer Gambit

In this chapter I'll teach you how to draw negotiations to a conclusion very effectively. You don't have to use it when the other person is negotiating in good faith with you. You use it only when you feel that the other side is simply grinding away to get the last penny off your price. Or when you know that the other person wants to do business with you, but she's thinking, "How much would I be making per hour, if I spent a little more time negotiating with this person?"

Let's say that a group of friends got together and bought a cabin in the mountains to use for a vacation home. There's a whole group who have all gone in together on the investment, and they're sharing the use of it. One partner drops out of the syndication, and your neighbor comes to you and tells you about the cabin in the mountains. Your initial reaction to this is, "This sounds fantastic. I'd love to do something like that." However, you're smart enough to play the Reluctant Buyer Gambit (see Chapter 5).

You say, "I appreciate your telling me about that, but I just don't think we'd be interested right now. I'm so busy I don't think we'd have the time to get up there. But look, just to be fair to you, what is the very lowest price that you would sell a share in the home for?"

He's been studying negotiating too, and he's learned that you should never be the first one to name the price. So he says, "We have a committee that decides on the price (the Higher Authority Gambit, see Chapter 7) and I don't know what that price would be. I can take them a proposal, but I don't know what the reaction would be."

When you press him a little more, he finally says, "I'm pretty sure that they're going to be asking $10,000."

This is a lot less than you expected. You were willing to go to $15,000. So your initial reaction is to jump at it right away, but you're smart enough to remember to Flinch (see Chapter 3). You exclaim, "$10,000. Oh no, I could never go along with anything like that. That's way too much. Tell you what, $8,000 might interest me. If they're interested at $8,000, let me know, and we'll talk about it."

The next day he comes back and has decided to bring you into line by using the Withdrawing an Offer Gambit. He says, "Am I embarrassed about this. I know that we were talking $10,000 yesterday, but the committee decided last night that they wouldn't sell a share for less than $12,000."

This is psychologically devastating to you for two reasons:

1. Because you feel that you created the problem—you say, "Boy, I wish I'd never run into that Roger Dawson and his Power Negotiating because if I hadn't I would have nailed him down at $10,000 yesterday."

2. You've made the mistake of telling your family all about it. They're all excited about the home up in the mountains, and you've passed that critical point in the negotiations when you're prepared to walk away.

You say, "Joe what are you talking about? You said $10,000 yesterday, $12,000 today, is it going to be $14,000 tomorrow? What's going on here?"

He says, "I do feel bad, but that's what they (Higher Authority) decided."

You say, "Joe, come on."

So he says, "Well I do feel bad about this. Tell you what, let me go back to them one more time, let me see what I can do for you with them." (That's Good Guy/Bad Guy isn't it?) "If I can get it for you for the $10,000, are you interested?"

And you say, "Of course I'm interested. I want it." And he has sold you at full price and you may not have realized what he's done to you until it's too late.

Let me give you another example because it's a very powerful negotiating Gambit. Let's say that you sell widgets, and you quote the buyer a price of $1.80; the buyer offers you $1.60. You negotiate back and forth, and finally it looks as though he will agree to $1.72. What's going through the buyer's mind is, "I got him down from $1.80 to $1.72. I bet I can squeeze another penny out of him. I bet I can get this salesperson to $1.71."

So he says, "Look, business is really tough right now, I just can't do business with you on widgets unless you can bring the order in at $1.71."

He may be only baiting you, just trying it to see if he can get you down. Don't panic and feel you have to make the concession to stay in the game. The way to stop this grinding away process is to say, "I'm not sure if we can do that or not, but tell you what, if I can possibly get it for you I will." That's a subtle form of Good Guy/Bad Guy (see Chapter 14). "Let me go back, we'll re-figure it and see if we can do it. I'll get back to you tomorrow."

The next day you come back and pretend to withdraw the concession that you made the day before. You say, "I'm really embarrassed about this, but we've been up all night re-figuring the price of widgets. Somebody, somewhere down the line, has made a mistake. We had an increase in the cost of raw materials that the estimator didn't figure in. I know we were talking $1.72 yesterday, but we can't even sell it to you for that—$1.73 is the lowest price that we could possibly offer you on widgets."

What's the buyer's reaction? He's going to get angry and say, "Hey, wait a minute buddy. We were talking $1.72 yesterday, and $1.72 is what I want." And immediately the buyer forgets $1.71. The Withdrawing an Offer Gambit works well to stop the buyer grinding away on you.

Haven't we all had an appliance or car salesperson, when we were trying to force the price a little lower, say, "Let me go to my sales manager, and I'll see what I can do for you with him." Then he comes back and he says, "Am I embarrassed about this. You know that advertised special we were talking about? I thought that ad was still in effect, but it went off last Saturday. I can't even sell it to you at the price we were talking about."

Immediately you forget future concessions and want to jump on the bandwagon at the price you'd been talking about.

You can also employ this Gambit by withdrawing a feature of the offer, rather than by raising the price. Here are some examples:

- The appliance salesperson says to you, "I know we were talking about waiving the installation charge, but my sales manager is now telling me that at this price we just can't."

- The air-conditioner salesperson says to you, "I understand that we were talking about including the cost of building permits, but at a price this low, my estimators are telling me we'd be crazy to do that."

- You're a sub-contractor, and you say to your general contractor, "I know you requested 60-days terms, but at this price, we'd need payment in 30 days."

- You market computers, and you tell your customer, "Yes, I told you that we would waive the charge for training your people, but my people are saying that at this price, we'd have to charge."

Don't do it with something big because that could really antagonize the other person.

The Withdrawing an Offer Gambit is a gamble, but it will force a decision and usually make or break the deal. Whenever the other person uses this on you, don't be afraid to counter by insisting that the other side resolve its internal problem first, so that you can then resume the real negotiation.

Key points to remember:

- Withdrawing an Offer is a gamble, so use it only on someone who is grinding away on you.

- You can do it by backing off of your last price concession or by withdrawing an offer to include freight, installation, training, or extended terms.

- To avoid direct confrontation, make the Bad Guy a vague higher authority. Continue to position yourself as if on the other person's side.

Chapter 18

Ending Gambits: Positioning for Easy Acceptance

The Positioning for Easy Acceptance Gambit is very important, particularly if you're dealing with people who have studied negotiating. If they're proud of their ability to negotiate, you can get ridiculously close to agreement, and the entire negotiation will still fall apart on you.

When it does, it's probably not the price or terms of the agreement that caused the problem, it's the ego of the other person as a negotiator.

Let's say that you market advertising specialties such as rulers with a company's name on them or custom-printed baseball caps and T-shirts. You have made an appointment to meet with the manager at a local appliance store. What you may not realize is that just before you showed up in his office, the manager said to the owner of the store, "You just watch me negotiate with this advertising specialties representative. I know what I'm doing, and I'll get us a good price."

Now he's not doing as well as he hoped in the negotiation and he's reluctant to agree to your proposal because he doesn't want to feel that he lost to you as a negotiator. That can happen, even when the other person knows that your proposal is fair and it satisfies his needs in every way.

So when this happens you must find a way to make the other person feel good about giving in to you. You must Position for Easy Acceptance. Power Negotiators know that the best way to do this is to make a small concession just at the last moment. The size of the concession can be ridiculously small, and you can still make it work because it's not the size of the concession that's critical, but the timing.

So you might say, "We just can't budge another dime on the price, but I tell you what. If you'll go along with the price, I'll personally supervise the installation to be sure that it goes smoothly."

Perhaps you were planning to do that anyway, but the point is that you've been courteous enough to position the other person so that he can respond, "Well, all right, if you'll do that for me, we'll go along with the price." Then he doesn't feel that he lost to you in the negotiation, he feels that he traded off.

Positioning for Easy Acceptance is another reason why you should never go in with your best offer up front. If you have offered all of your concessions already, before you get to the end of the negotiation, you won't have anything left with which to position the other side.

Here are some other small concessions that you can use to position:

- You're selling a boat, so you offer to take the buyers out and show them how to sail it.
- If you sell office equipment, offer to inventory their supplies and set them up on an automatic reordering system.
- You're selling a car, so you offer to include the snow chains.
- Hold this price for 90 days in case they want to duplicate this order.
- You're hiring someone and can't pay them what they asked, but you offer to review it after 90 days.
- Offer forty-five-day terms instead of 30 days.
- Offer three years for the price of two on an extended service warranty.

Remember it's the timing of the concession that counts, not the size. The concession can be ridiculously small and still be effective. Using this Gambit, Power Negotiators can make the other person feel good about giving in to them.

Never, ever gloat. Never, when you get through negotiating, say to the other person, "Harry, you know, if you'd hung in there a little bit longer, I was prepared to do this and this and this for you." Harry's going to say unkind things about your mommy when you do that.

I realize that in the normal course of business you'd never be foolish enough to gloat over the other person because you felt you out-negotiated him. However, you get into trouble with this one when you're negotiating with someone you know really well. Perhaps you've been playing golf with this person for years. Now you're negotiating something. You both know you're negotiating and you're having fun playing the game. Finally he says to you, "All right. We're all agreed on this, and we're not going to back out, but just for my own satisfaction, what was your real bottom line there?" Of course you are tempted to brag a little, but don't do it. He will remember that for the next 20 years.

Always when you're through negotiating—congratulate. However poorly you think the other people may have done, congratulate them. Say, "Wow. Did you do a fantastic job negotiating with me. I realize that I didn't get as good a deal as I could have done, but frankly, it was worth it because I learned so much about negotiating. You were brilliant." You want the other person to feel that he or she won in the negotiations.

Have you ever watched attorneys in court? They'll cut each other to ribbons inside the courtroom. However, outside you'll see the district attorney go up to the defense attorney and say, "Wow, were you brilliant in there. You really were. True, your guy got 30 years, but I don't think anybody could have done a better job than you did." The district attorney understands that he'll be in another courtroom one day with that same defense attorney, and he doesn't want the attorney feeling that this is a personal contest. Gloating over a victory will just make the attorney more determined than ever to win the rematch.

Similarly, you will be dealing with that other person again. You don't want her remembering that she lost to you. It would make her only more determined to get the better of you in a rematch.

Key points to remember:

- If the other person is proud of his ability to negotiate, his egotistical need to win may stop you from reaching agreement.

- Position the other person to feel good about giving in to you with a small concession made just at the last moment.

- Because timing is more important than the size of the concession, the concession can be ridiculously small and still be effective.

- Always congratulate the other person when you get through negotiating, however poorly you think he or she did.

Chapter 19

Unethical Gambits: The Decoy

In the next six chapters I'm going to teach you the unethical gambits that people can use to get you to sweeten the deal. Unless you're so familiar with them that you spot them right away, you'll find that you will make unnecessary concessions just to get the other side to agree with your proposal. Many a salesperson has had to endure an embarrassing interview with a sales manager who can't understand why he made a concession. The salesperson tries to maintain that the only way to get the order was to make the concession. The truth was that the buyer out-maneuvered the salesperson with one of these unethical gambits.

There's no point in getting upset with the person who uses these unethical Gambits. Power Negotiators remember to concentrate on the issues (see Chapter 72) and think of negotiating as a game. Unless the individual is Mother Theresa, he or she is simply doing what he or she is on this planet for, which is to get the best possible deal from you. You must be skilled enough to instantly recognize these unethical gambits and smoothly counter them.

The other side can use the Decoy Gambit to take your attention away from what the real issue is in the negotiation.

Perhaps you are selling custom gears to a large manufacturer of bulldozers located in Houston. You have been calling on this company for two years trying to get your foot in the door, but they have never been willing to budge from their existing supplier. However, today appears to be the day when all your persistence will pay off. The buyer offers to give you a large order providing that you can complete shipment in a 90-day period. Both of you know that it typically takes 120 days to design, engineer and manufacture a custom gear. The thought of getting the sale excites you, but you realize that a 90-day ship date is virtually impossible.

You check with the people at your plant, and they confirm that even 120 days would be a scramble and that non-recurring engineering costs will be $22,000. However much you fight for an accelerated production schedule, you can't get your people to budge. It's going to take 120 days and not a day less, even if you have to lose the order over it.

You return to present the proposal to the other side. You show him a price of $230,000 for the gears, plus $22,000 in non-recurring engineering costs, FOB your plant in Toledo, with shipment in 120 days.

The buyer insists that he must have delivery in 90 days to complete a large shipment they need to deliver to a construction project in Buenos Aires. The negotiation has taken on an air of two people desperately trying to solve a problem together, but nothing you can come up with seems to solve the problem. The negotiations appear to have stalemated.

Finally the buyer says, "Maybe there's something that would work. Let me check with my shipping people and see what they have to say. I'll be right back." He leaves the office for 15 minutes. Your mind is in a turmoil, thinking of the commission you'll lose if you can't put this sale together. By the time the buyer returns, you're almost frantic.

The buyer has a concerned look on his face and says, "I think I've found a way, but I need your help to put it together. My guy in shipping says that we can air freight the gears to Argentina, but we're going to have to pay off some customs people. To do this I need you to waive the engineering charges and air freight them to us in Houston at your expense."

Unless you're very careful, the relief of finding a solution to the problem will overwhelm you so much that you'll concede the $22,000 engineering charge and agree to pick up a $6,000 air freight bill. And it may be months before you realize that the buyer used the Decoy Gambit on you. Six months later you're sitting in a hotel coffee shop in Dallas talking to a friend of yours who sells sheet metal to the bulldozer company. He asks you how you got your foot in the door, and you tell him the story. Your friend says, "I don't believe what the buyer told you. It doesn't ring true to me. Those people are the best organized manufacturing plant in the business. They always work at least six months out. No way would they be ordering custom gears only 90 days out." Only then does it dawn on you that the shipment date never was the real issue. They could have lived with 120 days. The ship date was the Decoy issue. The buyer created the issue of an accelerated shipment date simply so that he could trade it off later for the real issue: Waiving the engineering charges and the freight.

Several years ago, an association hired me to do a seminar at John Portman's Peachtree Hotel in Atlanta. That's a Westin Hotel and a fabulous place. It's 73 stories high, one of the tallest hotels in the country and possibly the world. It's like a round tall tower with only 15 or so pie-shaped rooms on each floor.

As I walked into the hotel I was wondering what I could do to provide an illustration to the people who would be in the seminar the following day, to show how effective Power Negotiating can be. A room had been pre-arranged for me by the organization that had hired me, and I decided to see what I could do about negotiating down the price of the room. Rooms at the Peachtree then typically cost $135. They had given me a very good corporate rate of $75. Nevertheless, I determined to see what I could do and within 10 minutes got them to reduce the price of the room to $37.50.

I used the Decoy Gambit on them. They told me that they only had a twin-size room for me. If they had said they only had a full-size room, I would have asked for a twin bed, you understand. It didn't matter what it was, but I said "The association that hired me booked this room a month ahead of time. I am not going to accept a twin-size room." The desk clerk brought out the manager. He explained that they have 1,074 rooms in the hotel, guests already occupied 1,064 of them, so they only had 10 available, and I would have to settle for a twin-size room.

So, I used the Trading Off Gambit (see Chapter 13). I said, "Well, I might be willing to settle for a twin-size room, but if I do that for you, what will you do for me?" I thought possibly they might offer a free breakfast, or something like that. However, to my amazement he said, "We might be able to adjust the price of the room a little bit. How would half price be for you?"

I said, "That would be just fine." Then, as they gave me the key to the room, the manager said, "Let me check just a moment. We may be able to do something more for you." They made a telephone call and found out that they did have a queen-size room available. Maintenance had just finished redecorating it, and they weren't sure whether they had released it yet. So, I ended up getting a $135 queen-size room for only $37.50. (Other than giving me a neat story for the seminar, this didn't benefit me because the organization that hired me was paying for it, and they got the benefit of the reduction.)

The Decoy I used was that they only had twin-size rooms available, not king-sized. That wasn't the real issue at all, of course; what I wanted to accomplish was a reduced room rate. The size of the bed took their attention away from the real issue.

Watch out for people who lure you away from the real issue with the Decoy Gambit. Stay focused and isolate the objection. "Is that the only thing that's bothering you?" Then go to Higher Authority and Good Guy/Bad Guy: "Let's get something in writing, and take it to my people and I'll see what I can do for you with them." Then turn the tables: "We may be able to accelerate the shipment, but it's going to increase the non-recurring engineering charges."

Chapter 20

Unethical Gambits: The Red Herring

The Red Herring Gambit is a further twist on the Decoy Gambit. With the Decoy, the other person raises a phony issue to get concessions on a real issue. With the Red Herring, the other person makes a phony demand that he will subsequently withdraw, but only in exchange for a concession from you. If the Red Herring distracts you, it will deceive you into thinking that it's of major concern to the other side when it may not be.

Red herring is an English fox-hunting expression. England has many very vocal animal-rights activists, and their prime target has been fox-hunting, a sport that Oscar Wilde called "the unspeakable in pursuit of the uneatable." To which the lord of the hunt, resplendent in his red hunting jacket, with a matching nose pickled by too much port wine, would reply, "What nonsense. The fox is proud to die."

Herrings that have been dried and salted become dark red in color, like smoked salmon. The English call such red herrings "bloaters." Opponents of fox-hunting found that if they dragged a bloater across the path of the hunt its smell would mask the trail of the fox and confuse the dogs. When it happens the hunt master will cry, "Those blighters have faulted my hounds." In this way the phrase red herring became part of the English language and came to mean the raising of an issue that would divert and confuse opponents. When President Harry Truman faced increasing charges from Congress that Communists had infiltrated his administration, he responded by saying, "It's just a red herring to get the minds of the voters off the sins of the 80th Congress."

The classic example of the use of a red herring came during the Korean War armistice talks. Very early in the talks the parties concerned agreed that each side would be represented at the table by officials of three neutral countries, along with their own national negotiators. The South Korean side selected Norway, Sweden, and Switzerland as their three neutral negotiators. The North Koreans chose Poland and Czechoslovakia, but couldn't seem to choose a third. They suggested that the talks start, and they would identify a third country later.

What they were really doing was leaving an opening for the Red Herring Gambit. When the time came and they had set the stage, they announced their selection for the third country: The Soviet Union. The international outcry was unanimous: "The Soviet Union? Now wait a minute. The Soviet Union isn't a neutral country."

The North Koreans responded by saying that the Soviets were not directly involved in the conflict, and there was no reason for them to be considered biased.

They waged the battle of the Red (pardon the pun) Herring for quite a while, until the situation became absurd. What the North Koreans were using, beside the Red Herring Gambit, was a repetitive tactic that children everywhere understand.

"Dad," says Junior, "may I go to the movies tonight?"

Filled with paternal authority, the father says, "No son, I don't want you going to the movies tonight."

Junior pleads, "Why not, Dad?"

"Because you went to a movie last week."

"I know that, but why can't I go tonight?"

The father stands firm. "I don't want you going to the movies all the time."

"Why not, Dad? I don't understand."

By the time the father has repeated himself 10 or 12 times, he's forgotten why he was making such a big deal about Junior going to the movie in the first place. His reasoning seems to have lost validity, and he begins to think of himself as making a mountain out of a molehill.

That was the tactic the North Koreans were using to support their Red Herring Gambit. They continued to insist that they couldn't understand what the objection was to using the Soviet Union as a neutral third party, until the objections of the South Koreans seemed as ludicrous as the demands of the North Koreans. The negotiations had stalemated.

Just as it seemed that the pointless arguing would continue forever, the North Koreans announced that they would abandon their insistence on having the Soviets at the negotiating table, but they expected a reciprocal concession.

Both sides had agreed earlier that during the negotiations, neither side would rebuild their airstrips. The North Koreans realized later that this left them at a severe disadvantage because we could fly planes off aircraft carriers, but they needed their runways. So the North Koreans decided that it was time to use the Red Herring Gambit and suggested the Soviet Union as the third neutral country. Now it was time to name the price: They would concede and choose a different country to represent them, but only if the South Koreans would waive the restriction on rebuilding the airfields.

The North Koreans never seriously thought that we would agree to letting the Soviet Union be part of the negotiations. However, they were able to magically create a bargaining issue out of thin air and then trade it off later for an issue about which they really cared.

When the other person is creating a red herring issue that she will try to trade off later, keep your eye on the real negotiating issues and don't let her link it to a concession you're reluctant to make.

Chapter 21

Unethical Gambits: Cherry Picking

Cherry Picking is a gambit that a buyer can use against a seller with devastating effect, unless the seller is a Power Negotiator and knows his or her options. Let's imagine that you're getting bids from contractors on a remodelling job at your house. It involves adding a second story office over your garage. You ask three contractors to submit bids and ask each of them to break down their bids by component.

Contractor "A" bids:		Contractor "B" bids:		Contractor "C" bids:	
Framing	$19,200	Framing	$17,200	Framing	$18,400
Flooring	$2,400	Flooring	$2,900	Flooring	$2,800
Roofing	$6,300	Roofing	$6,800	Roofing	$7,300
Carpentry	$4,300	Carpentry	$4,100	Carpentry	$4,100
Carpeting	$1,750	Carpeting	$1,950	Carpeting	$2,150
Plumbing	$1,800	Plumbing	$1,600	Plumbing	$1,600
Painting	$1,100	Painting	$1,500	Painting	$1,300
Total	**$36,850**	**Total**	**$36,050**	**Total**	**$37,650**

Which bid should you take? Contractor "A" at $36,850, contractor "B" at $36,050, or contractor "C" at $37,650? If the choice seems obvious to you, you are probably overly-obsessed with price. If the workmanship, the reliability, the start date, the completion date, and the quality of materials and sub-contractors used is of no importance to you, then you'd obviously choose contractor "B." However, there is much more than price for you to consider, and the best bid for you may be the highest.

A Cherry Picker can do better than that. He or she would go to Contractor "B" and say, "You are close on your bid, but you're high on flooring by $500 and carpentry by $200. If you'll match contractor "A" on those two items I'll give you the job." This would cause the general contractor to go back to his flooring and carpentry sub-contractors and get them to rework their bids. You can understand why contractors don't like to break down their bids into components.

You could also Cherry Pick on the terms of a proposal. Let's say that you're buying a piece of land in the country, and the seller is offering it for sale at $100,000 with 20 percent down and the balance due over ten years with 10 percent interest added. You might ask the owner to quote his or her lowest price for an all-cash deal. He or she might agree to $90,000 for all cash. Then you ask what the lowest interest rate would be for a 50 percent down transaction. The owner quotes you 7 percent. Then you Cherry Pick the best features of both components of the deal and offer $90,000 with 20 percent down and the balance carried by the owner with 7 percent interest added.

Buyers clearly love Cherry Picking whereas sellers hate it.

There's no question that information is the key to effective Cherry Picking and this takes time. However, if you're thinking of acquiring a new piece of equipment for your company you should shop around and accumulate information before you make a decision. Call up companies and have all their salespeople come in and make a presentation to you. You'll find that one has a good point in a particular area, perhaps a fast shipment. Another has a low price and a third has a good guarantee. So, from all these interviews, you piece together the ideal piece of equipment.

Then you go back to the one you like best and say, "I'd like to buy your equipment except that I want to get the longer guarantee." Or "I want to get the faster shipping." In this way you create the type of deal and the kind of contract that you want.

So buyers should push for itemized contracts whereas sellers should avoid it. Because Cherry Picking is to me an unethical gambit, the perpetrator is less likely to do it to someone he knows and trusts than he is to a comparative stranger. So sellers can forestall this tactic by building a personal relationship with the buyer.

Another way to handle people who might want to Cherry Pick you is to forestall the Gambit. Let's say that you're a contractor who is trying to sell a remodelling job to a homeowner, and you know she's going to talk to all the other contractors in town—how do you forestall it?

The answer is to know more about your competition than they'll ever learn. So the homeowner says, "I want to check with some other people before I make my final decision."

You respond, "I absolutely agree with you." Always agree up front, right? Salespeople should always agree with any objection however ridiculous it is and then work to turn it around. "I absolutely agree with you. You should check with other companies before you make a decision. But look, let me save you some time. Have you talked to Ted Smith over at ABC Construction? He uses XYZ cabinets which have this feature, this feature and this feature; but they don't have this. Then if you talk to the national department store company down at the mall, the salesperson who'll come out will be Fred Harrison, and he'll tell you about model number such and such ..."

By the time you've gone through letting her know how much you know about the competition, she's going to think, "Why on Earth do I need to waste my time talking to all these other people, when this person knows more than I'll ever learn."

To defend yourself against Cherry Picking, always consider the alternatives of the other side before making a concession. The fewer alternatives the other side has, the more power you have. If you as a seller refuse to budge on your price, then you force the buyer to pay more from another supplier or use multiple suppliers. In the case of the home remodelling job, this would mean that the homeowner would have to bypass you as the general contractor and contract with each sub-contractor separately. This may require more knowledge or expertise than the other side possesses or may create so much extra work and pressure that it is not worth the savings.

Chapter 22

Unethical Gambits: The Deliberate Mistake

The Deliberate Mistake is a very unethical tactic, and, as with any con job, it requires a victim who also lacks ethics. The seller baits the hook when she prepares a proposal and deliberately leaves out or under-prices one of the elements—the car salesperson who runs an adding machine tape on the cost of the car but includes only the price of a tape player, when the car also has a CD player. If the buyer takes the bait, he starts thinking that he now has an opportunity to put one over on the car salesperson. He becomes eager to close the deal before the salesperson spots the mistake. This eagerness makes the buyer a sloppy negotiator, and he may end up paying more for the car than if he had pointed out the mistake. Apart from that, the salesperson still has the option of "discovering" the mistake before the buyer consummates the sale and, with an accusing look, shames the buyer into paying the extra amount.

The counter-gambit may sound high-minded, but it's obvious. Never try to get away with anything. If your greed doesn't cost you at that moment, it will certainly catch up with you later on down life's road. Instead, point out the mistake and say, "I assume that you're not charging me for the CD player because you're trying to get me to make a decision now?"

A variation of the Deliberate Mistake is the Erroneous Conclusion close. Using this method, the salesperson asks a question of the buyer, but deliberately draws an erroneous conclusion. When the buyer corrects the salesperson, she finds she has made a commitment to buy. For example, the car salesperson says, "If you did decide today, you wouldn't need to take delivery today would you?" The buyer responds, "Well, of course we'd want to take it today."

The real estate salesperson says, "You wouldn't want the sellers to include the refrigerator would you?" The buyers hadn't been thinking of doing that, but the refrigerator looks better than theirs so they reply, "Do you think they would include it?" The salesperson responds with, "Let's include it in our offer and see what happens."

The boat salesperson says, "You wouldn't expect us to include a CB would you?" The buyer sees an opportunity to get something for nothing and responds, "I sure would."

Chapter 23

Unethical Gambits: The Default

The Default Gambit is one that involves a unilateral assumption that obviously works to the advantage of the side proposing it, such as the company that sends a payment check to a vendor after having deducted two and a half percent. Attached is a note that says, "All of our other vendors discount for payment within 15 days, so we assume you will too." Or, the salesperson who writes a potential buyer: "Because I haven't heard from you on your choice of options, I will ship the deluxe model unless I hear from you within ten days."

The Default Gambit preys on busy or lazy people; it assumes that rather than take action the other side will take the easy way out and let you get away with it. Once you have failed to respond, the law of precedent comes into play. When you finally do object the perpetrator is able to say, "But you've never had a problem with it in the past."

As with all unethical gambits, call the other side on it and gently explain that you expect to see a higher level of ethics from them in the future.

Chapter 24

Unethical Gambits: Escalation

I once knew a man who became very wealthy after he sold his real estate franchise to a large corporation. He had been one of the original purchasers of a territory when real estate franchising was new, and the founder of the company was running around the country trying to sign up anyone who believed in his concept. Many years later a huge New York corporation had bought the master franchise and was starting to buy back the territorial franchises. After attending one of my Secrets of Power Negotiating seminars, he asked me to join him for a drink and asked me, "Roger, have you ever heard voices speak to you when you're negotiating?" Not wanting to admit it if I had, I asked him what he was talking about. He told me that after he had agreed to sell his territorial franchise to the new corporate owners for what he first thought was a huge amount of money, he started to have second thoughts. Because his was the first franchise the corporation was buying back they flew him to New York for a signing ceremony to be followed by a press conference at which they would announce the corporation's plans to buy back all the franchises. "The night before the ceremony I had trouble sleeping," he told me. "I lay on my bed wondering whether I was doing the right thing. Suddenly I heard a voice talking to me."

"What was it saying," I asked him, half expecting a humorous punch line.

"It said, 'Joey, you're not getting enough money.' So the next morning I went down and asked for another half million dollars and got it."

What Joey was describing was a classic case of escalation—raising demands after both sides have reached agreement. Of course it's outrageous and unethical, but just as Joey thought he heard voices telling him to do it rather than accept responsibility for his actions, the perpetrators often don't see any harm in cutting the best deal by any means possible. So why is anyone ever allowed to get away with such outrageous behavior? All too often, the other side swallows its pride and concedes just as easily as that corporation conceded the extra half million. In that case, the corporation paid rather than face the humiliation of having to call off the press conference. In other cases, the other side has simply become too emotionally involved in the purchase to back out.

The history of big business is full of stories of people who extorted a little more out of a deal simply because they had enough leverage to do so. Frankly I have mixed emotions about how to respond. My heart tells me that if people do that, you should call their bluff and walk away from the deal on principle. However, I also believe in keeping emotions out of a negotiation. If that New York corporation was able to pay the extra half million and still have it be a good deal (and it was still a *very* good deal) then they were right to swallow their pride and pay the money.

Fortunately, the history of big business is also full of stories of people who would not sell their honor at any price, like the rancher who shook hands on a deal to sell his land in Orlando, on the morning of the day that the *Orlando Sentinel* broke the news that Walt Disney was secretly buying up all the land to create Walt Disney World. The rancher could have held out and made millions more, but his sense of honor stopped him from doing it.

When Henry Hollis sold the Palmer House hotel in Chicago to Conrad Hilton, he shook hands on Hilton's first offer of $19,385,000. Within a week he received offers of more than a million dollars above that, but he never wavered on his word. As Hilton said in his autobiography, "I have done business with a great many men in my time. I do not think I have ever had a greater experience than dealing with this perfect gentleman. I felt throughout that I was watching a master in the greatest traditions of American business."

There are some responses to escalation other than swallowing your pride or walking away. You might try these:

- Protecting yourself with Higher Authority (see Chapter 7). Tell them that their suggestion does not offend you, but that your board of directors will never re-negotiate a deal once it has been made, and they will force you to walk away. Then Position for Easy Acceptance (see Chapter 18) by telling them that although you cannot budge on the price, you might be able to offer them something of value in another area.

- Escalating your demands in return. Tell them that you are glad that they want to reopen the negotiations because your side has been having second thoughts also. Of course you would never renege on a deal, but since they have chosen to negate the original proposal, your price has now gone up also.

It is better to avoid Escalation than to have to deal with it. Avoid it by these techniques:

- Tying up all the details up front. Don't leave anything to "we can work that out later." Unresolved issues invite Escalation.

- Building personal relationships with the other parties that makes it harder for them to be ruthless.

- Getting large deposits so that it's harder for them to back out.

- Building win-win negotiations so that they don't want to back out.

Chapter 25

Unethical Gambits:
Planted Information

Returning from a speaking engagement, I was discussing that day's Presidential press conference with my seatmate. "I don't believe he's telling us the truth," he told me. "I met a man who knew someone who works at the White House, and he told me that the President did know all about it all along. He's covering something up." What amazed me about this was that I found myself believing what this man was telling me, rather than believing what I had earlier heard the President of the United States say at the press conference. Why? Because we always tend to believe information that we have obtained surreptitiously.

Planted information can be an astoundingly powerful influencer.

A salesman is making an impressive presentation to a board of directors. He is surrounded by flip charts and audio visual aids. He is fervently making a plea that they go with his company because it offers the best value in the marketplace. He believes that no competitor can undercut his prices and feels confident that he can close the sale at his asking price of $820,000—until he sees one of the directors pass a note to another director who nods and lays the note on the table in front of him. Curiosity gets the better of the salesman. He has to see what's on that note. He finishes his presentation, then approaches the table and dramatically leans toward them. "Gentlemen, do you have any questions?" Out of the corner of his eye he can now see the note. Even reading upside down, he can see that it says, "Universal's price is $762,000. Let's go with them."

The chairman of the board says, "I do have one question. Your price seems high. We're obligated to go with the lowest price that meets our specifications.

Is $820,000 the best you can do?" Within minutes the salesman has lowered his price by $58,000.

Was the note real or was it Planted Information? Even though it was just an unsubstantiated note scrawled on a piece of paper, the salesperson believed it because he obtained the information surreptitiously. Even if they had planted it, could the salesperson cry foul later? No, because they didn't tell him that the competition's bid was $762,000. He obtained the information surreptitiously, and he must accept responsibility for his assumptions.

Simply knowing about planted information will help you to diffuse this unethical tactic. Any time that you are negotiating based only on information that the other side has chosen to tell you, you are extremely vulnerable to manipulation. When the other side may have planted the information for you to discover, you should be even more vigilant.

Chapter 26

Negotiating Gambits— Principles: Get the Other Side to Commit First

In the next seven chapters, I'm going to teach you the fundamental principles of negotiation—the things that apply to every negotiation, every time. They may not be as direct and as clear-cut as the negotiating gambits that I've taught you, but if you'll completely absorb what I'll teach you in the next few chapters, you'll see how smoothly things can go together for you and just how much fun negotiation can be when you do it right.

Unlike the Gambits that are used as the need arises, these principles are always at work for you and will help you smoothly get what you want.

Power Negotiators know that you're usually better off if you can get the other side to commit to a position first. Several reasons are obvious:

- Their first offer may be much better than you expected.
- It gives you information about them before you have to tell them anything.
- It enables you to bracket their proposal (see Chapter One). If they state a price first, you can bracket them, so if you end up splitting the difference, you'll get what you want. If they can get you to commit first, they can then bracket your proposal. Then if you end up splitting the difference, they get what they wanted.

To a neophyte negotiator this may sound all wrong. Let's say that you have a neighbor who has a motorboat parked in his driveway. He's lived there for five years, and you can't recall him ever taking it out on the lake. If you can get it for a good price, you'd consider buying it. Asking him how much he wants for his boat may seem like a bad idea. What if he gets the impression he has a live one on his hands and deliberately inflates the price. Let's say a fair price is $10,000, but you're hoping to steal it for $5,000. When you approach him, he gets greedy and says, "That boat is in brand-new condition. I haven't even taken the cover off it in five years. I wouldn't take a penny less than $15,000." You could argue that in letting him state his price first, you have expanded the negotiating range and made it harder for you to reach your goal. You can't even bracket that range. If he wants $15,000 and you're willing to pay only $5,000, you'd have to ask him to pay you $5,000 to take it off your hands to accurately bracket. If it seems that getting him to go first was a mistake, you're forgetting that you can do several things to get him to modify that opening offer without having to state your offer first. You can use these approaches:

- Plead poor. "Mike, I don't think for a moment that I can afford to buy your boat from you, but I did notice that you never use it, and I thought you might just want to sell it to me at a give-away price."

- Apply the pressure of Higher Authority. "Mike, my wife is going to kill me for even asking you this, but ..."

- Use the power of competition. "Mike, I've been looking at a boat similar to yours that seems like a real bargain, but before I go ahead I thought I'd see what you would want for yours."

By using these approaches you modify Mike's aspirations without having to commit to a position.

The less you know about the other side or the proposition that you're negotiating, the more important the principle of not going first becomes. If the Beatles' manager Brian Epstein had understood this principle he could have made the Fab Four millions more on their first movie. United Artists wanted to cash in on the popularity of the singing group, but was reluctant to go out on a limb because UA didn't know how long the Beatles would stay popular. They could have been a flash in the pan that fizzled out long before their movie hit the screens. So UA planned it as an inexpensively made exploitation movie and budgeted only $300,000 to make it. This was clearly not enough to pay the Beatles a high salary, so UA planned to offer the Beatles as much as 25 percent of the profits. The Beatles were such a worldwide sensation in 1963 that the producer was very reluctant to ask them to name their price first, but he had the courage to stay with the rule. He offered Epstein $25,000 up front and asked him what percentage of the profits he thought would be fair.

Brian Epstein didn't know the movie business and should have been smart enough to play Reluctant Buyer (see Chapter 5) and use Good Guy/Bad Guy (see Chapter 14). He should have said, "I don't think they'd be interested in taking the time to make a movie, but if you'll give me your very best offer, I'll take it to them and see what I can do for you with them." Instead his ego wouldn't let him play dumb (see Chapter 27), so he assertively stated that they would have to get 7.5 percent of the profits or they wouldn't do it. This slight tactical error cost the group millions when the director, Richard Lester, to everyone's surprise, created a brilliantly humorous portrait of a day in the group's life that became a world-wide success.

If both sides have learned that they shouldn't go first, you can't sit there forever with both sides refusing to put a number on the table, but as a rule you should always find out what the other side wants to do first.

Apart from price, you're always better off to have the other person bring a proposal to you than you are to take one to them. Some crafty negotiators go to incredible lengths to make it look as though the other side approached them when the reverse was true. Movie producer Sam Goldwyn once wanted to borrow a contract actor from Darryl Zanuck, but couldn't reach Zanuck because he was in a meeting. After many tries to reach Zanuck, an exasperated Goldwyn finally insisted that the call be put through. When Darryl Zanuck finally picked up the phone, Sam Goldwyn, who had initiated the call, blithely said, "Darryl, what can I do for you today?"

Chapter 27

Negotiating Gambits— Principles: Acting Dumb Is Smart

To Power Negotiators, smart is dumb and dumb is smart. When you are negotiating you're better off acting as if you know less than everybody else, not more. The dumber you act, the better off you are unless your apparent I.Q. sinks to a point where you lack any credibility.

There is a good reason for this. With a few rare exceptions, human beings tend to help people that they see as less intelligent or informed, rather than taking advantage of them. Of course there are a few ruthless people out there who will try to take advantage of weak people, but most people want to compete with people they see as brighter and help people they see as less bright. So the reason for acting dumb is that it diffuses the competitive spirit of the other side. How can you fight with someone who is asking you to help them negotiate with you? How can you carry on any type of competitive banter with a person who says, "I don't know, what do you think?" Most people, when faced with this situation, feel sorry for the other person and go out of their way to help him or her.

Do you remember the TV show *Columbo*? Peter Falk played a detective who walked around in an old raincoat and a mental fog, chewing on an old cigar butt. He constantly wore an expression that suggested he had just misplaced something and couldn't remember what it was, let alone where he had left it. In fact, his success was directly attributable to how smart he was—by acting dumb. His demeanor was so disarming that the murderers came close to wanting him to solve his cases because he appeared to be so helpless.

The negotiators who let their egos take control of them and come across as sharp, sophisticated negotiators commit to several things that work against them in a negotiation. These include being the following:

- A fast decision maker who doesn't need time to think things over.
- Someone who would not have to check with anyone else before going ahead.
- Someone who doesn't have to consult with experts before committing.
- Someone who would never stoop to pleading for a concession.
- Someone who would never be overridden by a supervisor.
- Someone who doesn't have to keep extensive notes about the progress of the negotiation and refer to them frequently.

The Power Negotiator who understands the importance of acting dumb retains these options:

- Requesting time to think it over so that he or she can thoroughly think through the dangers of accepting or the opportunities that making additional demands might bring.
- Deferring a decision while he or she checks with a committee or board of directors.
- Asking for time to let legal or technical experts review the proposal.
- Pleading for additional concessions.
- Using Good Guy/Bad Guy to put pressure on the other side without confrontation.
- Taking time to think under the guise of reviewing notes about the negotiation.

I act dumb by asking for the definitions of words. If the other side says to me, "Roger, there are some ambiguities in this contract," I respond with, "Ambiguities...ambiguities...hm, you know I've heard that word before, but I'm not quite sure what it means. Would you mind explaining it to me?" Or I might say, "Do you mind going over those figures one more time? I know you've done it a couple of times already, but for some reason I'm not getting it. Do you mind?" This makes them think: What a klutz I've got on my hands this time. In this way I lay to rest the competitive spirit that could have made a compromise very difficult for me to accomplish. Now the other side stops fighting me and starts trying to help me.

Be careful that you're not acting dumb in your area of expertise. If you're a heart surgeon, don't say, "I'm not sure if you need a triple by-pass or if a double by-pass will do." If you're an architect, don't say, "I don't know if this building will stand up or not."

Win-win negotiating depends on the willingness of each side to be truly empathetic to the other side's position. That's not going to happen if both sides continue to compete with each other. Power Negotiators know that acting dumb diffuses that competitive spirit and opens the door to win-win solutions.

Chapter 28

Negotiating Gambits—
Principles: Don't Let the
Other Side Write the Contract

In a typical negotiation you verbally negotiate the details, then put it into writing later for both parties to review and approve. I've yet to run across a situation where we covered every detail in the verbal negotiation. There are always points that we overlooked when we were verbally negotiating that we must detail in writing. Then we have to get the other side to approve or negotiate the points when we sit down to sign the written agreement—that's when the side that writes the contract has a tremendous advantage over the side that doesn't. Chances are that the person writing the agreement will think of at least a half-dozen things that did not come up during the verbal negotiations. That person can then write the clarification of that point to his or her advantage, leaving the other side to negotiate a change in the agreement when asked to sign it.

Don't let the other side write the contract because it will put you at a disadvantage.

This applies to brief counter-proposals just as much as it does to agreements that are hundreds of pages long. For example, a real estate agent may be presenting an offer to the sellers of an apartment building. The seller agrees to the general terms of the offer, but wants the price to be $5,000 higher. At that point either the listing agent who represents the seller or the selling agent who represents the buyer could pull a counter-proposal form out of his or her briefcase and write out a brief counter-offer for the seller to sign that the selling agent will present to the buyer for approval. It doesn't have to be complicated: "Offer accepted except that price is to be $598,000," will suffice.

If the listing agent writes the counter-offer, however, she might think of some things that would benefit her seller. She might write: "Offer accepted except that price to be $598,000. Additional $5,000 to be deposited in escrow upon acceptance. Counter-offer to be accepted upon presentation and within 24 hours."

If the selling agent were to write the counter-offer, he might write: "Offer accepted except that price is to be $598,000. Additional $5,000 to be added to the note that the seller is carrying back."

These additions are probably not big enough to be challenged by either a seller or a buyer who is eager to complete the transaction, however, they substantially benefit the side who wrote the brief counter-offer. If the person who writes a one paragraph counter-offer can affect it so much think how much that person could affect a multi-page contract.

Remember that this may not just be a matter of taking advantage of the other side. Both sides may genuinely think that they had reached agreement on a point whereas their interpretations may be substantially different when they write it out. A classic example of this is the Camp David accord, signed by President Carter, President Anwar Sadat of Egypt, and Prime Minister Menachem Begin of Israel. After 13 frustrating days of negotiating at Camp David where they all felt until the last moment that their efforts were futile, they reached what they thought was a breakthrough to agreement. Excitedly they flew helicopters to Washington and with massive publicity signed the accord. In the East Room, the normally unemotional Menachem Begin turned to his wife and said, "Mama, we'll go down in the history books tonight." That may be so, but the truth is that many years later, hardly any of the elements of the agreement had gone into effect. Their enthusiasm led each of them to think that they had reached agreement when they really hadn't.

If you are to be the one writing the contract, it's a good idea to keep notes throughout the negotiation and put a check mark in the margin against any point that will be part of the final agreement. This does two things:

1. It reminds you to include all the points that you wanted.

2. When you write the contract you may be reluctant to include a point in the agreement unless you can specifically recall the other side agreeing to it. Your notes will give you the confidence to include it even if you don't remember it clearly.

If you have been team negotiating, be sure to have all the other members of your team review the contract before you present it to the other side. You may have overlooked a point that you should have included or you may have misinterpreted a point. It's common for the lead negotiator to let her enthusiasm overwhelm her to a point that she feels that the other side agreed to something when it was less than clear to more independent observers.

I'm not a big believer in having attorneys conduct a negotiation for you because so few of them are good negotiators. They tend to be confrontational negotiators because they're used to threatening the other side into submission, and they are seldom open to creative solutions because their first obligation is to keep you out of trouble, not make you money. Remember that in law school they are not taught how to make deals, only how to break deals. In our litigious society there isn't much point in making an agreement that won't hold up in court, however, so it's a good idea to have the agreement approved by your attorney before you have it signed. In a complicated agreement what you prepare and have the other side sign may be no more than a letter of intent. Have the attorneys work on it later to make it a legal document. It's better that you devote your energy to reaching agreement.

If you have prepared an agreement that you think the other side may be reluctant to sign, you may be smart to include the expression "Subject to your attorney's approval," to encourage them to sign it.

Once the verbal negotiations are over, get a memorandum of agreement signed as quickly as possible. The longer you give them before they see it in writing, the greater the chance that they'll forget what they agreed to and question what you've prepared.

Also make sure they understand the agreement. Don't be tempted to have them sign something when you know they're not clear on the implications. If they don't understand and something goes wrong, they will always blame you. They will never accept responsibility.

I find it helpful to write out the agreement I want before I go into the negotiations. I don't show it to the other side, but I find it helpful to compare it to the agreement that we eventually reach, so that I can see how well I did. Sometimes it's easy to get excited because the other side is making concessions that you didn't expect to get. Then your enthusiasm carries you forward and you agree to what you feel is a fantastic deal. It may be a good deal, but unless you have clearly established your criteria up front it may not be the deal that you hoped to get.

Power Negotiators know that you should always try to be the one that writes the contract. When the verbal negotiations are over, it's time for someone to put everything in writing and the person who gets to put it in writing has definite power in the negotiations. There are bound to be a half-dozen little details that you didn't think of when you were verbally negotiating, that need to be specified in the written contract.

If you're the one who gets to write the contract, you can write those to your favor. Then it's up to the other person to negotiate them out when it comes to signing the contract. So try to be the one who writes the contract.

I'll say to the other people, "Look, we need to put this down in writing. But let's not go to a lot of expense on this. I have an attorney on retainer, it won't cost either one of us anything for me to have my attorney do it." Even if I had to pay the attorney to do it, I still think I'd be better off to be the one who is writing the contract.

Chapter 29

Negotiating Gambits— Principles: Read the Contract Every Time

In this age of computer-generated contracts, it's a sad fact of life that you have to reread a contract every time it comes across your desk.

In the old days, when contracts were typewritten, both sides would go through it and write in any changes, and then each negotiator would initial the change. You could glance through the contract and quickly review any change that you had made or to which you had agreed. Nowadays with computer-generated contracts we're more likely to go back to the computer, make the change, and print out a new contract.

Here's the danger. You may have refused to sign a clause in a contract. The other side agrees to change it and says they'll send you a corrected contract for your signature. When it comes across your desk you're busy, so you quickly review it to see that they made the change you wanted and then turn to the back page and sign it. Unfortunately, because you didn't take the time to reread the entire contract, you didn't realize that they had also changed something else. Perhaps it was something blatant such as changing "F.O.B. factory" to "F.O.B. job site." Or it may be such a minor change in wording that you don't discover it until years later when something goes wrong, and you need the contract to enforce some action. By then you may not even remember what you agreed to, and you can only assume that because you signed it you must have agreed to it.

Yes, I agree with you—you have a wonderful case for a lawsuit that the other side defrauded you—but why expose yourself to that kind of trouble? In this age of computer-generated contracts you should read the contract all the way through, every time it comes across your desk for signature.

Chapter 30

Negotiating Gambits—
Principles: Funny Money

There are all kinds of ways of describing the price of something. If you went to the Boeing Aircraft Company and asked them what it costs to fly a 747 coast to coast, they wouldn't tell you "Fifty-two thousand dollars." They would tell you eleven cents per passenger mile.

Salespeople call that breaking it down to the ridiculous. Haven't we all had a real estate salesperson say to us at one time or another, "Do you realize you're talking 35¢ a day here. You're not going to let 35¢ a day stand between you and your dream home are you?" It probably didn't occur to you that 35¢ a day over the 30-year life of a real estate mortgage is more than $7,000. Power Negotiators think in real money terms.

When that supplier tells you about a 5¢ increase on an item, it may not seem important enough to spend much time on. Until you start thinking of how many of those items you buy during a year. Then you find that there's enough money sitting on the table to make it well worth your while to do some Power Negotiating.

I once dated a woman who had very expensive taste. One day she took me to a linen store in Newport Beach because she wanted us to buy a new set of sheets. They were beautiful sheets but when I found out that they were $1,400, I was astonished and told the sales clerk that it was the kind of opulence that caused the peasants to storm the palace gates.

She calmly looked at me and said, "Sir, I don't think you understand. A fine set of sheets like this will last you at least 5 years, so you're really talking about only $280 a year." Then she whipped out a pocket calculator and frantically started punching in numbers. "That's only $5.38 a week. That's not much for what is probably the finest set of sheets in the world."

I said, "That's ridiculous."

Without cracking a smile, she said, "I'm not through. With a fine set of sheets like this, you obviously would never sleep alone, so we're really talking only 38 cents per day, per person." Now that's really breaking it down to the ridiculous.

Here are some other examples of funny money:

- Interest rates expressed as a percentage rather than a dollar amount.
- The amount of the monthly payments being emphasized rather than the true cost of the item.
- Cost per brick, tile, or square foot rather than the total cost of materials.
- An hourly increase in pay per person rather than the annual cost of the increase to the company.
- Insurance premiums as a monthly amount rather than an annual cost.
- The price of land expressed as the monthly payment.

Businesses know that if you're not having to pull real money out of your purse or pocket, you're inclined to spend more. It's why casinos the world over have you convert your real money to gaming chips. It's why restaurants are happy to let you use a credit card even though they have to pay a percentage to the credit card company. When I worked for a department store chain, we were constantly pushing our clerks to sign up customers for one of our credit cards because we knew that credit card customers will spend more and they will also buy better quality merchandise than a cash customer. Our motivation wasn't entirely financial in pushing credit cards. We also knew that because credit card customers would buy better quality merchandise, it would satisfy them more, and they would be more pleased with their purchases.

So when you're negotiating by all means break the investment down to the ridiculous because it does sound like less money, but learn to think in real money terms. Don't let people use the Funny Money Gambit on you.

Chapter 31

Negotiating Gambits—
Principles: People Believe
What They See in Writing

The printed word has great power over people. Most people believe what they see in writing; even if they won't believe it when they just hear about it.

The Candid Camera people did a stunt to prove that a number of years back; you may remember seeing it on television. They posted a sign on a road next to a golf course in Delaware that said, "Delaware Closed." Allen Funt stood by the sign in a rented trooper's uniform. He wasn't allowed to speak to the people as they came up, only point up at the sign.

What happened amazed me. People were coming to a screeching halt and saying things like, "How long's it going to be closed for? My wife and kids are inside."

People believe what they see in writing. That's why I'm such a big believer in presentation binders. When you sit down with someone and you open up the presentation binder and it says, "My company is the greatest widget manufacturer in the world." Then you turn another page and it says, "Our workers are the greatest craftsmen in the business." You turn another page and start showing them reference letters from all your previous jobs.

They find it believable even when they know you just came from the print shop with it.

This is how hotels are able to get people to check out of the rooms on time. Holiday Inns used to have a terrible time getting people to check out of their rooms at 12 noon, until the Inns learned the art of the printed word and posted those little signs on the back of the door. Now 97 percent of the guests check out of their rooms on time, without any question at all, because the written word is so believable.

So every chance you get, put things in writing. For example, if you have salespeople selling for you and you have to put a price change into effect, be sure that they have it in writing. Because there's a world of difference between them sitting with a potential customer and saying, "We're having a price increase at the start of next month, so you should make a commitment now," and them saying, "Look at this letter I just got from my boss. It indicates that we're having a price increase on July 1st." Always show it to people in writing whenever you can. If you're negotiating by phone, back up what you're saying by also faxing them the information.

If you sell big ticket items and don't have a method of creating computer-generated proposals, I'd suggest that you stop everything and go get a computer system right now. It'll pay for itself on the first job. Many years ago I was in Australia on a lecture tour and a fire broke out on the second floor of my home in California. When I returned I had three contractors bid on repairing the damage. Two of them scrawled out bids by hand. They both bid around $24,000. The third contractor prepared a very comprehensive bid by computer. Every little detail was spelled out in detail. But his bid was $49,000—more than twice as much. I accepted the higher bid because the Power of the Printed Word was so great that I just didn't trust the hand-written bids.

What's the bottom line? Because people don't question what they see in writing, you should always present written backup evidence to support your proposal. If the negotiation includes expectations that the other side will meet certain requirements, it also helps to confirm those requirements in writing.

Chapter 32

Negotiating Gambits— Principles: Concentrate on the Issues

Power Negotiators know that they should always concentrate on the issues and not be distracted by the actions of the other negotiators. Have you ever watched tennis on television and seen a highly emotional star like John McEnroe jumping up and down at the other end of the court. You wonder to yourself, "How on Earth can anybody play tennis against somebody like that? It's such a game of concentration, it doesn't seem fair."

The answer is that good tennis players understand that only one thing affects the outcome of the game of tennis. That's the movement of the ball across the net. What the other player is doing doesn't affect the outcome of the game at all, as long as you know what the ball is doing. So in that way, tennis players learn to concentrate on the ball, not on the other person.

When you're negotiating, the ball is the movement of the goal concessions across the negotiating table. It's the only thing that affects the outcome of the game, but it's so easy to get thrown off by what the other people are doing, isn't it?

I remember once wanting to buy a large real estate project in Signal Hill, California, that comprised eighteen four-unit buildings. I knew that I had to get the price far below the $1.8 million that the sellers were asking for the property, which was owned free and clear by a large group of real estate investors. A real estate agent had brought it to my attention, so I felt obligated to let him present the first offer, reserving the right to go back and negotiate directly with the sellers if he wasn't able to get my $1.2 million offer accepted.

The last thing in the world the agent wanted to do was present an offer at $1.2 million—$600,000 below the asking price—but finally I convinced him to give it a try and off he went to present the offer. By doing that he made a tactical error. He shouldn't have gone to them; he should have had them come to him. You always have more control when you're negotiating in your power base than if you go to their power base.

He came back a few hours later, and I asked him, "How did it go?"

"It was awful, just awful. I'm so embarrassed," he told me. "I got into this large conference room, and all of the principals had come in for the reading of the offer. They brought with them their attorney, their CPA, and their real estate broker. I was planning to do the silent close on them." (Which is to read the offer and then be quiet. The next person who talks loses in the negotiations.) "The problem was, there wasn't any silence. I got down to the $1.2 million, and they said: 'Wait a minute. You're coming in $600,000 low? We're insulted.'" Then they all got up and stormed out of the room.

I said, "Nothing else happened?"

He said, "Well, a couple of the principals stopped in the doorway on their way out, and they said: 'We're not gonna come down to a penny less than $1.5 million.' It was just awful. Please don't ever ask me to present an offer that low again."

I said, "Wait a minute. You mean to tell me that, in five minutes, you got them to come down $300,000, and you feel bad about the way the negotiations went?"

See how easy it is to get thrown off by what the other people are doing, rather than concentrating on the issues in a negotiation. It's inconceivable that a full-time professional negotiator, say an international negotiator, would walk out of negotiations because he doesn't think the other people are fair. He may walk out, but it's a specific negotiating tactic, not because he's upset.

Can you imagine a top arms negotiator showing up in the White House, and the President saying, "What are you doing here? I thought you were in Geneva negotiating with the Russians."

"Well, yes, I was, Mr. President, but those guys are so unfair. You can't trust them and they never keep their commitments. I got so upset, I just walked out." Power Negotiators don't do that. They concentrate on the issues, not on the personalities. You should always be thinking, "Where are we now, compared to where we were an hour ago or yesterday or last week?"

Secretary of State Warren Christopher said, "It's okay to get upset when you're negotiating, as long as you're in control, and you're doing it as a specific negotiating tactic." It's when you're upset and out of control that you always lose.

That's why salespeople will have this happen to them. They lose an account. They take it into their sales manager, and they say, "Well, we lost this one. Don't waste any time trying to save it. I did everything I could. If anybody could have saved it, I would have saved it."

So the sales manager says, "Well, just as a public relations gesture, let me give the other side a call anyway." The sales manager can hold it together, not necessarily because he's any brighter or sharper than the salesperson, but because he hasn't become emotionally involved with the people the way the salesperson has. Don't do that. Learn to concentrate on the issues.

Chapter 33

Negotiating Gambits— Principles: Always Congratulate the Other Side

When you're through negotiating you should always congratulate the other side. However poorly you think the other people may have done in the negotiations, congratulate them. Say, "Wow—did you do a fantastic job negotiating that. I realize that I didn't get as good a deal as I could have done, but quite frankly it was worth it because I learned so much about negotiating. You were brilliant." You want the other person to feel that he or she won in the negotiations. And, let me repeat myself, you never want to gloat.

One of my clients is a large magazine publishing company that has me teach Power Negotiating to its sales force. When I was telling the salespeople how they should never gloat in a negotiation, the founder of the company jumped to his feet and said, "I want to tell you a story about that." Very agitated, he went on to tell the group, "My first magazine was about sailing, and I sold it to a huge New York magazine publisher. I flew up there to sign the final contract, and the moment I signed it and thanked them, they said to me, 'If you'd have been a better negotiator, we would have paid you a lot more.' That was 25 years ago and it still burns me up when I think about it today. I told them that if they had been better negotiators, I would have taken less." Let me ask you something. If that magazine publisher wanted to buy another one of his magazines, would he start by raising the price on them? Of course he would. However harmless it may seem, be sensitive to how you're reacting to the deal. Never gloat and always congratulate.

When I published an earlier book on negotiating, a newspaper reviewed it and took exception to my saying that you should always congratulate, saying that it was clearly manipulative to congratulate the other side when you didn't really think that they had won. I disagree. I look upon it as the ultimate in courtesy for the conqueror to congratulate the vanquished. When the British army and navy went down the Atlantic to recapture the Falkland Islands from the Argentinians, it was quite a rout. Within a few days the Argentinian navy lost most of its ships and the victory for the English was absolute. The evening after the Argentinian admiral surrendered, the English admiral invited him on board to dine with his officers and congratulated him on a splendid campaign.

Power Negotiators always want the other parties thinking that they won in the negotiations. It starts by asking for more than you expect to get. It continues through all of the other Gambits that are designed to service the perception that they're winning. It ends with congratulating the other side.

Section Two

Why Money Isn't as Important as You Think

In this section I'm going to spend some time talking about my pet subject: that when you're negotiating, money is way down the list of things that are important to the other side.

First, we'll talk about something that you may find hard to believe, but it's something of which I've become convinced—that people want to spend more, not less, and that the price concerns salespeople more than the people to whom they sell.

Then I'll teach you all the things that are more important to people than money.

Finally, I'll teach you some techniques to find out how much they'll pay.

Chapter 34

People Want to Pay More, Not Less

After almost two decades of training salespeople, I have become convinced that price concerns salespeople more than it does the people to whom they sell. I'll go even further than that—I think that customers who may be asking you to cut your price are secretly wishing that they could pay more for your product. Hear me out before you dismiss this as being imbecilic.

I was the merchandise manager at the Montgomery Ward store in Bakersfield, California, back in 1971. Although Bakersfield was not a large town, the store ranked 13th in volume in a chain of more than 600 stores. Why did it do so well? In my opinion it was because the head office left us alone and allowed us to sell to the needs of the local population. For example, we did a huge business in home air conditioners because of the outrageously hot summers. In Bakersfield, it's not unusual for it to be 100 degrees at midnight. In those days an average blue-collar home in that city cost around $30,000. The air conditioners that we would install in these homes might cost $10,000 to $12,000. It was very hard for me to get new salespeople started selling in that department because they had a real resistance to selling something that cost more money than they had ever made in a year. They simply didn't believe that anybody would spend $12,000 to put an air conditioner in a $30,000 home. The customers were willing to pay it, as was illustrated by our huge sales volume, but the salespeople weren't willing to support these decisions because they thought it was outrageously expensive.

However, if I could get salespeople to where they began to make big money and they installed air conditioners in their own homes, suddenly they didn't think it was so outrageous any more, and they would dismiss the price objection as if it didn't exist.

Beginning stockbrokers have the same problem. It's very hard for them to ask a client to invest $100,000 when they don't know where lunch money is coming from. Once they become affluent, their sales snowball.

So I believe that price concerns salespeople more than any customer. This is demonstrated by the experience of one of my clients who is a designer and supplier of point-of-purchase sales aids and displays. He tells me that if three products are on a shelf in a store—let's say three toasters—and the features of each are described on the carton, the customers will most frequently select the highest price item—*unless* a salesperson comes along to assist them with the selection. When that happens, the salesperson, who is probably working for minimum wage, is unable to justify spending money on the best and manages to talk the customer down to the low-end or middle-of-the-line toaster.

The key element here is the description on the carton. You must give customers a reason for spending more money, but if you can do that, they want to spend more money, not less. I think that spending money is what Americans do best. We love to spend money. We spend six trillion dollars a year in this country, and if we could walk into a store and find a salesclerk who knew anything about the merchandise, we'd spend seven trillion dollars a year. And that's when we're spending our own hard earned after-tax dollars. What if you're asking someone who works at a corporation to spend the company's money? There's only one thing better than spending your own money, and that's spending someone else's money. If that weren't enough, remember that corporate expenditures are tax deductible, so Uncle Sam is going to pick up 40 percent of the bill.

So I believe that we've had it all wrong for all these years. When we're trying to sell something to somebody she doesn't want to spend less money, she wants to spend more. However, you do have to do two things:

1. You must give her a reason for spending more.

2. You must convince her that she could not have gotten a better deal than the one you're offering her.

That second point is where Power Negotiating comes in, because everything I teach is designed to convince the other people that they won the negotiation and that they couldn't have done better. Let's face it, does what you pay for something really matter? If you're going to buy a new automobile, does it matter if you spend $20,000 or $21,000? Not really, because you'll soon forget what you paid for it, and the slight increase in payments is not going to affect your lifestyle. What really matters is the feeling that you got the best possible deal. You don't want to go to work the next morning and have everybody crowded around to admire your new car when somebody says, "How much did you get it for?"

You say, "I worked out a terrific deal. I got them down to $21,000."

"You paid what?" he replies. "My friend bought one of those, and he paid only $20,000. You should have gone to Main Street Auto Mall." That's what hurts—the feeling that you didn't get the best deal.

The objection that every salesperson hears most is the price objection. "We'd love to do business with you, but your price is too high." Let me tell you something about that. It has nothing to do with your price. You could cut your prices 20 percent across the board and you'd still hear that objection. I trained the salespeople at the largest lawnmower factory in the world. You probably own one of their products because they manufacture most of the low-end private label lawn mowers that discount and chain stores sell. Nobody can undercut their production cost on lawn mowers. They have it down to such a science that if you bought one of their mowers at Home Depot and you tipped the kid who carried it to your car a dollar, the kid made more on the lawnmower than the factory did. That's how slim their profit margins are. However when I asked them to tell me the number one complaint they hear from the buyers at stores, guess what they told me? You got it. "Your prices are too high."

You hear that complaint all the time because the people you're selling to study negotiating skills too. They meet in groups at their conventions and sit around in the bars saying things like, "Do you want to have fun with salespeople? Just let them go through their entire presentation. Let them take all the time they want. Then when they finally tell you how much it costs, lean back in your chair, put your feet up on the desk and say, 'I'd love to do business with you, but your prices are too high.' Then try not to laugh as they stammer and stutter and don't know what to say next."

Instead of letting this kind of thing work you up into a sweat, adopt the attitude that negotiating is a game. You learn the rules of the game, you practice, practice, practice until you get good at it, then you go out there and play the game with all the gusto you can muster. Negotiating is a game that is fun to play when you know what you're doing and have the confidence to play it with vigor.

The next time you're trying to get somebody to spend money remember that they really want to spend more money with you, not less. All you have to do is give them a reason and convince them that there's no way they could get a better deal.

Chapter 35

Things That Are More Important Than Money

A reporter at a press conference once asked Astronaut Neil Armstrong to relate his thoughts as Apollo 11 approached the moon. He said, "All I could think of was that I was up there in a spaceship built by the lowest bidder." A cute line, but he was falling prey to a popular misconception that the government must do business with anybody who bids the lowest price. Of course that's not true, but it's amazing how many people believe it. I hear it all the time at my *Secrets of Power Negotiating* seminars: "What can we do when we have to deal with the government? They have to accept the lowest bid."

I once found myself sitting next to a Pentagon procurement officer on a flight to the East Coast, and I raised this point with him. "All the time I hear that the government has to buy from the lowest bidder. Is that really true?"

"Heavens no," he told me. "We'd really be in trouble if that were true. Cost is far from the top of the list of what's important to us. We're far more concerned with a company's experience, the experience of the workers and the management team assigned to the product, and their ability to get the job done on time. The rules say that we should buy from the lowest bidder who we feel is capable of meeting our specifications. If we know that a particular supplier is the best one for us, we simply write the specifications to favor that supplier."

Of course, that is the key to selling to government agencies, whether it be the city, county, state, or federal government. If you want to do business with any level of government, you should become known as the most knowledgeable person in your industry, so that when the agencies start to prepare bid specifications, they welcome your advice on what they should specify. Fortunately, the trend is away from this type of direct bidding and toward the government agency hiring a private sector project manager to supervise the work. By inserting this middle person, they avoid the obligation to let bids and instead let the middle person negotiate the best deal.

So even with the federal government, price is far from the most important thing. When you're dealing with a company that doesn't have legal requirements to put out a request for bids, it's far from the top of the list. Just for the fun of it, review the following list of things that are probably more important than price to buyers.

- The conviction that they are getting the best deal you're willing to offer.

- The quality of the product or service. This is an interesting one because I frequently hear from salespeople that they sell an item that has become a commodity, and it doesn't matter which source the buyer uses and that the buyer wants only the lowest price. Baloney. If that were true 90 percent of companies supplying such products or services would be out of business. If that were true, the only company that could exist in the market place would be the one offering the lowest price, and that's a nonsensical proposition.

- The terms that you offer. Many large companies make more on the financing of their product than they do the sale of the product. I recently leased a top-of-the-line luxury automobile and became convinced that making the car was only a small part of what this company did. The real money was in financing the lease or the purchase.

- The delivery schedule that you offer. Can you get it to them when they need it and be counted upon to keep on doing that? Do you offer a just-in-time delivery system? Are you willing to let them warehouse the product and bill them as they use it?

- The experience you have in delivering the product or service. Are you familiar with their type of company and the way they do business? Are you comfortable with that kind of relationship?

- The guarantee that you offer and, in general, how well you stand behind what you do. I once paid several hundred dollars to buy a product from a Sharper Image store. After a few months a part on it broke, and I called their 800 number to see if they would take care of the problem. After listening to me only long enough to understand what the problem was, the operator said, "If you'll give me your address I'll FedEx a replacement part to you."

  I said, "Don't you need to know when and where I bought it? I'm not sure that I can find my receipt."

"I don't need to know any of that," he told me. "I just want to be sure that you're happy with what you bought." When a company stands behind what they do to that extent, am I really going to worry about whether they have the lowest price or not? Of course not.

- Return privileges. Will you take it back if it doesn't sell? Will you inventory their stock and do that automatically for them?

- Building a working partnership with you and your company. The old adversarial relationship between vendor and customers is disappearing as astute companies realize the value of developing a mutually beneficial partnership with their suppliers.

- Credit. A line of credit with your company may be more important than price, especially to a start-up company or in an industry where cash flow is cyclical, and you could take up the slack during the lean months.

- Your staff. When the contract calls for something to be made (aerospace, construction) or a service to be performed (legal, audit or accounting work, computer services) other factors may be more important than price:

  - The quality of the workers that you will assign to the job.

  - The level of management that you will assign to oversee the work.

  - The ability and willingness to tailor your product and packaging to their needs.

- The respect that you will give them. Many times a company will move from a large vendor to a smaller one because they want to be a substantial part of the vendor's business to have more leverage.

- Peace of mind. AT&T keeps my telephone business even though they are more expensive than Sprint and MCI and have never pretended that they aren't. I stay with them because the service has been trouble free and simple to use for many years, and I have more important things concerning me than switching long distance companies to save a few pennies a call.

- Reliability. Can they trust that the quality of your product and service will stay high?

Chapter 36

Finding Out How Much
a Seller Will Take

In the two previous chapters, I made the point that money isn't the most important thing to consider when you're buying or selling. Now let's take a look at some techniques to find out the seller's lowest price. When you are buying, the negotiating range of the seller ranges from the wish price (what they're hoping you'll pay) all the way down to the walk-away price (at anything less than this they will not sell at all). The same is true in reverse with the buyer. How do we uncover the seller's walk-away price? Let's say that your neighbor is asking $15,000 for his pickup truck. Here are some techniques you can use to uncover his lowest price.

- Ask. That may seem incredibly naive, but if he's not a good negotiator he may just tell you what's on his mind. Of course a Power Negotiator won't fall for that, but many people will. If he's a Power Negotiator, he will automatically turn the tables on you by saying, "I think $15,000 is a very fair price, but if you want to make me an offer somewhere close to that, I'll talk it over with my wife (Higher Authority—see Chapter 7). What is the best price you would offer me?"

  Of course the way that you ask for his lowest price makes a big difference. Try these approaches:

  "I'm really interested only in a pickup truck for occasional use, not one as fine as yours. I'm looking at one that the owner's asking only $5,000 for. However, I thought I'd be fair to you and ask you what the least you'd take would be."

  Or the Reluctant Buyer approach (see Chapter 5): After spending a lot of time looking it over and asking questions you say, "I really appreciate all the time you've taken with me on this, but unfortunately its not what I was looking for. But I wish you the best of luck with it." Then, when you're halfway into your car to leave you say, "Look, I really want to be fair to you because you spent so much time with me, so just to be fair to you, what is the very lowest price you would let it go for?"

- Drop out of contention, but tell him you have a friend who might be interested. You might say, "Thanks for showing it to me but it's really not what I'm looking for. However, I do have a friend who's looking for something like this, but he doesn't have much money. What's the very least you'd take?"

- Nibble for a finder's fee. "If my friend did buy it from you, would you give me a $500 finder's fee?"

- Offer something in return to see if it will cause them to lower the price. "Would you take less if I let you borrow it once in a while?"

- Have other people make super-low offers to lower the expectation of the seller. This is unethical of course, but I'll tell you about it so that you will recognize it when it's used against you. If the seller has high hopes of getting $15,000 for his truck, your offer of $10,000 may sound like an insult. However if he's had only two offers so far, one for $7,000 and the other for $8,000, when you come along and offer him $10,000, he may jump at it.

- Make a low offer subject to the approval of a higher authority. "My buddy and I are going in on this so I'll have to run this by him, but would you take $10,000?"

Now let's take a look at some techniques that a seller could use to find out how much a buyer is willing to pay. Let's say that you sell switches to computer manufacturers. Here are some techniques you could use:

- Raise their top offer by hypothesizing what your higher authority might be willing to do. Perhaps they buy similar switches now for $1.50 and you're asking $2.00. You might say, "We both agree we have a better quality product. If I could get my boss down to $1.75, would that work for you?" Protected by Higher Authority, it doesn't mean that you have to sell them to him for $1.75. However, if he acknowledges that $1.75 might be workable, you have raised his negotiating range to $1.75 so that you're only 25¢ apart instead of 50¢.

- Determine their quality standards by offering a stripped down version. "We may be able to get down below $1.50 if you don't care about copper contacts. Would that work for you?" In this way you probably get them to acknowledge that price isn't their only concern. They do care about quality.

- Establish the most they can afford by offering a higher quality version. "We can add an exciting new feature to the switch, but it would put the cost in the $2.50 range." If the buyer shows some interest in the feature you know that they could pay more. If he or she says, "I don't care if it's diamond plated. We can't go over $1.75," you know that fitting the product to a price bracket is a critical issue.

- Remove yourself as a possible vendor. This disarms the buyer and may cause him to reveal some information that he wouldn't if they thought you were still in the game. You say, "Joe, we love doing business with you, but this item is just not for us. Let's get together on something else later." Having disarmed Joe in this way, a little later you can say, "I'm sorry we couldn't work with you on the switches, but just between you and me what do you realistically think you can buy them for?" He may well say, "I realize that $1.50 is a lowball figure, but I think I'll get somebody to come down to around $1.80."

As you can see from all we've talked about here, there's a lot to be said about the subject of price. Power Negotiators know not to exacerbate the price problem by assuming that price is uppermost in the other person's mind. Also, it is ludicrous to say that what you sell is a commodity, and you have to sell for less than your competitor's price for you to get the sale.

Section Three

Negotiating Pressure Points

Louis (Satchmo) Armstrong used to tell this story about his early days as a musician: "One night this big, bad-ass hood crashes my dressing room in Chicago and instructs me that I will open in such-and-such a club in New York the next night. I tell him I got this Chicago engagement and don't plan no traveling and I turn my back on him to show I'm so cool. Then I hear this sound: SNAP! CLICK! I turn around, and he has pulled this vast revolver on me and cocked it. Jesus, it looks like a cannon and sounds like death! So I look down at that steel and say, 'Weelllll, maybe I do open in New York tomorrow.' " As Al Capone once said, "You can get much farther with a kind word and a gun than you can with a kind word alone."

Pulling a gun on someone during a negotiation is the crudest pressure point of them all. I imagine that it's remarkably effective, but there's never a need for you to do it. In this section I'll teach you some pressure points that you can use that are just as effective and far more acceptable. Many of them you could use with the brutality of pulling a gun on someone, but usually you're better off to be far more subtle. If you have the power, you don't have to flaunt it.

Chapter 37

Time Pressure

Vilfredo Pareto never studied the time element in a negotiation, yet the Pareto principle reveals the incredible pressure that time can put on a negotiation.

Pareto was an economist in the nineteenth century. Born in Paris, he spent most of his life in Italy, where he studied the balance of wealth as it was distributed among the populace. In his book, *Cours d'economie politique*, he pointed out that 80 percent of the wealth was concentrated in the hands of 20 percent of the people.

The interesting thing about the 80/20 rule is that it surfaces repeatedly in apparently unrelated fields. Sales managers tell me that 80 percent of their business is done by 20 percent of the salespeople. Eventually it occurs to them that they should fire the 80 percent and just keep the 20 percent. The problem with that is that the 80/20 then reapplies itself to the remainder, and you're back with the same problem—only with a smaller sales force.

Schoolteachers tell me that 20 percent of the children cause 80 percent of the trouble. In seminars 20 percent of the students ask 80 percent of the questions.

The rule in negotiating is that 80 percent of the concessions occur in the last 20 percent of the time available to negotiate. If demands are presented early in a negotiation, neither side may be willing to make concessions, and the entire transaction might fall apart. If, on the other hand, additional demands or problems surface in the last 20 percent of the time available to negotiate, both sides are more willing to make concessions.

Think of the last time that you bought a piece of real estate. It probably took about 10 weeks from the time you signed the initial contract to the time you actually became the owner of the property. Now think of the concessions that were made. Isn't it true that during the last 2 weeks when things came up to be renegotiated, both sides became more flexible?

Some people are unethical enough to use this against you. They hold out, until the last minute, elements of the negotiation that could have been brought up earlier and resolved simply. Then when you're getting ready to finalize the arrangements these problems come up because they know you'll be more flexible under time pressure.

Tie up all the details up front

One thing this tells you is that you should always tie up all the details up front. Don't leave anything to, "Oh well, we can work that out later." A matter that appears to be of little importance up front can become a very big problem under time pressure.

I remember being in Kalispell, Montana, to do a seminar for the Montana graduates of the Realtors' Institute. These are the highest trained residential real estate people in the state. We were doing an all-day seminar on Power Negotiating, and during the break an agent came up to me and said, "Perhaps you can help me. I have a big problem. It looks as though I'm going to lose a big part of my commission on a very large transaction."

I asked her to tell me more, and she said, "A couple of months ago a man came into my office and wanted me to list his $600,000 home. Well, I had never listed anything that large before, and I guess I didn't express as much confidence as I should have, because when he asked me how much commission I would charge, he flinched, and I fell for it. I told him six percent. He said: 'Six percent. That's $36,000! That's a lot of money.' So I said: 'Look, if you have to come down much on the price of the property, we'll work with you on the commission.' That's all I said, and I never gave it a second thought.

"As luck would have it, I ended up not only getting the listing, but I found the buyer as well. He didn't have to come down much on the price, so now I have almost the full $36,000 commission coming into my office, and the property is due to close next week. Yesterday he came into my office and said: 'I've been thinking about the amount of work that you had to do on that sale…' " Remember the value of services always appears to diminish rapidly after those services have been performed (see Chapter 8). " '…you remember you told me that you'd work with me on the commission?'

"I said, 'yes.'

"'Well, I've been thinking about the amount of work you had to do, and I've decided that $5,000 would be a very fair commission for you.' "

$5,000 when she was due $36,000. She was almost panic stricken. This illustrates that you shouldn't leave anything to "We can work that out later" because a little detail up front can become a big problem later on, when you're under time pressure.

That story also illustrates how we always think we have the weaker hand in negotiations—whichever side we're on. In fact, the real estate agent in Montana was in a very strong position, wasn't she? As I explained to her, she had a written contract for the six percent. If anything, she had verbally modified it with a vague comment that wouldn't hold up in court anyway. So in fact she had all the power, but didn't think she had any.

However, why expose yourself to that kind of problem? Tie up all the details up front. When the other side says to you, "We can work that out later, it's not going to be a big problem," bells should start to ring and lights should start to flash. Don't let people do that to you.

People become flexible under time pressure

The next thing that Power Negotiators have learned about time is that people become flexible under time pressure.

When do your children ask you for something? Just as you're rushing out of the door, right? When my daughter Julia was attending the University of Southern California, she lived in a sorority house and would sometimes come home for the weekends and need money for books. When would she ask me? Seven o'clock on a Monday morning, just as she was racing out the door she'd say, "Dad, I'm sorry, I forgot; I need $60 for books."

I'd say, "Julia, don't do this to me. I teach this stuff. How come you've been home all weekend, and we didn't have a chance to talk about it before?"

"Oh sorry, Dad, I just didn't think about it until I got ready to go, but I'm late now, I've got to get on the freeway, or I'll be late for class. If I can't get my books today, I won't be able to get my assignment in on time. So please, can I have the money now, and we'll talk next weekend?"

Not that children are that manipulative, but instinctively, over all those years of dealing with adults, they understand that under time pressure people become more flexible.

It's interesting to look at international negotiations and how time pressure has affected the outcome. Remember the Vietnam peace talks that were held in Paris? You'll recall that in the spring of 1968, Lyndon Johnson had announced that he wouldn't run for reelection and would devote all his time to the peace talks. He was very eager to reach a peace agreement before November, when his vice-president, Hubert Humphrey, would be running for election. He sent our negotiator, Averell Harriman, to Paris with clear instructions: Get something done, get it done fast, right now. Texas style.

Averell Harriman rented a suite at the Ritz Hotel in Paris on a week-to-week basis. The Vietnamese negotiator Xuan Thuy rented a villa in the countryside for two and half years. Then the Vietnamese proceeded to spend week after week after week talking to us about the shape of the table.

Did they really care about the shape of the table? Of course not. They were doing two things. Number one they were projecting, very successfully, that they were not under any time pressure. They'd been in the war for 30 years or so, and another year or two here and there wouldn't bother them one way or the other. Second, they were trying to push us up against our November deadline, which they did very successfully. On November 1st, only five days before the election, Johnson called a halt to the bombing of Vietnam. Under that kind of time pressure, it was a wonder that he didn't give everything away.

When you're negotiating with people, never reveal that you have a deadline.

Let's say for example, that you have flown to Dallas to resolve a negotiation with a hotel developer, and you have a return flight at 6 o'clock. Sure, you're eager to catch that flight—but don't let the other people know. If they do know you have a 6 o'clock flight, be sure to let them know you also have a 9 o'clock backup flight or, for that matter, you can stay over for as long as it takes to work out a mutually satisfactory arrangement.

If they know you're under time pressure, they could delay the bulk of the negotiations until the last possible minute. Then there's a real danger that you'll give things away under that kind of time pressure.

In my Power Negotiating seminars I set up exercises so the students can practice negotiating. They may have 15 minutes to complete a negotiation, and I impress on them the importance of reaching agreement within that time period. As I walk around the room eavesdropping on the progress of the negotiations, I can tell that during the first 12 minutes they have trouble making any progress. Both sides are stonewalling the issues and there is very little give and take. At 12 minutes, with 80 percent of the time used up, I take the microphone and tell them they have only 3 minutes left. Then I continue periodic announcements to keep the time pressure on them and end with a countdown of the seconds from 5 to zero. It's very clear to see that they make 80 percent of the concessions in the last 20 percent of the time available to negotiate.

What to do when both sides are approaching the same time deadline

An interesting question is raised when both sides are approaching the same time deadline. This would be true if you lease your office space for example. Let's say that your five-year lease is up in six months, and you must negotiate a renewal with your landlord. You might think to yourself, "I'll use time pressure on the landlord to get the best deal. I'll wait until the last moment to negotiate with him. That will put him under a great deal of time pressure. He'll know that if I move out, the place will be vacant for several months until he can find a new tenant." That seems like a great strategy until you realize that there's no difference between that and the landlord refusing to negotiate until the last minute to put time pressure on you.

So there you have a situation in which both sides are approaching the same time deadline. Which side should use time pressure and which side should avoid it? The answer is that the side that has the most power could use time pressure, but the side with the least power should avoid time pressure and negotiate well ahead of the deadline. Fair enough, but who has the most power? The side with the most options has the most power. If you can't reach a negotiated renewal of the lease, who has the best alternatives available to them?

To determine this you might take a sheet of paper and draw a line down the middle. On the left side, list your options in the event you are unable to renew the lease. What other locations are available to you? Would they cost more or less? How much would it cost you to move the telephones and print new stationery? Would your customers be able to find you if you move?

On the right hand side of the page, list the landlord's options. How specialized is this building? How hard would it be for him to find new tenants? Would they pay more or would he have to rent it for less? How much would he have to spend on improvements or remodeling to satisfy a new tenant?

Now you must do one more thing. You must compensate for the fact that whichever side of the negotiating table you're on, you always think you have the weaker hand. After all you know all about the pressure that's on you, but you don't know about the pressure that's on the landlord. One of the things that makes you a more powerful negotiator is understanding that you always think you have the weaker hand and learning to compensate for that. So when you list each side's alternatives in this way, you'll probably end up with the conclusion that the landlord has more alternatives than you do. So compensate for that, but if you do so and clearly the landlord still has more alternatives than you do, he's the one who has the power. You should avoid time pressure and negotiate the lease renewal with plenty of time to spare. If clearly you have more alternatives available to you than the landlord does, put him under time pressure by negotiating at the last moment.

In September 1994, former President Jimmy Carter, along with Senator Sam Nunn and former Chief of Staff Colin Powell flew to Haiti to see if they could get General Cedras to give up power without our having to invade the country to force him out. At the end of the second day of negotiations President Clinton called President Carter to tell him that he had already started the invasion, and Carter had 30 minutes to leave the country. Isn't that an ultimate example of applying time pressure to a negotiation? The only problem was that Clinton was putting time pressure on the wrong side. We had all the power in that negotiation because we had all the options. It should have been Carter putting time pressure on Cedras, not Clinton putting time pressure on Carter.

When negotiations drag on, people become more flexible

The longer you can keep the other side involved in the negotiation, the more likely the other side is to move around to your point of view. The next time you're in a situation in which you're beginning to think that you'll never budge the other side, think of the tug boats in the Hudson River off Manhattan. A tiny tugboat can move that huge ocean liner around if it does it a little bit at a time. However, if the tugboat captain were to back off, rev up its engines, and try to force the ocean liner around, it wouldn't do any good. Some people negotiate like that. They reach an impasse in the negotiations that frustrates them, so they get impatient and try to force the other side to change their mind. Think of that tugboat instead. A little bit at a time, it can move the liner around. If you have enough patience you can change anybody's mind a little bit at a time.

Unfortunately, this works both ways. The longer you spend in a negotiation the more likely you are to make concessions. You may have flown to San Francisco to negotiate a large business deal. At 8 o'clock the next morning, you're in their office feeling bright, fresh, and determined to hang in and accomplish all of your goals. Unfortunately, it doesn't go as well as you hoped. The morning drags on without any progress, so you break for lunch. Then the afternoon passes, and you've reached agreement on only a few minor points. You call the airline and reschedule for the midnight red-eye flight. You break for supper and come back determined to get something done. Look out. Unless you're very careful, by 10 o'clock you'll start making concessions that you never intended to make when you started that morning.

Why does it work that way? Because your subconscious mind is now screaming at you, "You can't walk away from this empty handed after all the time and effort you've spent on it. You have to be able to put something together." Any time you pass the point where you're prepared to walk away, you have set yourself to lose in the negotiations (more about this later in Chapter 39). A Power Negotiator knows that you should disregard any time or money that you have invested in a project up to any given point. That time and money is gone whether you strike a deal or not. Always look at the terms of a negotiation as they exist at that moment and think, "Disregarding all the time and money we've poured into this deal up to now, should we go ahead?" Never be reluctant to pull the plug if it doesn't make sense any more. It's much cheaper to write off your investment than it is to plow ahead with a deal that isn't right for you just because you have so much invested in it. That's one of the things that makes Donald Trump such a powerful negotiator—he's not afraid to pull the plug on a deal that no longer makes sense. For example, he spent $100 million dollars to acquire the site for Television City on the west side of Manhattan. He spent millions more designing plans for the project that would include a 150-story tower, the world's tallest, and a magnificent television studio to which he hoped to attract NBC. However, when he couldn't negotiate the right tax concessions from the city, he shelved the entire project. You have to look at a negotiation in the same way. Forget what you've already invested and examine whether it stills looks good the way things stand at the moment.

Time is comparable to money. They are both invested, spent, saved, and wasted. Do invest the time to go through every step of the negotiation, do use time pressure to gain the advantage, and don't yield to the temptation to rush to a conclusion. Power Negotiators know that time is money.

Chapter 38

Information:
A Valuable Asset

Why do countries send spies into other countries? Why do professional football teams study the replays of their opponents' games? Because knowledge is power, and the more knowledge one side is able to accumulate about the other, the better chance that side has for victory.

If two countries go to war, the country that has the most intelligence about the other has the advantage. That was certainly true in the Persian Gulf War—the C.I.A. spies had photographed every building in Baghdad, and we were able to completely take out their communication systems in the first few bombing runs.

Governments spend billions of dollars finding out about the other side before they'll go into an arms control talk. It was interesting to see Henry Kissinger being interviewed before a summit meeting. "Mr. Kissinger," the interviewer said, "do you think it's possible our negotiators know what the other side will propose at the talks, before they actually propose it?" He said, "Oh, absolutely—no question about it. It would be absolutely disastrous for us to go into a negotiation not knowing in advance what the other side was going to propose."

Can you imagine the cost of getting that kind of information? The budget of the C.I.A. is top secret, but experts think it is almost $4 billion a year, even now that the Cold War is over. So if governments think it's important enough to spend that kind of money doesn't it make sense that we at least spend a little time before we go into negotiations to find out more about the other side?

If two companies are planning to merge, the company that knows the most will usually end up with the better deal. If two salespeople are vying for an account, the salesperson who knows more about the company and its representatives stands a better chance of being selected for the account.

Despite the obviousness of the important role that information plays in a negotiation, few people spend much time analyzing the other side before starting a negotiation. Even people who wouldn't dream of skiing or scuba diving without taking lessons will jump into a negotiation that could cost them thousands of dollars without spending adequate time gathering the information they should have.

Rule One: Don't be afraid to admit that you don't know

If you're a homeowner, think back to when you bought your present home. How much did you know about the sellers before you made an offer? Did you know why they were selling and how long they had been trying to sell? Did you find out how they had arrived at their asking price? How much did you know about their real needs, their real intentions in the negotiation? Very often even the listing agent doesn't know, does he? He's been in direct contact with the sellers since they listed the property, but when asked about the objectives of the sellers, he will very often reply, "Well, I don't know, I know they want cash out, so they're not willing to carry back paper, but I don't know what they're going to do with the cash. I didn't think it was my place to ask."

In my all-day and two-day seminars, I have the students break into teams of negotiators with some assigned as buyers and others as sellers. I give them enough information to complete a successful negotiation. In fact, I purposely give each side discoverable strengths and weaknesses. I tell each side that if the other side asks them a question to which they have been given an answer they may not lie. If one side unearthed only half of these carefully planted tidbits of information, that side would be in a powerful position to complete a successful negotiation.

Unfortunately, no matter how many times I drill students on the importance of gathering information—even to the point of assigning ten minutes of the negotiation for only that—they are still reluctant to do a thorough job.

Why are people reluctant to gather information? Because to find things out, you have to admit that you don't know, and most of us are extraordinarily reluctant to admit that we don't know. Let me give you a quick exercise to prove this point. I'm going to ask you six questions, all of which you can answer with a number, but instead of having you try to guess the right number,

I'll make it easier for you by asking you to answer with a range. So if I asked you how many states there are, instead of saying 50, you'd say, "Between 49 and 51." If I asked you for the distance from Los Angeles to New York, you might be less sure so you'd say, "Between 2,000 and 4,000 miles." You could say from one to a million and be 100 percent sure of course, but I want you to be 90 percent sure that the right answer falls within the range you give. Do you have the idea? Here are the questions:

    1. How many provinces are there in Canada?
       Between ___ and ___.

    2. How many wives did Brigham Young have?
       Between ___ and ___.

    3. How much did we pay Spain for Florida in 1819?
       Between ___ and ___.

    4. How many Perry Mason novels did Erle Stanley Gardner write?
       Between ___ and ___.

    5. How many eggs do chickens lay each year in the United States?
       Between ___ and ___.

    6. What is the length of Noah's Ark in feet according to Genesis?
       Between ___ and ___.

Here are the answers:

    1. There are ten provinces in Canada (and two territories).

    2. Brigham Young, the Mormon leader, had 27 wives.

    3. We paid $5 million for Florida.

    4. Erle Stanley Gardner wrote 75 Perry Mason novels.

    5. About 67 billion eggs are laid in the United States each year.

    6. Noah's Ark was 450 feet long. According to Genesis 6:15, the ark was 300 x 50 x 30 cubits, and a cubit equals 18 inches.

How did you do? Did you get them all right? Probably not, but think how easy it would have been to get them all right. All you would have had to do is to admit that you didn't know and make the range of your answer huge. You probably didn't do that because just like everyone else, you don't like to admit that you don't know.

So the first rule for gathering information is "don't be overconfident." Admit that you don't know and admit that anything you do know may be wrong.

Rule Two: Don't be afraid to ask the question

I used to be afraid to ask questions for fear that the question would upset the other person. I was one of those people who say, "Would you mind if I asked you?" or "Would it embarrass you to tell me?" I don't do that any more. I ask them, "How much money did you make last year?" If they don't want to tell you, they won't. Even if they don't answer the question, you'll still be gathering information. Just before General Schwarzkopf sent our troops into Kuwait, Sam Donaldson asked him, "General, when are you going to start the land war?" Did he really think that the General was going to say, "Sam, I promised the President that I wouldn't tell any of the 500 reporters that keep asking me that question, but since you asked I'll tell you. At 2:00 A.M. on Tuesday we're going in"? Of course Schwarzkopf wasn't going to answer that question, but a good reporter asks anyway. It might put pressure on the other person or annoy him so that he blurts out something he didn't intend to. Just judging the other person's reaction to the question might tell you a great deal.

As I travel around the country, I'm always looking for bargains in real estate. Several years ago I was in Tampa and noticed a For Sale By Owner classified advertisement that offered a waterfront home on an acre of land for $120,000. To someone who lives in Southern California, as I do, it seemed like an incredible bargain. If you could find an acre of waterfront land here it would sell for many millions. So I called the owner to get more information. He described the property, and it sounded even better. Then I said, "How long have you owned it?" That's a normal question that very few people would have trouble asking. He told me that he'd owned it for three years. Then I asked, "How much did you pay for it?" That's a question that many people certainly would have trouble asking. They might think that it would upset the other person and make him angry. There was a long pause on the other end of the line. Finally he responded, "Well, all right, I'll tell you. I paid $85,000." Immediately I knew that this wasn't the great deal that it appeared to be. It has been a very flat real estate market in Tampa, and he hadn't improved the property. So I learned a great deal from asking that one question. What if he had refused to answer the question, if he had told me that it wasn't any of my business what he paid for it, would I still have been gathering information? Of course I would. What if he'd lied to me? What if he'd said, "Let's see, what did we pay for it? Oh, yes, we paid $200,000. We're really losing money." If he'd have lied to me like that, would I still be gathering information? Of course. So don't be afraid to ask the question.

Sometimes people are involved in a conflict negotiation, and they're afraid to ask the other side what they want. Many years ago I worked for a small department store in northern California that was part of a large nation-wide chain. This company's policy stopped any employee from saying no to a customer. If a clerk or manager didn't feel that a customer's complaint was justified, they would transfer the complaint up the customer-service ladder. This meant that if a customer kept complaining to this company without getting satisfaction for his or her complaint, the problem would eventually work its way to the chairman of the board at the head office in Chicago.

An elderly couple had bought a Franklin stove from the company's catalog. They had installed it themselves and, according to their complaint letter, the stove had malfunctioned, blackening the walls of their home and burning a hole in their carpet.

Everyone who tried to deal with this complaint assumed that it would be very expensive to satisfy this couple, so everyone was reluctant to admit blame and offer a settlement. The letter made its way from desk to desk until it came to rest on the desk of the regional vice-president. The last thing he wanted to do was let the complaint reach the head office in Chicago, so he wrote to me, requesting that I visit the couple and take some pictures so that they could estimate the cost of a settlement.

I drove out to their little home in the countryside and met this elderly couple. They were a sweet, trusting couple who had bought a stove out of the catalog and were genuinely disappointed at the results. The husband calmly showed me how soot from the chimney had blackened the outside of his home. Then he took me inside to show me the hole in their carpet caused by hot coals falling from the stove. He quickly convinced me that the stove had malfunctioned, and the problem wasn't in the way they had installed it.

Fearing that we would be talking about a settlement of several thousand dollars, I starting with a question that I assumed many of our people had asked them before: "Exactly what do you think our company should do for you? How can we compensate you for this?"

To my surprise, the husband answered, "You know, we're retired and have a lot of time on our hands. The wall is a mess, but we can certainly clean it up. It's really no problem at all. However, we are concerned about the hole in our carpet. It's quite large, but we really don't expect you to replace the entire carpet. If we had a scatter rug that we could put over the hole, that would take care of it."

He was asking for so little that it stunned me. Then I recovered enough to say, "Do you mean to tell me that if we gave you a scatter rug, that would solve the problem?"

"Oh, yes," he answered, "we'd be very happy with that."

So we all got into my car and drove straight to the store, where I helped them choose a beautiful rug to put over the hole in their carpet. I got them to sign a complete release form confirming that the settlement satisfied them and sent it off to the regional vice-president.

Several days later I got a letter from the vice-president congratulating me on "what was obviously a masterful job of negotiating." That was nonsense, of course; I had solved the problem merely by asking what nobody had the courage to ask before: "What exactly is it you want?"

This lesson served me well in the coming years as I worked my way up the corporate ladder. I was able to easily solve customer complaint problems simply because I bothered to get adequate information, starting with "What do you want?"

When I later became president of a large real estate company, I started using the lesson to solve the problem of buyers who were not happy with the home they'd bought. The sellers of the home had usually moved out of the area, leaving the company—and me—to solve the problem.

I would sit my visitors down in my office and with a large piece of paper in front of me, ask, "Please, I would like to know exactly what your complaints are and exactly what you think we should do for you in each instance."

"Well," they would say, "the light switch in the living room doesn't work." I would write on the paper, "Light switch in living room." I would continue to ask them if there was anything else until they had aired all of their grievances and carefully written them down on my paper.

When they ran out of complaints, I would draw a line across the sheet under the last item and show the paper to them. Then I'd negotiate what we would or wouldn't do for them. Most people are willing to compromise, and if I offered to send out a plumber to fix the leaking faucet, they would be willing to replace the light switch in the living room. With this method, what they wanted was clear from the beginning; they had laid all of their cards out, face up, and I was in the controlling position because I could decide what my response would be.

Doing it the other way is foolish, but it's the way most people who handle complaints do it. They ask what the problem is and then handle it item by item. The homeowners complain that the light switch doesn't work and because that's not an expensive item, the person handling the complaint says, "No problem, we'll take care of it." The homeowners would immediately think that it would be easy to get more concessions and keep thinking of other things that were wrong. In negotiating terms that's called escalating the demands. By asking them to commit first to a list of demands, you put parameters on the demands.

If you want to learn about another person, nothing will work better than the direct question. In my own experience—now that I'm no longer afraid to ask—I've met only a few people who were seriously averse to answering even the most personal questions. For example, how many people get offended when you ask them, "Why were you in the hospital?" Not very many.

It's a strange fact of human nature that we're very willing to talk about ourselves, yet we're reticent when it comes to asking others about themselves. We fear the nasty look and the rebuff to a personal question. We refrain from asking because we expect the response, "That's none of your business." Yet how often do we respond that way to others?

If you ever want to win a bet with someone, bet that you can walk up to a stranger and get him or her to tell you what brand of underwear he or she is wearing. Of course, it will help immensely if you approach that stranger with a clipboard in your hand and explain that you're taking a survey. If people tell you things like that on the street, why should you be nervous about asking the questions you need answered in a negotiation?

As president of a real estate company, I wanted to encourage our agents to knock on doors searching for leads. Real estate people call it farming. I found our agents very reluctant to do it. So I eventually formulated a plan where I would take each one of our 28 office managers out separately knocking on doors, and we would play the information game. I would say, "Okay, I'm going to knock on the first door, and I'm going to see how much information I can get from these people. You knock on the second door—see if you can get more information than I did."

It was amazing to see the amount of information the people would volunteer to a stranger on the doorstep. I could get them to tell me where they worked, where their wives worked, sometimes how much money they made, how long they'd been in the property, how much they paid for it, how much their loan payments were, and so on. People are often eager to volunteer information if we'll only ask.

Asking for more information in your dealings with others will not only help you to be a better negotiator, it will also be a major factor in helping you get what you want out of life. Asking questions is a good habit for you to adopt. Just ask. Sounds easy doesn't it? Yet most of us are so squeamish about asking someone a question.

When you get over your inhibitions about asking people, the number of people willing to help you will surprise you. When I wanted to become a professional speaker, I called up a speaker I admired, Danny Cox and asked him if I could buy him lunch. Over lunch he willingly gave me a $5,000 seminar on how to be successful as a speaker. Whenever I see him today, I remind him of how easy it would have been for him to talk me out of the idea. Instead, though, he was very encouraging. It still astounds me how people who have spent a lifetime accumulating knowledge in a particular area are more than willing to share that information with me without any thought of compensation.

It seems even more incredible that these experts are very rarely asked to share their expertise. Most people find experts intimidating, so the deep knowledge that they have to offer is never fully used. What a senseless waste of a valuable resource—all because of an irrational fear.

Rule Three: Ask open-ended questions

Power Negotiators understand the importance of asking and of taking the time to do it properly. What's the best way to ask? Rudyard Kipling talked about his six honest serving men. He said,

> I keep six honest serving-men.
> (They taught me all I knew);
> Their names are What and Why and When
> and How and Where and Who.

Of Kipling's six honest serving men, I like Why the least. Why can easily be seen as accusatory. "Why did you do that?" implies criticism. "What did you do next?" doesn't imply any criticism. If you really need to know why, soften it by rephrasing the question using what instead: "You probably had a good reason for doing that. What was it?" Learn to use Kipling's six honest serving men to find out what you need to know.

You'll get even more information if you learn how to ask open-ended questions. Close-ended questions can be answered with a yes or a no or a specific answer. For example, "How old are you?" is a closed-ended question. You'll get a number and that's it. "How do you feel about being your age?" is an open-ended question. It invites more than just a specific-answer response.

"When must the work be finished by?" is a closed-ended question. "Tell me about the time limitations on the job," is an open-ended request for information.

Here are four open-ended Gambits you can use to get information.

First try repeating the question. They say, "You charge too much." However, they don't explain why they feel that way, and you want to know why. You repeat the question, "You feel we charge too much?" Very often they'll come back with a complete explanation of why they said that. Or if they can't substantiate what they said, if they were just throwing it out to see what your response would be, maybe they'll back down.

The second Gambit is to ask for feelings. Not what happened, but how did they feel about what happened? You're a contractor, and your foreman says, "Did they ever cuss me out when I showed up on the job. The air was turning blue." Instead of saying, "What caused that?" try saying, "How did you feel about that?" Maybe the response you get will be, "I probably deserved it. I was an hour late, and they did have three truckloads of concrete sitting there, waiting for me."

The third Gambit is ask for reactions. The banker says, "The loan committee usually requires a personal guarantee from small business owners." Instead of assuming it's the only way you're going to get the loan, try saying, "And what's your reaction to that?" She may come back with, "I don't think it's necessary, as long as you'll guarantee to maintain adequate net worth in your corporation. Let me see what I can do for you with them."

The fourth Gambit is to ask for restatement. They say, "Your price is way too high." You respond, "I don't understand why you say that." Chances are that instead of repeating the same words, they'll come back with a more detailed explanation of the problem.

So let's recap the four open-ended Gambits for gathering information.

1. Repeat the question. "You don't think we can meet the specifications?"

2. Ask for feelings, "And how do you feel about that policy?"

3. Ask for reactions, "What was your response to that?"

4. Ask for restatement, "You don't think we'll get it done on time?"

Rule Four: Where you ask the question makes a big difference

Power Negotiators also know that the location where you do the asking can make a big difference. If you meet with people at their corporate headquarters, surrounded by their trappings of power and authority and their formality of doing business, it's the least likely place for you to get information.

People in their work environment are always surrounded by invisible chains of protocol—what they feel they should be talking about and what they feel they shouldn't. That applies to an executive in her office, it applies to a salesperson on a sales call, and it applies to a plumber fixing a pipe in your basement. When people are in their work environments, they're cautious about sharing information. Get them away from their work environments and information flows much more freely. And it doesn't take much. Sometimes all that it takes is to get that vice-president down the hall to his company lunch room for a cup of coffee. Often that's all it takes to relax the tensions of the negotiation and get information flowing. And if you meet for lunch at your country club, surrounded by your trappings of power and authority, where he's psychologically obligated to you because you're buying the lunch, then that's even better.

Rule Five: Ask other people—not the person with whom you will negotiate

If you go into a negotiation knowing only what the other side has chosen to tell you, you are very vulnerable. Others will tell you things that the other side won't, and they will also be able to verify what the other side has told you.

Start by asking people who've done business with the other side already. I think it will amaze you—even if you thought of them as competition—how much they're willing to share with you. Be prepared to horse trade information. Don't reveal anything that you don't want them to know, but the easiest way to get people to open up is to offer information in return. People who have done business with the other side can be especially helpful in revealing the character of the people with whom you'll be negotiating. Can you trust them? Do they bluff a great deal in negotiations or are they straightforward in their dealings? Will they stand behind their verbal agreements or do you need an attorney to read the fine print in the contracts?

Next ask people further down the corporate ladder than the person with whom you plan to deal. Let's say you're going to be negotiating with someone at the main office of a nationwide retail chain. You might call up one of the branch offices and get an appointment to stop by and see the local manager. Do some preliminary negotiating with that person. He will tell you a lot, even though he can't negotiate the deal, about how the company makes a decision, why one supplier is selected over another, the specification factors considered, the profit margins expected, the way the company normally pays, and so on. Be sure that you're "reading between the lines" in that kind of conversation. Without you knowing it, the negotiations may have already begun. For example, the branch manager may tell you, "They never work with less than a 40 percent markup," when that may not be the case at all. And never tell the branch manager anything you wouldn't say to the people at his head office. Take the precaution of assuming anything you say will get back to them.

Next take advantage of peer-group sharing. This refers to the fact that people have a natural tendency to share information with their peers. At a cocktail party, you'll find attorneys talking about their cases to other attorneys, when they wouldn't consider it ethical to share that information with anyone outside their industry. Doctors will talk about their patients to other doctors, but not outside their profession.

Power Negotiators know how to use this phenomenon because it applies to all occupations, not just in the professions. Engineers, controllers, foremen and truck drivers; all have allegiances to their occupations, as well as their employers. Put them together with each other and information will flow that you couldn't get any other way.

If you're thinking of buying a used piece of equipment, have your driver or equipment supervisor meet with his counterpart at the seller's company.

If you're thinking of buying another company, have your controller take their bookkeeper out to lunch.

You can take an engineer from your company with you to visit another company and let your engineer mix with their engineers. You'll find out that unlike top management—the level at which you may be negotiating—engineers have a common bond that spreads throughout their profession, rather than just a vertical loyalty to the company for which they currently work. So all kinds of information will pass between these two.

Naturally, you have to watch out that your person doesn't give away information that could be damaging to you. So be sure you pick the right person. Caution her carefully about what you're willing to tell the other side and what you're not willing to tell—the difference between the open agenda and your hidden agenda. Then let her go to it, challenging her to see how much she can find out. Peer-group information gathering is very effective.

Rule Six: Use questions for reasons other than gathering information.

Although the primary reason for asking questions is to gather information, there are many other purposes for asking questions:

- *To criticize the other side:* Have you resolved the delivery problems you were having? How did that consumer law suit work out? Why did you close your Atlanta office after only six months of operation? Why did Universal pull their business from you? Is the FTC investigation going forward? You may already know the answers to these questions or the answer may be unimportant to you.

- *To make the other side think:* Are you sure that expanding into Puerto Rico is the right thing to do? How comfortable are you with your new advertising agency? How would your people react to your doing business with us? Doesn't giving all of your business to that vendor make you nervous?

- *To educate them:* Were you at the association meeting where we got the packaging award of the year? Did you see the review of our product in *Newsweek*? Were you aware that we have a new plant in Bangkok? Were you aware that our vice-president used to be president of Universal?

- *To declare your position:* You're aware that experts regard our delivery system as the best in the industry? Why would we be willing to do that? Do you know anybody else who believes that? Then why do 95 percent of our customers continue to increase the size of their orders?

- *To get a commitment:* Which model would work best for you? How many should we ship you? Will you want the deluxe packaging or the mail-order packaging? How quickly will you want delivery?

- *To pull the two sides closer together (used by mediators and arbitrators):* So can we both agree on that? What would happen if I could get them to agree to a five percent increase? But what would you do if they decide to picket your stores? You don't really expect them to go along with that, do you?

I think of the information gathering process as rather like the game of battleship that I used to play when I was a youngster. You can buy electronic versions of it in toy stores today, but when I was growing up in England after World War II, no toys were being manufactured. We had to entertain ourselves with little games that we could create without having to buy anything, and the game of battleship was great fun. My cousin Colin and I would sit at the table across from each other and build a barrier between us so that we couldn't see the piece of paper that was in front of the other person. We usually constructed the barrier with a pile of books. Each of us would take a piece of paper and draw a hundred different squares marked with the alphabet down one side and numbers along the bottom. Onto this graph we would draw our fleet of battleships, cruisers, and destroyers. My cousin couldn't see where I had located mine, and I couldn't see where he had located his. Then we would attempt to bomb each other's fleets by calling out the graph number. When we made a successful hit, we would mark the position on our chart and in doing so gradually build up a picture of the other person's hidden fleet.

The parallel here is that the hidden piece of paper in negotiations is the other person's hidden agenda. By judicious questioning, you should try to find out as much as you possibly can about that person's hidden agenda and recreate it on your side so that you know exactly where he's coming from and what he's trying to achieve.

Power Negotiators always accept complete responsibility for what happens in the negotiations. Poor negotiators blame the other side for the way they conducted themselves. Many years ago, I was conducting a negotiating seminar in the San Fernando Valley, and comedian Slappy White was in the audience. During the break I told him how much I admired comedians. "It must be fun to be successful like you," I told him, "but coming up through those comedy clubs with all their hostile audiences must be sheer hell."

"Roger," he told me, "I've never had a bad audience."

"Oh, come on, Slappy," I replied. "When you were starting out, you must have had some awful audiences."

"I've never had a bad audience," he repeated. "I've only had audiences that I didn't know enough about."

As a professional speaker, I accept that there is no such thing as a bad audience, there are only audiences about which the speaker doesn't know enough. I've built my reputation on the planning and research that I do before I'll get up in front of an audience.

As a negotiator, I accept that there's no such thing as a bad negotiation. There are only negotiations in which we don't know enough about the other side. Information-gathering is the most important thing we can do to assure that the negotiations go smoothly.

Chapter 39

Being Prepared to Walk Away

Of all the negotiating pressure points, this one is the most powerful. It's projecting to the other side that you will walk away from the negotiations if you can't get what you want. If there's one thing that I can impress upon you that would make you a ten times more powerful negotiator, it's this: Learn to develop walk-away power. The danger is that there's a mental point that you pass when you will no longer walk away.

There's a point you reach in the negotiations when you start thinking:

- I'm going to buy this car. I'm going to get the best price I possibly can, but I'm not leaving here until I get it.

- I'm going to hire this person. I'm going to get them for the lowest salary and benefits that I can, but I'm not going to let this person slip through my fingers.

- I have to take this job. I'm going to fight for the best pay and benefits I can get, but I have to take this job.

- I'm going to buy this house. I'll get the seller down as low as I can, but this is the one I want.

- I have to make this sale. I can't walk out of here without a commitment.

The minute you pass the point when you're willing to say, "I'm prepared to walk away from this," you lose in the negotiations.

So, be sure you don't pass that point. There's no such thing as a sale you have to make at any price, or the only car or home for you, or a job or employee that you can't do without. The minute you pass the point when you think there is, you've lost in the negotiations.

At seminars when people tell me that they made a mistake in negotiations, this is always a part of the problem. They passed the point where they were willing to walk away. Some place in relating the story, they'll say to me, "I made up my mind that I was going to get it," and I know that was the turning point in the negotiation. It was the point at which they lost.

Many years ago my daughter bought her first car. She went down to the dealer and test drove a really fine used car. She fell in love with the car, and they knew it. Then she came back and wanted me to go back down with her, to renegotiate a better price. Tough situation, right? On the way down there, I said, "Julia, are you prepared to come home tonight without the car?"

And she said, "No, I'm not. I want it, I want it."

So I told her, "Julia, you might as well get your checkbook out and give them what they're asking because you've already set yourself up to lose in the negotiations. We've got to be prepared to walk away."

We walked out of the showroom twice in the two hours that we spent negotiating and bought the car for $2,000 less than she would have paid for it.

How much money was she making while she was negotiating? Bearing in mind that I waived my normal fee? She was making a thousand dollars an hour. We'd all go to work for a thousand dollars an hour, wouldn't we? You can't make money faster than you can when you're negotiating.

You become a Power Negotiator when you learn to project to the other side that you will walk away from the job if you can't get what you want.

If you're the one who's selling something, be sure that you've built enough desire before you threaten to walk away. Obviously, if they don't particularly want your product or service yet and you threaten to walk away, you're going to find yourself standing on the sidewalk saying, "What happened?"

You should consider selling as a four-step process:

1. Prospecting. Looking for people who want to do business with you.

2. Qualifying. Can they afford to do business with you?

3. Desire building. Making them want your product or service above everybody else's.

4. Closing. Getting the commitment. Walking away is a stage four Gambit. You use it after you've built desire, and you're going for the commitment.

Please remember that the objective is to get what you want by threatening to walk away. The objective is not to walk away. Don't say, "Roger, you'd be so proud of me. I just walked away from a million-dollar sale." It's like General Patton saying to his troops, "Keep the objective clear. The objective is not for you to die for your country. It's for you to get the other poor bastard to die for his country."

In a heavy situation, when there's a big issue at stake, don't threaten to walk away without the protection of Good Guy/Bad Guy. Don't do it alone. You should have a Good Guy left behind. Then, if you threaten to walk away and they don't say, "Hey, wait a minute, where are you going? Come on back, we can still put this together." If they don't say that, then you still have the Good Guy left behind, who can say, "Look. He's just upset right now. I think we can still put this together, if you can be a little bit more flexible in your pricing."

Developing walk-away power

You develop walk-away power by increasing your alternatives. Remember that the side with the most options has the most power. So if you've found the home of your dreams, and are planning on making an offer on it, here's what you should do: You should find a couple of other homes that you'd like just as well. That way you'll be a tougher negotiator when you're dealing with the seller of the first home. Instead of thinking that this is the only home in which you'd be happy, you're thinking, "No problem. If I don't get a good price on this one, I'd be just as happy with one of the other two that I've picked out." It doesn't mean that you're not going to get the first one. It just means that when you give yourself options, you give yourself power.

If you're trying to buy a boat from an owner, first find two more boats that would make you just as happy. The side with the most options has the most power. If you are the only buyer with whom the seller is dealing, and you have three boats that would make you equally happy, you have enormous power as a negotiator.

How to project walk-away power

Let me tell you how to project walk-away power by telling you how a real estate broker used it on me.

I owned a couple of properties in Long Beach, California—that's about 50 miles from where I live. I wasn't that familiar with the marketplace, and I was having trouble finding a good real estate agent to handle it for me. Finally, I heard about Walter Sanford, a real estate broker who seemed to be very aggressive in the way he went about business. He seemed to be the kind of person that I wanted to have representing me in the sale of this property.

I called him up and said: "I've got a couple of properties very close to your real estate office. I'd like you to list them for me. His response was: "I might be prepared to represent you. When can you come to my office so that we can talk about it?" I liked that. He clearly was familiar with Power Negotiating. Number one, he was prepared to walk way from the listing. He didn't take the typical real estate attitude of "Wow, for two listings I'll drop everything and come right now." He said: "I might be prepared to represent you." Second, he knew that you should always try to negotiate in your own territory. He was a lot better off if he could talk me into coming to his office than if he came to my home to discuss it. Third, he was starting the process of getting me to follow instructions. If you can get people to start doing what you ask them to do, even if it's a very small thing, you start to take command of the relationship. A momentum begins to build that ends up with: "Bear down, the fourth copy's yours."

I made an appointment for three or four days later and went to his office to meet with him. Meanwhile, he had checked out the properties and prepared a couple of information folders with his suggested selling prices. These prices were way below what I had hoped the properties were worth.

By this point, however, I had developed a lot of confidence in him and was thinking, "Well, he does know the territory a lot better than I do. Either I trust him or I don't. I'll go along with his proposed listing prices."

Then he said to me: "Roger, you do understand that I won't work with anything less than a nine-month listing, don't you?"

I said: "Wait a minute, Walter. Nine months when we've never worked together before? I don't think I'm prepared to take my property off the market for nine months."

What he did next was very bright. He stood up, closed the folders that he'd been consulting and reached across the desk with his hand extended, saying, "Mr. Dawson, I'm very sorry, but I guess we won't be doing business together after all."

He was prepared to walk away from the listings if he couldn't get what he wanted. Where did that put me? Now I was in the position of having to negotiate with him to get him to accept the listings.

Of course, he had no idea that he was dealing with such a great negotiator. I was able to get him all the way down to six months on those listings. Which is what he wanted in the first place.

I admired that—you should always ask for more than you expect to get—so that you set up a climate in which the other person can win in the negotiations.

The key issue here is to communicate to the other side that you're prepared to walk away. What will typically happen for you is what happens when you're in the stores in Mexico. When you're prepared to walk out of the store, they will come racing out after you.

Power Negotiators know that learning to communicate subtly to the other side that you're prepared to walk away is the most powerful Gambit of them all.

Chapter 40

Take It or Leave It

In the last chapter I told you that projecting that you're prepared to walk away is the most powerful pressure point of them all. If you use it, however, be sure that you're gentle when you tell them that you're prepared to walk away. Remember that the objective is to get what you want by projecting that you're prepared to walk away. The objective is not to walk away—any idiot can do that.

If you're too blunt in the way you project this, you may antagonize them, so be careful. Don't use that obnoxious expression "take it or leave it." Even people of good will who feel that they're willing to meet your demands may recoil if you use that. Instead use more subtle expressions such as, "Sorry, but that has to be my walk-away price." Or, "We never deviate from our published price list."

The take it or leave it approach in union negotiations even has a name—Boulwarism. Lemuel Boulware was chief of labor relations for General Electric during the fifties and sixties. His negotiating method was to make one offer that he thought was fair to the company, the union and the stockholders and never deviate from it. This take it or leave it attitude obviously creates bad feelings because it doesn't give the union negotiators a chance to have a win for their members. I'm sure it didn't escape Boulware's attention that if the union took the first offer, the members would begin to wonder why they needed a union. In 1964, the National Labor Relations Board found GE guilty of not bargaining in good faith. Even worse, Boulware's intransigence caused 13 unions to join in a walk-out against the company in 1969.

A great way to be firm without being offensive is to use the Higher Authority Gambit. Who could take offense when you say, "I'd love to do better, but the people back at the head office won't let me."

I knew a man once who owned a small hotel in Manhattan. One of the problems he faced was friends who wanted to stay and not have him charge them. He solved the problem by establishing a mother-in-law rate. They would call up to see if he had a room free, and he would say, "I tell you what I'll do. I'll give you my mother-in-law's rate. This is what she pays when she stays here. Nobody stays for less." In that way he was firmly telling them "No freebies," but he was doing it in a very diplomatic way.

Responding to Take It or Leave It

When somebody uses the blunt take it or leave it approach on you (and it may be more subtly expressed, such as, "That's our price, we don't negotiate"), you have three options:

1. Call his bluff. Tell him that your higher authority insists on concessions and if that remains their position, there's no way that you can put this together. Perhaps you walk out and hope that they'll call you back.

   Before you consider this drastic response consider whether the other negotiator has much to lose from your walking away. If it's a sales clerk in a retail store who is not on commission, he probably has little, if anything, to lose and will let you walk. I never had any luck negotiating price with communists, for example, because profit was not a motivating factor for them. Even if I bribed them, there was nothing they could spend money on anyway. I remember checking into a hotel in East Berlin a few weeks after the wall had come down, but while the city was still in communist hands. It was four o'clock in the morning, and I had just driven in from Zermatt, Switzerland—a monstrous drive. Frankly I was lost and didn't even realize that I was in East Berlin until the desk clerk refused to budge on the room rate. My initial suggestion was that, since it was already 4:00 A.M. he not charge for the first night, and I would pay for the following night. He refused. I tried for 50 percent off the first night and finally 25 percent off, all to no avail. Eventually he said, "Maybe they do that in West Berlin, but we don't do it here."

   I said, "Wait a minute, I'm in East Berlin? How did I get here? I didn't see any wall."

"The wall is down," he bluntly told me. Well, I had heard *that* news, but I always thought that the wall was a huge thing, several feet thick. I could swear that I'd seen pictures of people standing on top of the thing. I didn't realize that it was mainly poured concrete slabs stood up on end that were comparatively easy to remove. Consequently I had driven past where it used to be without seeing any sign of it. Once I knew that I was dealing with a communist, I gave up trying to get a concession from him. He had no incentive in his system that would make him want to please me.

So before you walk out consider how much the other person has to lose by letting you do that. If they have nothing to lose, you probably won't get anywhere by walking out.

2. Go over the person's head. That doesn't always mean demanding to see his boss or calling his boss to complain. A gentler way is to ask, "Who is authorized to make an exception to the rule?" A little stronger would be to say, "Would you mind checking with your supervisor and seeing if you can get her to make an exception to the rule? I'm sure that if anybody could get her to do it, it would be you." Even stronger would be, "Would you mind if we talked to your supervisor about this?"

3. Find a face-saving way for the other person to modify his or her intransigent position. This is the most desirable way to handle "take it or leave it" of course. It is especially effective if the other negotiator has something to gain by finding a way around the impasse, which would be true if you're dealing with the owner of a business or someone on commission. "I can understand why you feel so strongly," you say, "but surely if I were willing to pay you a bonus, you'd be willing to make an exception to the rule, wouldn't you, Joe?" Or you might try, "Joe, let me ask you something. What would it take for you to change your position on that, just a little bit and just this one time?"

Chapter 41

The Fait-Accompli

Fait-Accompli is a French expression that roughly means "it is done." If you have ever sent someone a check for less than they're asking and marked the back of the check "Payment in full is acknowledged," you have used the Fait-Accompli Gambit. It means that one negotiator simply assumes the other will accept the assumed settlement rather than go to the trouble of reopening the negotiations. It works on the principle that it's a lot easier to beg forgiveness than it is to get permission.

In California and many other states, Fait-Accompli became so common in the auto repair industry that we passed laws against it. Before that it was common for service stations to fix your car without getting your approval of the estimate, figuring that there wasn't much you could do about it once they had fixed the car, and they could hold it until you paid for it.

A friend of mine owns a billboard company in Asheville, North Carolina. He was negotiating with a farmer who had let trees grow on his property until they obscured one of Mike's billboards, reducing its commercial value to zero. Mike tried to negotiate a good faith payment in return for the farmer letting him trim back the trees, but the farmer demanded an outrageous amount of money because he thought that Mike had no options. Mike decided to use the Fait-Accompli Gambit on him. One morning he had four of his workers sneak onto the farmer's property and fire up their chain saws in unison. Before the farmer could reach for his shotgun, the trees were down and his workers were back over the fence and driving off. Later in the day Mike went by to apologize for the misunderstanding and was able to reach a much more reasonable settlement with the farmer.

The Fait-Accompli Gambit does not engender warm feelings from one side to another. When *Batman* movie producers Peter Guber and Jon Peters were offered key positions at Sony Studios in 1989, they were already under contract to Warner Brothers. They decided to sign anyway and present the Fait-Accompli to Steve Ross, their boss at Warner. He went ballistic at the way they had handled this and decided to fight them on it. It ended up costing them over $500 million to buy out their contract. It was a bad choice of negotiating tactic because Ross probably would have released them without penalty if they had not antagonized him so much. What does this teach you? Don't use a Fait-Accompli unless you don't care how the other side reacts because it won't endear you to them.

Sometimes Fait-Accompli is done so outrageously that you have to smile at the nerve of the person who does it to you. When I was young, I lent an expensive camera to an older man who had been an important mentor to me. He promptly pawned it and sent me the pawn ticket. Attached was a note that said, "Sorry about this, but I had to have the money. This is a very important lesson for you to learn in life—don't trust *anybody*."

More recently a speaker's agent booked me to do a speech and collected the speaking fee from the company, but didn't send me my share, which was over $6,500. He told my business manager that he had spent the money to pay his creditors who were turning nasty. When pressed for a reason for stealing from me like this, he said, "I just figured that Roger was rich and didn't need the money nearly as much as I did." His audacity stunned and amused us so much that we let him make payments to us.

More subtle forms of Fait-Accompli are effective ways of putting pressure on the other side. If you have been overcharged, sending them a check for the correct amount with a "paid in full" endorsement on the back may be a lot simpler than arguing the point with them. If you are signing a contract and disagree with any of the points, make the changes and send the corrected contract back to them. They may well accept the changes rather than take the trouble to reopen the negotiations.

Chapter 42

The Hot Potato

The next pressure point is the Hot Potato. That's when somebody wants to give you his or her problem and have you make it your problem. It's like tossing you a Hot Potato at a barbecue.

What Hot Potatoes do you get tossed?

Do you ever hear: "We just don't have it in the budget"? Whose problem is it that they didn't budget properly for your fine product or service? It's their problem, right? Not yours. But they'd like to toss it to you and make it yours.

How about: "I can't authorize that"? Whose problem is it that he hasn't developed the trust of the people to whom he reports? It's his, right? Not yours. But he'd like to toss it to you and make it yours.

If you're a contractor, customers have probably called you to say: "I need you to move my job up. If you're not here first thing in the morning, this entire project comes to a screeching halt." Whose scheduling problem is that? Theirs, right, not yours. But what they'd like to do is toss you their problem and make it yours.

What you should do is what the international negotiators would tell you to do when the other side tries to give you its problems. I've found out from my study of international negotiations that exactly the same principles apply— the same rules that applied for the negotiators in Geneva during the arms control talks also apply to you when the other side is putting pressure on you. The same things apply, and the same responses are appropriate.

Here's how the international negotiators would tell you to respond to the Hot Potato: Test it for validity right away. This is what international negotiators do when the other side tries to give them their problem. You have to find out right away whether it really is a deal killer that they've tossed you or simply something they threw on to the negotiating table to judge your response.

You must jump on it right away. Later on is too late. If you work on their problem they soon believe that now it's your problem and it's too late to test it for validity.

I used to be president of a 28-office real estate company in Southern California. In real estate we used to get tossed the Hot Potato all the time such as from the buyer who would come into one of our offices and say: "We have only $10,000 to put down." Even in blue-collar areas that would be a very low down payment. Our real estate agent could possibly work with it, but it would be tough.

I would teach the agents to test it for validity right away—to tell the buyers, "Maybe we can work with $10,000. But let me ask you this: If I find exactly the right property for you, in exactly the right neighborhood, the price and terms are fantastic, your family is going to love it, your kids are going to love having their friends over to play but it takes $15,000 to get in—is there any point in showing it to you or should I just show it to my other buyers?"

Once in a great while they would respond, "Don't you speak English? Watch my lips: $10,000 is it and not a penny more. I don't care how good a buy it is."

But 9 times out of 10 they would say, "Well, we didn't want to touch our Certificate of Deposit, but if it's a really good buy we might. Or maybe Uncle Joe would help us with the down payment." Immediately the agent found out that the problem the buyers tossed her was not the deal killer that it had appeared to be.

If you sell home furnishings one of your customers might say, "We've got $20 a square yard for carpeting and that's it." If you catch that Hot Potato, instead of tossing it back you will probably start thinking of cutting prices right away—if you assume that what they told you was final. But instead you test for validity up front, saying, "If I could show you a carpet that would give you double the wear and still be looking good five years from now, but cost only 10 percent more, you'd want to take a look at it, wouldn't you?" Nine times out of 10, they'll say, "Sure, we'll take a look at it," and immediately you know that the price issue is not the deal buster that it appeared to be.

Another way to counter the Hot Potato of "We don't have it in the budget" is to simply say, "Well, who has the authority to exceed the budget?"

Sometimes you'll kick yourself at what happens next. They'll say, "Well, that would take a vice-president to authorize that."

And you say: "Well, you want to do it, don't you? Why don't you call the vice-president and see if you can get an okay to exceed the budget?"

And he'll pick up the phone and call the vice-president and argue for an okay. Sometimes, it's that simple. But you have to test for validity right away.

I remember doing a seminar for the Associated General Contractors of Alaska. They put me up at the Anchorage Hilton, and on my departure day I needed a late checkout. There were two young women standing right next to each other behind the registration desk, and I said to one of them: "Would you give me a 6 o'clock checkout from my room, please."

She said, "Mr. Dawson, we could do that for you, but we'd have to charge you for an extra half-day."

I said, "Who would have the authority to waive that charge?"

And she pointed to the woman standing next to her and said: "She would." The woman standing right next to her!

So I leaned over and said to the other woman: "And how would you feel about that?"

She said: "Oh, sure. That would be fine. Go ahead."

Another way to handle the *We don't have it in the budget* Hot Potato is to ask them when their budget year ends. I trained the 80 salespeople at one of the top health maintenance organizations in California. A few weeks before the meeting, the training director called me and suggested we have dinner so that she could fill me in on how the company operates. Because I figured that she was going to pay for dinner I picked the top French restaurant in Orange County, and we had a great dinner. As dessert was served, I said, "You know what you should do? You should invest in a set of my cassette tapes for each of your salespeople so that they have the advantage of a continuous learning process." As I said that, I was mentally computing that 80 salespeople at $65 per set of tapes would be another $5,200 income on top of the speaking fee to which they'd already agreed.

She thought about it and said, "Roger, that probably would be a good idea, but we just don't have it in the budget."

I need to make a confession here. I'm very ashamed of what I thought next, but I want to share it with you because it may help you if you've ever had the same shameful thought. I thought, "I wonder if I cut the price she would say Yes." Isn't that a shameful thought? She hadn't said a thing about the tapes costing too much. She hadn't told me that she might be tempted if I lowered my price. She had simply told me that she didn't have it in the budget.

Fortunately I caught myself in time and instead did what I teach, which is to test for validity. I asked, "When does your budget year end?" This was August and I thought that she would tell me December 31.

To my surprise she said, "At the end of September."

"So you would have it in the budget on October 1?"

"Yes, I suppose that we would."

"Then, no problem. I'll ship you the tapes and bill you on October 1, fair enough?"

"That would be fine," she told me. In less than 30 seconds I had made a $5,200 sale because I knew that when she tossed me what was essentially her problem, I should test for validity.

I was feeling so good about this that when the waiter brought the bill, I slid my credit card into the leather case. He took it away, and she quietly said, "Roger, we were thinking of paying for dinner." I thought, "Roger, there are days when nothing goes right. You suffer through those. This is a day when nothing can go wrong, so why not relish it?" So I called the waiter back and told him that we gave him the wrong credit card.

Look out for people giving you their problems. You have enough of your own, don't you? It's like the businessman who was pacing the floor at night. He couldn't sleep, and his wife was also getting frantic. "Darling, what's bothering you, why don't you come to bed?" He said, "Well, we have this huge loan payment due tomorrow, and the bank manager is a good friend of ours. I just hate to face him and say that we're not going to have the money to pay him."

So his wife picked up the phone and called their friend the bank manager and said, "That loan payment we have coming due tomorrow, we don't have the money to pay it."

The husband exploded. He said, "What did you do that for? That's what I was afraid of."

And she said: "Well, dear, now it's his problem, and you can come to bed."

Don't let other people give you their problems.

Chapter 43

Ultimatums

Ultimatums are very high profile statements that tend to strike fear into inexperienced negotiators. Terrorists are holding a plane full of hostages, and tell negotiators that unless their demands are met, they will start shooting hostages at noon on the following day. Jimmy Carter used to say that the worst nightmare of his Presidency was that the Iranians who had taken the hostages in the embassy in Tehran would start shooting them one at a time until he met their demands.

An ultimatum is a powerful pressure point, but it has one major flaw as a gambit: If you say that you are going to shoot the first hostage at noon tomorrow, what had you better be prepared to do at noon tomorrow? Right. Shoot the first hostage. Because if 12:01 rolls around and you haven't done that, you have just lost all of your power in the negotiation. Of all the terrorist actions during the Reagan years, the one that failed most miserably was the hijacking of the Italian cruise ship *Achille Lauro* by four heavily armed Palestinians. The hijackers announced that they would start shooting the passengers unless Israel released 50 Palestinian prisoners. Although the hijackers quickly killed a 69-year-old passenger in a wheelchair who had challenged them, they never followed through on their threat to kill the other passengers. When they found that Israel would not release the prisoners, the hijackers settled instead for what they thought would be safe passage through Egypt.

The same weakness applies to an ultimatum in a business negotiation. If you tell a supplier that unless she can deliver by noon tomorrow, you will go with her competitor, what had you better be prepared to do at noon tomorrow? Right. Go with her competitor. Because if the deadline passes and you haven't done that, you have just lost all of your power in the negotiation. You should only use ultimatums as a pressure point if you are willing to follow through. Don't bluff because all the other side has to do is wait through your deadline to find out that you were only bluffing and your threat had no teeth in it.

When you understand the weakness in using ultimatums as a pressure point, you can easily figure out that the strongest counter-gambit is to call their bluff and let the deadline pass. There are other less blatant responses, however. If someone gives you an ultimatum, you have four ways to respond, and I list them here in increasing levels of intensity:

1. Test the ultimatum as soon as you can. They tell you that the shipment must be there by noon tomorrow. Test the ultimatum by asking if having a partial shipment there by noon would solve their problem. Could you air-freight enough for them to keep their assembly line going and surface-ship the balance?

2. Refuse to accept the ultimatum. Tell them that you have absolutely no idea if you can make that deadline or not, but that they can be assured that you're doing everything humanly possible to get it done.

3. Play for time. Time is the coin of the realm when one side is threatening the other with an ultimatum. The longer they go without carrying out the threat, the less likely they are to follow through with the threat. So terrorist negotiators always play for time. This happens in hostage negotiations where the perpetrators are demanding a getaway helicopter or car. The police negotiator plays for time by saying that he needs to get the governor's approval or that the getaway car is on its way, but it's stuck in traffic. As time passes, the scales tip dramatically in favor of the negotiators.

4. Bluff your way through and let the ultimatum pass. If it works, it's the best alternative because it not only solves this immediate crisis, but it also lets them know that you're not going to let them push you around in the future. Bluffing takes courage, however, and you shouldn't do it capriciously. Get all the information you can about the situation. The key thing to find out is whether anything has changed. Since you signed the contract with them, has a new supplier appeared who could supply them on time and for less money? If you have a contract or an option to buy, have they had a better offer from someone else? If nothing else has changed, you may be safe in taking the chance. What you're trying to uncover, of course, is if they want to continue the relationship with you or if the ultimatum is their method of getting you out of the picture.

Section Four

Negotiating With Foreigners

At my Secrets of Power Negotiating seminars, I almost always get asked about negotiating with foreigners. It seems that just about everyone has had a frustrating experience dealing either with a foreigner in a foreign country or a person of foreign origin who lives in this country.

Because I'm an immigrant from England, although I've been here more than 30 years and a citizen for more than 20 years, I can relate to the difficulty of dealing with foreigners. Along with my experience of moving here and adapting to the American way of doing things, I have traveled also to 94 other countries around the world.

Because of my background, I know how different America is from any other country on Earth. America is deceptively different to foreigners because many of them have had a great deal of exposure to American culture from watching our movies and television shows. Movies and television don't reveal what is in the American heart and mind, however, and that is what determines our approach to business.

Conversely, we tend to look at foreigners and think we understand them. True, they may dress in Western business suits and speak our language, but that doesn't mean that their traditional values and mind-sets have changed. They may prefer American music and American movies, but their beliefs in their way of life and the values they place on their traditions are as strong as ever.

I believe that underneath all of our apparent similarities, there lie enormous differences in our approaches to business. In this section I'll try to unravel some of the mysteries of negotiating with foreigners.

Chapter 44

The American Art of the Deal

New York real estate investor Donald Trump wrote a best-selling book, *The Art of the Deal,* that detailed many of his real estate negotiations—with remarkable scorn for the people that he had outsmarted. Of course, not everyone in this country is as ruthless as Donald Trump, but the title and the premise of the book illuminate the overriding concern of most American negotiators—the cutting of the deal. We do live in a very deal conscious environment.

I suppose that sociologists would tell you that we concentrate more on cutting the deal than other nations because we are such a mobile and diverse society that we have little sense of roots. Instead of trusting the people and the way things are done, as is common around the world, we place all of our trust in creating an unbreakable deal. "Will it hold up in court?" we demand, as though anyone who doesn't consider the possibility of having to defend the deal in court is naive.

Sociologists would also point out that this is a fairly recent change in the fabric of our society. During the first half of the twentieth century, we still looked to community pressures to enforce our obligations. To renege on a deal was unthinkable because of the dishonor that it would bring us in our community. We also had our religious community to police any thoughts of reneging on a commitment. It would be unthinkable to let down our priest, minister, or rabbi. Also, before television commandeered our leisure time, we belonged to many community organizations. We did not stray far because the members of our Lions, Kiwanis, or Optimist clubs—or the members of our PTA, Masonic or Elks lodges—might ostracize us. Sadly, that way of life is lost to us as the twentieth century accelerates to a close. Now what is left to us is the deal and an all-too-common resort to the courts to enforce the deal at all costs. The deal is finite, the deal is static, the deal has been made and cannot be changed.

Most foreigners completely reject our dependence on the deal. Should they choose to sign a contract at all, it is simply an expression of an understanding that existed between the parties on a particular date. It is a formal expression of a relationship that now exists between the parties. As with any other relationship, it must mold itself to changing conditions.

Most Americans are astounded to learn that you can sign a contract in Korea and have it mean nothing six months later. "But we signed a contract," the Americans howl.

"Yes," their Korean counter-part patiently explains, "we signed a contract based on the conditions that existed six months ago when we signed it. Those conditions no longer exist, so the contract we signed is meaningless."

"Foul," cries the American. "You are trying to cheat me." Not at all. What seems to us to be disreputable action is not to them, and we should not attempt to paint it as such. It is merely their way of doing things.

Americans are often delighted to find that they had so little trouble getting their Arab trading partners to sign a contract. Then they are horrified to find out that in the Arab world signing the contract announces the start of the negotiations, not the end. A signed contract means less in Arabian culture than a letter of intent does in ours. I am not putting this down, and you should not either. What we should do is recognize that different nationalities and cultures have different ways of doing things and it behooves us to learn, understand, and appreciate those ways.

It will come as no surprise to you to learn that Americans resort to legal action more quickly and frequently than any other people on Earth. This would be laughable to a businessman in India where the civil legal system is close to nonexistent. It would take five years to have a civil case heard and most realistic people suggest that you forget it because it's questionable that the system will even be functioning five years from now. Even the chief justice of India has said in public that the system is about to collapse.

In America, legal action is so common that companies continue to do business with a company that is suing them. We see it as a normal way to resolve a dispute and no reason for rancor. In most foreign countries there is such a loss of face involved in being sued by another company that they will refuse to deal in any way with a company that is suing them.

The word context describes the degree of importance attached to the relationship between the parties, as opposed to the details of the contract. When the relationship is paramount we call it a high context negotiation. When the deal is the thing we call it a low context negotiation. Different nationalities place greater or lesser importance on context—the environment in which the proposal is made. These cultures are listed from high context to low context: Orient, Middle East, Russia, Spain, Italy, France, England, United States, Scandinavia, Germany, Switzerland.

The first thing we should learn about negotiating with foreigners is that the deal is not the major issue to them. They put far more trust in the relationship between the parties. Is there good blood between the parties? If there is only bad blood, no amount of legal maneuvering will make the relationship worthwhile. While you are trying to hammer out the fine points of the deal, they are spending time assessing the fine points of your character.

Chapter 45

Getting Down to Business with Foreigners

In the previous chapter, I told you that the major difference between the way that Americans negotiate and the way that foreigners negotiate is that the terms of the deal obsess most Americans, whereas foreigners focus on the relationship between the parties. In this chapter, I'll concentrate on the other major mistake that we make in dealing with foreigners—that Americans want to get down to business too quickly.

Nobody gets down to business faster than Americans do. Typically we exchange a few pleasantries to ease any tension and then get right down to hammering out the details of the deal. We socialize afterwards. Foreigners may take days, weeks, or even months before they feel comfortable moving from the getting-to-know-you stage to the point where they feel good about doing business.

When the Shah of Iran fell from power, the real estate company that I ran in Southern California did a huge amount of business with Iranians (they prefer to be called Persians) who were fleeing the new regime, often with millions in cash to invest. Often I would watch our people make the mistake of trying to talk business too soon, which caused the Iranians to distrust them. Quickly we learned that they wanted to sit and drink tea for several hours as they sized us up.

If you fly to Japan to conduct business, you may have to socialize for many days before they feel that it's appropriate to talk business. (Be careful, however, that they're not just trying to push you up against a time deadline. At my seminars many people have told me that their joy at being treated so well soon turned to chagrin as they realized how difficult it would be to get down to business at all. They have told me horror stories of not being able to negotiate until they were in the limousine on the way back to the airport. It's a two hour ride out to Narita Airport, but that is negotiating under excessive time pressure. Terrified at the thought of going home empty handed, they went straight to their bottom line.)

So we see that Americans fall into two major traps when dealing with foreigners. We over-emphasize the deal and don't attach enough importance to the relationship of the parties, and we get down to business too quickly. The two are closely related, of course. Building a relationship with the other side to where you feel comfortable with them takes time. Enlarging on that relationship to the point where you trust the other person, and don't have to rely on the contract being airtight, takes a great deal of time.

Chapter 46

Negotiating Characteristics of Americans

Let's first take a look at the characteristics of the typical American who negotiates with foreigners, and then in the following chapter we'll look at the characteristics of foreign negotiators.

We tend to be very direct in our communications

We use expressions such as "What's your bottom line?" or "How much profit would you make at that figure?" Or we try to shift the emphasis of the negotiations by saying, "Let's lay our cards on the table," or "Let's wrap this one up tonight." Although I recommend this kind of directness when negotiating with other Americans because it puts pressure on the other side, realize that to foreigners it may seem too blunt and such bluntness may offend them.

We resist making outrageous initial demands

This goes back to our hope that we can "cut the deal" and "get out of Dodge." Because we want to blitz the negotiations and wrap them up quickly, we tend to think in much shorter time frames than foreigners. We're thinking we can conclude the negotiations in hours, while they're thinking it will take many days. Although a foreigner may be comfortable making an outrageous initial demand because he knows that the price and terms will change enormously as the days go by, we see that as slowing the negotiations down or drawing us into endless haggling.

We are more likely to negotiate alone

It's not unusual to find a lone American negotiator showing up at an international negotiation, fully empowered to do business. (She may be able to put together a team of three if it includes her interpreter and driver.) Then when she is led into the negotiating room she finds that she is faced with a team of

10 or 12 from the other side. This is not good for the American, because she will feel psychologically overwhelmed unless the negotiating teams are roughly the same size. However, the effect of this on the foreign team concerns me more. Foreigners may interpret a lone negotiator as "They're not serious about making a deal at this meeting because if they've only sent one negotiator, this must be only a preliminary expedition." Or foreigners get the impression that the American is merely gathering information to take back to her team of negotiators. Unless the American understands this and takes pains to explain that she is the entire negotiating team and that she is empowered (up to a point) to negotiate the deal, she may not be taken seriously.

Americans are uncomfortable with emotional displays

The English are the most uncomfortable, of course, but Americans also see displaying emotions in public as a weakness. If an American wife starts to cry, her husband instantly assumes that he has done something devastatingly cruel to her. In the Mediterranean countries, the husband simply wonders what ploy his wife has concocted. This fear of an emotional reaction causes Americans to be tentative in their negotiations with foreigners, and if the other side does explode with anger at one of our proposals, we tend to overreact. Instead, we should merely see it as a negotiating ploy that might be perfectly acceptable in their culture.

We tend to expect short term profits

Beside wanting to conclude the negotiations before we have built a relationship with the other side, we also expect quick results from the deal that we cut. We look at quarterly dividends while foreign investors are looking at ten-year plans. To many foreigners this comes across, unfairly I think, as a "fast-buck" mentality. Where they are looking to build a long term relationship with us, we appear to concentrate only on profits, and this can be offensive to them.

We are less likely to speak a foreign language

There's no question that English is becoming the business language of the world. Conferences in Europe are typically conducted in English now because it is the common-denominator language. Most European business people can speak two foreign languages, and one of them is always English. Most Oriental business people can at least understand English even if they cannot speak it well. Sadly, hardly any Americans can speak German or Japanese. If we do know a foreign language, it is probably Spanish or French.

To realize how arrogant this may appear to foreigners, you have only to think of how frustrated you became when you first dined in a Parisian restaurant. When the waiter didn't appear to speak any English, you probably thought as I did: "This is a tourist restaurant. They must get English-speaking people in here all the time. Why is he being so difficult by refusing to speak

English?" Unfortunately, this attitude is all too prevalent with American business people. Any expectation that "If they want to do business with us they should learn our language," can come across as irritatingly arrogant to a foreigner. We should always appear surprised and delighted that they speak even a few words of our language. We should always make an effort to speak a few words of their language, even if it's only to say Good morning and Thank you.

We are uncomfortable with silence

Americans hate silence. Fifteen seconds of silence to us seems like an eternity—do you remember the last time the sound went out on your television? You were probably thumping the top of the set within 15 seconds. Particularly to Asians, who are comfortable with long periods of meditation, this impatience appears to be a weakness and a weakness that they can take advantage of. When dealing with foreigners, don't be intimidated by long periods of silence. See it as a challenge to not be the next one to talk. After an extended period of silence, the next person to talk loses. The next person to open his or her mouth will make a concession.

We hate to admit that we don't know

As I discussed in Chapter 38 on the importance of gathering information, Americans hate to admit that they don't know. This is something that foreigners know and can use to their advantage. You don't have to answer every question. You are perfectly entitled to say, "That's privileged information at this stage." Or simply tell them that you don't know or are not permitted to release the information they seek. Not every question deserves an answer.

Please permit me to do a little flag waving here. People around the world still admire and respect Americans and particularly American business people. They trust us and see us as straightforward in our business dealings. This I believe. In this chapter I have not been pointing out the shortcomings of Americans dealing with foreigners. I have been teaching you only how Americans are misperceived by foreign negotiators. Fair enough?

Chapter 47

Negotiating Characteristics of Foreigners

There's an old joke that the restaurants in heaven have a German manager, a French maitre d', English waiters, and an Italian cook. On the other hand, the restaurants in hell have an Italian manager, a German maitre d', French waiters, and an English cook. Comedian George Carlin says, "If there's a heaven, there are German mechanics, Swiss hotels, French chefs, Italian lovers, and British police. If there's a hell, there are Italian mechanics, French hotels, British chefs, Swiss lovers, and German police." These are stereotypes, sure, but it would also be wrong to ignore national business characteristics in the name of avoiding any stereotyping.

Let's take a look at the negotiating characteristics of foreigners. I would be guilty of massive stereotyping if I implied that all people from these countries or of these national backgrounds had these tendencies. However, it's realistic enough to assume that a large percentage of people from these countries behave this way. So it's well worth being aware of the propensities and observing the foreigners with whom you're negotiating to see if they do fit the mold.

English

Be sensitive to national origin. Great Britain includes England, Wales, and Scotland. The United Kingdom also includes Northern Ireland. Of the four countries that compose the United Kingdom, or UK, 82 percent are English, so unless they have a brogue, you can assume that they are English. English people prefer to be called English, not British. Part of this sensitivity comes from massive immigration problems. Until the 1960s, anyone who was born in one of the colonies (which included 60 percent of the land surface of the Earth at one time) carried a British passport and was free to emigrate to England. A refrain you will frequently hear is, "I don't wish to be called British. If you are British, you might be from just about anywhere. I am English."

Make appointments well in advance, because the English live by their calendars. Be punctual, but never early. Ten minutes late is better than one minute early for social engagements.

The English are excessively polite. Remember that there are 60 million Britons jammed into a country half the size of Oregon, and most of them live in the counties surrounding London. In such a crowded country it is important to have boundaries on one's behavior. Understanding this is the key to understanding the English. If someone on a crowded train started to play a saxophone off key, it is unlikely that anyone would protest. In America that person would get yelled down. This is why you will see such outrageous styles of dress and hair styles on young people in England. It appears to an outsider that a youth with spiky orange hair wearing a leather outfit with chrome studs can exist in harmony with a bowler-hatted banker who carries an umbrella year-round and has a handkerchief stuffed up his sleeve. This is deceptive. They don't approve of each other's behavior—they are just too polite to protest.

You will find it rare for an English person to ask you a personal question. Although it's acceptable in America to open a conversation with, "What do you do?" or "Where do you live?" that would be a hopeless invasion of privacy to an English person. Because they are excessively polite, they would answer the question if you asked them, but would never reciprocate by asking you what you do.

England is still a very class-conscious society, although that is changing rapidly. Indicative of the change is that Margaret Thatcher and John Major were the first two prime ministers who did not come from the upper classes. You will still run into a great deal of class consciousness especially with older people. If they are evasive about where they live, for example, don't press them because they may feel self-conscious about living in a working class suburb.

The English don't feel as comfortable talking to strangers as Americans do. The proper way to initiate a conversation with a stranger in England is to mention the weather with an innocuous comment such as "Nice day today," or "Might get some rain later." If the response is an unintelligible one syllable that sounds like "Hurrumph" they are not being impolite, they simply don't feel comfortable talking to you at that time. If they want to pursue a conversation, they will respond with an equally innocuous response such as

"My roses need some rain," or "Wouldn't be surprised to see rain at this time of year. Wouldn't be surprised at all." You may then start a conversation, but remember to not ask them any personal questions.

It's okay to decline the offer of tea or coffee, whereas in many parts of the world it's an insult.

Be aware that the English view Americans with suspicion. We are seen as too slick for English tastes. They are somewhat wary of getting involved with Americans for fear of getting bamboozled by a fast talker.

The English business executive does not move at the frantic pace of the American executive. I remember having lunch with my nephew when he worked for Lloyds of London. He took me to an old tavern in the City (equivalent to our Wall Street) that had been serving lunches in that location for more than 700 years. We sat at a long bench-type table with a group of three English businessmen. They had several gin and tonics before lunch and then launched into a huge roast beef and Yorkshire pudding meal washed down with two bottles of red wine. After a large dessert, they ordered brandies. I put on my best American accent and said to one of them, "Excuse me, buddy, could I ask you something? Do you go back to work after a big lunch like that?" His reply told a great deal about the English attitude toward work and success. He politely said, "Here in England we have a different approach to success than do you chaps in the States. Here we consider that success in business entitles us to work less hard. You chaps think that success requires you to work even harder."

French

I have never had the trouble with French people that most Americans seem to have. I think that much of that comes from Americans being exposed to only Parisians. Paris is to the French what New York is to Americans. It's a pressure cooker of frantic business activity—a very competitive environment—so naturally they come across as less courteous than we would prefer. Apart from Paris, French people are warm and friendly. Even in Paris I find that people treat you very much as you treat them. If you have a chip on your shoulder and are expecting to find them hostile that's exactly what you will get. If you are excited and eager to meet them and explore their culture, you'll find people who are eager to share with you.

Remember that the French pride themselves on their language skills. Even those who speak a few words of English may be reluctant to do so because they don't want to speak it poorly. It's not because they have the attitude, "If you want to speak to me, you must learn my language."

In negotiations when the French say Yes, they mean maybe. When they say No, it means "Let's negotiate."

The French are logical thinkers, so sell with logic and reason rather than an appeal to emotion.

As with the English, the French value principle over result. Making a fast buck is not reason enough to violate their traditional way of doing business.

Be punctual, because to be late is an insult to the French.

Shake hands briefly when you meet them. Kissing cheeks is for only close friends.

Call all adult women Madame, even if they're single.

Above all, don't ruin a good meal by trying to talk business. A French lunch can last two hours and can be an exquisite experience. Unless your host starts talking business, stay away from it. You'll be doing yourself far more good by showing them how much you appreciate their cuisine.

Germans

Germany (and the German-speaking part of Switzerland) is a low context country; Germans put their emphasis on the deal rather than the relationship of the parties or the environment in which they signed the contract. Germans are one of the few nationalities to expect more detailed contracts than Americans. They really are masters of the detailed deal that, once they have hammered it out, they will never change.

Shake hands firmly when you arrive and when you leave.

Don't put your hands in your pockets when you're talking business, as it seems too casual to them.

Germans appear formal and aloof at first. It takes them a long time to get relaxed with you.

Germans place great emphasis on titles. Use yours if you have one and respect theirs. Address people as Herr, Frau, or Fräulein followed by their professional designation if they have one, for example: Herr Doctor Schmitt, or Frau Professor Schmitt.

Southeast Asians

Asians are very relationship-based. They far prefer to trust the person with whom they negotiate rather than the contract they signed.

In Thailand and other southeast Asian countries, you may be greeted with a slight bow and both hands pointed toward you with palms together. You should respond with the same greeting but hold your hands level with or slightly higher than theirs. The height of the hands indicates the respect that the person has for the person they are meeting. Someone meeting a servant may hold his or her hands well below their waist. Someone meeting a holy person, or a great leader, might touch his hands to his forehead. Don't get carried away, but indicate respect by holding your hands a little higher than theirs.

Asians often consider promises made during the negotiation as being made to the individuals who negotiated, not to the organization.

Americans call the signing of an agreement "the closing." Asians consider it an opening of the relationship. With Asians it is very important to convey that you consider the signing of the contract a beginning not an ending.

Do not expect eye contact because they think it's impolite. It's not a sign of shiftiness. Many a Vietcong soldier suffered at the hands of American troops because they couldn't look the American in the eye. The American assumed that this meant the Vietcong was lying.

Koreans

Koreans also look at the agreement as a starting point, not the final solution. They don't understand how any agreement can be expected to anticipate every possible eventuality, so they see a contract as an expression of an understanding on the day that the contract was signed. If conditions change, they don't feel bound by the contract they signed. Your response to this should not be to place less emphasis on the contract, but to draft a contract that is flexible enough to move with changing conditions. If you can predict a shift in conditions, rather than resisting it, you should accept that it could happen and provide penalties and rewards for the way each side responds to the changing conditions.

Koreans don't believe in fault. They consider that if they fail to stick with the agreement, it is an act of God. Unfortunately, they may have planned to take advantage of you with this.

Chinese

The Chinese have a saying "He ging, he li, he fa." It means first examine the relationship between the parties, then look at what is right, and only then worry about what the law says.

Many Chinese now shake hands when they meet Americans, but first wait to see if they offer their hands. The traditional greeting is a slight bow from the shoulders that is almost an exaggerated nod and is much less pronounced than the Japanese bow, which is from the waist.

Be low key in your approach because loud behavior easily offends the Chinese.

The Chinese do business based on building a relationship with you, but they are not above using this as a pressure point and accusing you of breaking a friendship if you hesitate to go ahead with the project.

I spent two weeks in China when it was still under tight communist control and my observation was that every Chinese person is an entrepreneur at heart and loves to bargain and haggle. Expect them to start high and be willing to make concessions. You should do the same and not be offended by what appears to you to be grinding you down on price. Have fun and enjoy the bargaining.

Japanese

In Japan they are reluctant to say no. Yes to them means only that they heard you. So don't ask questions that they can answer with a yes or no; ask open-ended questions. "When can you do that," is better than, "Can you do that."

It is impolite for a Japanese person to say No to an elder. However Westernized they may have become they still have trouble with this. I know a man who owns a large fencing company. He sold out to a Japanese concern and now reports to a business executive who is younger than he. "Roger," he told me, "I've been dealing with him for years now, and I have never known him to turn down a proposal that I made to him. The problem is that I can never tell whether he likes the proposal or is so uncomfortable saying No to an older man that he would rather approve it."

When the Japanese say "it will be difficult" they mean no.

The opening position that the Japanese take depends on how well they know you. If they don't know you or your industry well they will start high, not to take advantage of you, but because they learn about you by judging your reaction. It's called the "banana no tataki uri" approach to negotiating, a term that refers to the way that banana vendors would ask an outrageously high price from people they didn't know and then lower it quickly if the buyer protested. It sounds unethical to us, but it does make sense. You don't know the negotiating style of the stranger. He may be accustomed to hard bargaining. If you start high, you will quickly learn about him and take a different approach the next time you do business with him.

In my book *The Confident Decision Maker* (William Morrow 1993), I devoted a chapter to explaining how the Japanese make decisions. Here are some key points:

They make decisions in large groups, so we have trouble figuring out who is making the decision. The truth is that no one person is making the decision. They consider defining the problem to be far more important than searching for the right answer. The group is there to absorb information and feels that once they fully understand the situation, the choice will be obvious. So each member of the group will give their input, starting with the lowest-ranking person and moving up to the top.

Japanese executives see their job as requiring them to come up with creative ideas, not to be held accountable for the results. Whereas we prefer to have one person make the final decision so that they can be held accountable, the Japanese let the entire group collectively make the decision. When everyone has given all of their input the choice may be obvious to the group. If it is still not obvious they may retreat, knowing that they need to absorb more information. This makes Americans frustrated because they feel that nothing is happening. The good part of all this is that once they do decide to go ahead, everybody is on board and fully committed to the course of action.

Russians and Ukrainians

I spent two weeks in the Soviet Union when Gorbachev was trying to push through reforms. Frankly I doubted that they would ever make a transition to a free market economy because the Russians are not entrepreneurial at heart. Understand that the communist system removed all incentives from their way of life. Banning religion meant that there was no moral incentive to do good in their society. Banning profitable private enterprise meant that there was no financial incentive to do good. Remember that for 70 years they lived under a system where everybody worked for the government—there was no other employer. Money was almost meaningless to them because even if they had any there wasn't anything to buy with it. (President Reagan loved to tell the story of the Russian who saved all his life for an automobile and got a permit from the government to buy one. He took the money and the permit down to the car showroom and said, "When do I get my car?" "You will get your car in exactly seven years," they told him. "Seven years?" "Yes, on this day seven years from now you will get your car." "Will it be in the morning or the afternoon?" "Comrade, we are talking seven years. What difference does it make?" "Because on that day, in the morning, the plumber has promised to come.") Although some Russians have taken to capitalism like a duck to

water, for many it is a difficult transition, so don't expect them to be motivated by profit the way that we would be.

Russians are not afraid to make tough initial demands.

They have a very bureaucratic mind-set, so they are not afraid to say they
don't have the authority.

They can say No endlessly to test your resolve.

They are self centered. They're not interested in win-win.

If Russians say that something would be inconvenient, they mean that it
would be impossible. It took me a while to figure this out, and I'm still not
sure why it is, but presumably it's because of a misunderstanding in transla-
tion. For example, I asked the desk clerk at our Moscow hotel to move us to
a larger room. She told me, "That would be inconvenient." I took that to
mean that if I pushed harder I could get her to do it. Not at all. She was
telling me that it was impossible. It took me nearly 15 minutes to move us to
a suite!

Middle Easterners

Be sensitive to ethnic differences when you're negotiating in the Middle
East. Above all don't refer to them as Arabs unless they come from the Arabian peninsula, which includes Saudi Arabia, Iraq, Jordan, and the Gulf
States. Egyptians do not appreciate being called Arabs, and Iranians are horrified because they are proud to be Persians.

Do expect to spend a great deal of time, perhaps many days, getting to
know the person before he feels comfortable negotiating with you.

When people from the Middle East sign a contract, they see it as the start of
negotiations, not the end. They sign the contract first and then negotiate. Most
Americans who do business there understand this and call them "contract col-
lectors." It's important to understand this and not see it as devious, it's simply
the way they do things. A contract to them means less than a letter of intent does
to us.

In their world the ground floor is where shopkeepers ply their trade and
shopkeepers are a lower class than business people. Don't insult your Middle
East trading partners by asking them to do business in a ground floor office.
The higher floor you are on the more they see you as having prestige.

Don't be offended if they show up late for an appointment, or perhaps
don't even show up at all. Appointments are not the firm commitments that
they are in this country, and time in general is not prized the way that we
value it.

Gifts

You will often be overwhelmed with hospitality and gifts by the foreigners with whom you'll be negotiating. This is an overt attempt to win your favor, and you must deal with it. Rather than giving offense by refusing their favors, the best plan is to reciprocate, which eliminates the personal obligation that may have been created. And you have twice the fun.

Section Five

Understanding the Players

In the previous sections, I've concentrated on how to play the negotiating game. Now I want to focus on the importance of understanding the other negotiator and realizing that it is a major key to Power Negotiating. People are different. They throw who they are into the negotiation. It affects the kind of strategy that they develop, it influences which of the Gambits they will use and how they will use them, and it determines their entire style of negotiating.

Remember that you're always dealing with an individual, not an organization, even if you are negotiating with a union boss who heads up a 10,000-member union. I don't blame you for assuming that the needs of his members dictate his actions, but I believe that his personal needs guide his actions just as much. A Secretary of State may have very explicit instructions from the President on how he should conduct international negotiations, but his personal needs may still dominate his actions. Understand the person and you can often dominate the negotiations.

First we'll take a look at you and see if you've got what it takes to be a Power Negotiator as I cover the Personal Characteristics, Attitudes, and Beliefs of Power Negotiators. Many people seem to think that some people are born with the characteristics that make them successful negotiators. "Oh, he's a born negotiator," you'll hear people say. You know that's not true, don't you? I challenge you to open up any newspaper in the land and show me a birth announcement that says, "A negotiator was born at St. Bartholomew's Hospital today." No, people are not born negotiators. Power Negotiating is a learnable skill.

In this section I'll teach how to feel comfortable with any style of negotiator so that you can easily read various negotiators and their approach to getting what they want. Then I'll show you how to adapt your style of negotiating to theirs.

Chapter 48

The Personal Characteristics of a Power Negotiator

To be a Power Negotiator you need to have or develop these personal characteristics:

- The courage to probe for more information.
- The patience to outlast the other negotiator.
- The courage to ask for more than you expect to get.
- The integrity to press for win-win solutions.
- The willingness to be a good listener.

Let's take a look at each of these.

The courage to probe for more information

Poor negotiators are always reluctant to question anything the other says, so they negotiate knowing only what the other side has chosen to tell them. Power Negotiators are constantly challenging what they know about the other side and, what is more important, the assumptions that they have made based on that knowledge. You should adopt many of the approaches of investigative reporters as you gather information. Ask the tough questions, the ones that you feel sure they won't answer. Even if they don't answer you will learn by judging their reaction to being asked. Ask the same question of several people to see if you get the same responses. Ask the same question several times during an extended negotiation to see if you get consistent answers. As you know, I devoted Chapter 38 to the importance of gathering information before and during the negotiation.

The patience to outlast the other negotiator

Patience is a virtue to a good negotiator. I remember going around the country on a press tour to promote an earlier book on negotiating. A couple of times I showed up at television stations, and the interviewer said to me, "You don't look like a negotiator." I knew what they meant and it didn't offend me. They meant, "We thought you'd look tougher, we thought you'd look meaner." Perhaps from seeing movies about union negotiators many people think of negotiators as tough, ruthless people who will pull any ruthless trick to trick the other side into losing. Nothing could be further from the truth. Good negotiators are very patient people who won't let time pressure bully them into making a deal that is not in everyone's best interests.

Remember what I told you in Chapter 37 about the Vietnam peace talks? Averell Harriman rented a suite at the Ritz Hotel in Paris on a week-to-week basis. The Vietnamese negotiator Xuan Thuy rented a villa in the countryside for two and half years. With your government, your people, and the world press breathing down your neck for results, it takes courage to show that much patience, but it's very effective.

The courage to ask for more
than you expect to get

Henry Kissinger says, "Effectiveness at the conference table depends upon overstating one's demands." Apart from projecting the willingness to walk away if you can't get what you want, I don't think that there is anything more important than understanding this principle and having the courage to apply it.

We all lack courage because we fear ridicule. Remember when I taught you about the Bracketing Gambit in Chapter One? I told you that you should make a super low offer, which brackets your objective, when you're buying something. Or, when you're selling something, make your initial proposal so high that it brackets your real objective. You should always advance your maximum plausible position. Sometimes that's hard to do. We simply don't have the courage to make those way-out proposals because we're afraid the other side will laugh at us. The fear of ridicule stops us from accomplishing many things with our lives. To be a power negotiator, you must get over that fear. You must be able to comfortably advance your maximum plausible position and not apologize for it. I'll teach you more about fear in Chaper 53 on Coercive Power.

The integrity to press for a win-win solution

Straight Up, by James Ramsey Ullman, is an excellent biography of young mountain climber John Harlin, who, at 30 years of age, died trying to climb the Eiger Mountain diretissima—straight up. The author, a famous chronicler of mountain climbing events, wrote about Harlin's life in the preface. He said, "Straight up is a way of serving a drink. It is also a way to climb a mountain and of living a life."

I believe that straight up is the way to negotiate. Often the opportunity to take quick advantage of a weakened opponent will tempt you. Often you'll be in a situation in which you know something that if the other knew, they wouldn't be so eager to settle. Having the integrity to push for a win-win solution even when you have the other side on the ropes is a rare and precious commodity. I don't mean by this that you make costly concessions to the other side because you're so charitable. I do mean that you continue to look for ways to make concessions to the other side that do not take away from your position.

The willingness to be a good listener

Only a good listener can be a win-win negotiator. Only a good listener can detect the other side's real needs in a negotiation. Here are some tips for being a good listener in preparing for and conducting the negotiation:

- Increase your concentration by thinking of listening as an interactive process. Lean forward. Tilt your head a little to show you're paying attention. Ask questions. Give feedback. Mirror what he or she said. Avoid boredom by playing mind games. Concentrate on what he or she is saying, not the style of delivery. You can do this by picking the longest word in a sentence or rephrasing what has just been said. Because you can listen four times faster than the speaker can speak, you need to do something or your mind will wander.

- Increase your comprehension of what's being said by taking notes right from the start of the conversation. Take a large pad of paper with you. Head it up with the date and the topic and start to keep brief notes on what's being said. Paper is cheaper than the time it takes to go back and get the details. This communicates to the other person that you care about what he's saying. An additional bonus is that when people see you're writing things down, they tend to be a lot more accurate in what they're telling you. Next, defer making judgment of the other person until he's through. If you immediately analyze someone as phony or manipulative or self-serving, you tend to shut him out and quit listening to him. So just hold off and wait until he's through before you evaluate.

- Improve your ability to evaluate what's said by asking the other person to present her conclusions first. Then if you don't agree with her completely, ask her to support her conclusions. Keep an open mind until she has. Be aware of your personal biases and be conscious of how they're coloring your reactions. If you know that you don't like attorneys, you can evaluate the information much more clearly when you're aware that this is causing you to distrust the person who's talking to you. Perhaps you're a person who can't stand people trying to hype you. You automatically resist what they have to say whether it's right or whether it's wrong, so be aware of that. It improves your ability to evaluate what they're saying. Learn to take notes with a divided note pad, one with a line down the middle. On the left you list the facts as they were presented, on the right you note your evaluation of what was said.

Chapter 49

The Attitudes of a Power Negotiator

The willingness to live with ambiguity

Power Negotiators relish the idea of going into a negotiation not knowing whether they'll come out as heros, or if they'll come out carrying their heads in their hands. This willingness to live with ambiguity requires a particular attitude.

People who like people are much more comfortable with ambiguity. People who prefer things have trouble with it. For this reason engineers, accountants and architects—members of those professions that depend on accuracy—have a tough time with negotiating. They don't like the push and the shove of it. They would rather have everything laid out in black and white.

Let me give you a little quiz to test your willingness to live with ambiguity:

1. If you're going to a party, do you first like to know who you're likely to meet there?

2. If your spouse is taking you to have dinner with friends at a restaurant, do you like to know exactly which restaurant you are going to?

3. Do you like to plan out your vacations to the smallest detail?

If you said Yes to all three of these, you have a major problem with ambiguity. To become a better negotiator I suggest that you force yourself to tolerate situations in which you don't know exactly what the outcome will be.

A competitive spirit

Good negotiators have an intense desire to win when they're negotiating. Seeing negotiating as a game is a big part of what makes you good at it. It's fun to walk into the arena and pit your skills against the skills of the other person.

It always amazes me that salespeople can be so competitive in sports and so gutless when it comes to handling buyers. A salesperson may enjoy playing racquetball so he sets up an early morning game with a buyer before he's scheduled to make a presentation to him. On the racquetball court he'll do everything he can—within the rules of the game—to beat the buyer. Then they shower and go to the office to negotiate the sale, and the moment the buyer mentions price, the salesperson rolls over and feels that he's at the buyer's mercy.

The more you think of negotiating as a game, the more competitive you'll become. The more competitive you become, the more courageous you become and the better you'll do.

No strong need to be liked

Power Negotiators are not restrained by the need to be liked. Abraham Maslow is famous for his pyramid of human needs, which showed our needs as:

1. Survival.

2. Security—the need to assure our continued survival.

3. Social—the need to be liked by others.

4. Self Esteem—the need to be respected by others.

5. Self Actualization—the need to feel fulfilled.

Power Negotiators are beyond stage three most of the time—they have surpassed the need to be liked. Negotiation, almost by definition, is the management of conflict or at least opposing viewpoints. People who have an exaggerated need to be liked will not be good negotiators because they fear conflict too much.

Does this mean that good negotiators are ruthless people who win because they don't care if the other person is losing? No, not at all. It does mean that the most important thing to them is to hammer away at the problem until a solution is found that everyone can live with.

Chapter 50

The Beliefs of a Power Negotiator

Negotiating is always a two-way affair

Power Negotiating is always a two-way affair. The pressure is always on the other person to compromise in the negotiations just as much as it is on you. For example, when you're walking into a bank to apply for a business loan, you may get very intimidated. You tend to look at that big bank, and you start thinking; "Why on Earth would a big bank like this want to lend little old me money?" You lose sight of the pressure that's on the other side. This bank spends millions of dollars a year in advertising to entice you to come in for a loan. There is tremendous pressure on the bank to get those deposits out in the form of loans. Many people at that bank have jobs that are dependent on their making loans.

So, a good negotiator learns to mentally compensate for the fact that we always think we have the weaker side in the negotiations. As she strides up to that loan officer's desk she thinks to herself, "I bet that loan officer just got a royal chewing out from his boss who told him, 'If you can't find somebody to lend money to today, we don't even need you around here anymore.' "

Remember when you've had a key employee come to you to ask for a raise in pay? What are you sitting there thinking? You're thinking: "I hope I don't lose him over this. He has done so well for me, all these years. He's so skilled in what he's doing. I have no idea where I'd find a replacement for him."

The employee is probably sitting there, thinking: "I hope this doesn't affect my career plan with the company. They've really been good to me over the years. Maybe I shouldn't push so hard. She's been so nice to me." You're both sitting there thinking that you have the weaker hand in the negotiation. Power Negotiators learn to mentally compensate for that.

Why does this happen? Because each side knows about the pressure that is on him or her but not about the pressure that is on the other side. For that reason each side typically thinks that it has the weaker hand.

Don't buy into it when a potential customer says to you: "I've got half a dozen other guys that will do it for less money and do it just as well." Don't buy into that. Something brought the other side to the negotiating table. The customer has pressure just as much as you have it on you.

The minute you believe that and learn to mentally compensate for it, you become a more powerful negotiator.

Negotiating is played by a set of rules

The second belief that makes you a good negotiator is that negotiating is a game that is played by a set of rules, just like the game of chess.

Perhaps when you read some of the Gambits in Section One, you thought: "Roger, you've never met some of the guys I have to deal with in my business. They make Attila the Hun look like Ann Landers. They're never going to fall for that kind of thing."

That's fair enough, but I want you to buy a little blue sky from me until you've had a chance to try them out. Time and time again, students of mine have told me: "I never thought that it would work, but it did. It's amazing." The first time you Flinch, Nibble, or use the Vise on the other person and walk out of the negotiations with $1,000 in your pocket that you didn't expect to get, you'll be a believer too.

I always remember training the employees of a large savings and loan in Southern California. At a local hotel they arranged an afternoon seminar followed by a cocktail party and a dinner. During the cocktail party I was standing talking to the president of the savings and loan when the maitre d' from the hotel came up with two bottles of wine in his arms. He asked the president if he would like wine served with the dinner. When asked, he told the president that wine cost $22.50 per bottle. The president was about to say okay when I said, "You'll have to do better than that." The maitre d' looked irritated, and the president looked shocked. The maitre d' finally said, "I tell you what. If you'll serve it for everybody, I'll give it to you for $15 a bottle."

The president's face lit up, and he was about to give his okay when I said, "We were thinking more like $10 a bottle." Which caused the maitre d' to respond: "I'm not going to negotiate the price of wine with you—$13.50 is absolutely the best I can do." Remember that the president had been in the seminar that afternoon and had heard me talk about the Vise Gambit, but until he saw it in action, I don't think he thought that it would work.

So buy some blue sky from me until you get a chance to get out there and try out these Gambits. The most important belief to have is that negotiating is a game that is played by a set of rules. If you learn the rules well, you can play the game well.

The word No is simply an opening negotiating position

To Power Negotiators the word No is never a refusal—it is simply an opening negotiating position. Remember that the next time you take a proposal in to somebody—perhaps your boss or a potential customer—and he explodes with rage and says, "Not you again, with another of your crazy ideas. How many times do I have to tell you that we're never going to do it. Get out of my office and quit wasting my time." When that happens remember that a Power Negotiator doesn't take it as a refusal (I know—it's close), she takes it only to be an opening negotiating position. She thinks to herself, "Isn't that an interesting opening negotiating position. I wonder why he decided to start with that approach."

Section Six

Developing Power Over the Other Side

Power. Control. Influence. That's really at the heart of any interpersonal situation, isn't it? In negotiating, the person with the most influence or power will gain the most concessions. If you allow other people to manipulate and intimidate you, it is your fault if you're not getting what you want out of life. If, on the other hand, you learn what influences people and how to use and counter specific methods, you can take control of any situation.

Developing personal power over the other side is an issue that is so critical to Power Negotiating that I'm going to devote all of this section to it.

In any negotiation one person always feels he's either the intimidator or the intimidatee. You always feel that you either have control of the other person or the other person has control over you. In this section I'm going to explain where that feeling comes from and how to deal with it.

At a seminar in Iowa a man approached me and said: "Roger, my wife took your Power Negotiating course, and I've never seen such a personality change in all my life. She has her own small business, and it wasn't doing that well. But once she studied up on Personal Power and your Negotiating Gambits, it's amazing to see the difference in her. She turned into a tiger and she really turned that business around."

I have always been fascinated by what causes one person to be influenced by another and for the last decade I have been absorbed with studying personal power. Now I've been able to pinpoint the key things that give you power over other people. In every situation in which one person exercises control over another, one or more of these factors have been called into play. Whether it is a drill sergeant harassing a private in boot camp or a parent trying to maintain control over an errant child, one or more of these basic power factors is being used.

Power has earned a nasty reputation, hasn't it? In a letter to Bishop Creighton, Lord Acton said that, "Power tends to corrupt and absolute power corrupts absolutely." Charles Colton said, "Power will intoxicate the best hearts, as wine the strongest heads. No man is wise enough, nor good enough to be trusted with unlimited power." However, I don't believe that power is inherently evil. It really isn't power that corrupts, is it? It's the abuse of power. You wouldn't say that water is bad because occasionally we have floods and people get killed. You wouldn't say that air is bad because we occasionally have hurricanes and things get damaged. So it's not power itself, it's the abuse of power that corrupts. There is tremendous power in the ocean's waves and yet every day hundreds of eager surfers ride the towering crests. Electricity has the power to light a child's room at night and the power to electrocute a convicted murderer. The power itself is independent of its use. The Pope has power over millions of people and so did Adolf Hitler. As George Bernard Shaw said, "Power does not corrupt man; fools, however, if they get into a position of power, corrupt power."

Power can be a very constructive force. When I talk about power, I am not referring to the wanton ruthlessness of a dictator, whether he be in politics or industry; I simply mean the ability to influence other people.

What I'm going to cover in this section are the things that people can do to you when they're negotiating with you to cause you to blink first at the negotiating table. Of course, these things are also what can give you power over the other side. Where does that ability come from? It comes from one or more of these eight elements.

Chapter 51

Legitimate Power

Legitimate Power goes to anyone who has a title. I think you'll agree that you are always a little more intimidated by someone who has the title of vice-president, or doctor, than you would be by someone who has no title. We gain Legitimate Power instantly because it goes to us the moment that the title is conferred upon us.

For example, the moment the Chief Justice swears in the President of the United States, the President receives the full power of the presidency, independent of any personal power that may have existed moments before. What a president does with that power from that point on makes all the difference. To strike a balance between appearing presidential and appearing close to the people—just a regular guy—is a delicate balance. When President Carter carried his own luggage into the White House, he started giving away his Legitimate Power. He gave away even more Legitimate Power when he turned the heat down in the White House to save energy. Perhaps the symbolism of being willing to share the burden of the energy crisis was important enough to lower the temperature, but none of us expected the First Lady to have to type her own letters with gloves on to stop her hands from freezing, as her husband forced her to do. President Reagan's use of limousines, state banquets, and helicopter rides to Camp David restored Legitimate Power to the presidency.

We knew that George Bush's career in politics was over when he taunted Bill Clinton and Al Gore with the titles of Bozo and Ozone Man. Barbara Bush wasn't the only one to be horrified at this un-presidential approach.

The sight of Bill Clinton jogging into McDonalds for an Egg McMuffin perhaps endeared him to millions of junk food fans, but it didn't help him in his negotiations with Congress and foreign leaders.

Titles influence people, so if you have a title, don't be afraid to use it. Don't be bashful about putting your title on your business cards and on your name plate. If the title on your business card says vice-president, you already have a head start over someone whose card says salesperson. When I ran the real estate company, I would let the agents who were farming a territory put Area Manager on their business cards. (Farming means that they had staked out an area of 500 homes, and they were knocking on doors and mailing newsletters to those homeowners to establish themselves as an expert in that community.) They told me that having the title Area Manager on their cards made a dramatic difference in the way people accepted them.

So if you don't have an impressive title on your business card, this may be something your company should review. The standard designations for territories are that an area manager reports to a district manager who reports to a regional manager, so regional vice-president appears to be the more impressive title. Occasionally I run into a company that designates titles the other way, and the area manager is in charge of the Western United States. I don't suggest that they change, but because it's traditionally done the other way, area manager tends to be a less impressive title than regional manager.

So if you have a title, use it on your business card, your letterhead, and your nameplate because titles do influence people.

Legitimate Power also tells you that you should have them come to you if possible, rather than negotiating in their territory where their trappings of power surround them. If you're taking them somewhere it should always be in your car because that gives you more control. If you're taking them to lunch it should be to your choice of restaurant, not to their favorite place where they would feel in control.

Here are five small things that Power Negotiators can do to build their Title Power:

1. Use your title if you have one. If you don't have a title, see if you can get one.

2. Use your initials. For example, describe yourself as J. R. Doe, rather than John Doe. People who don't know you must then call you Mr. Doe rather than calling you by your first name.

3. If possible, always negotiate in your office, in your surroundings, rather than in theirs. That way you're in your power base surrounded by the trappings of your title.

4. Always use your automobile when you're negotiating with people; don't let them drive. Real estate people always do that, don't they? When they're in your car, you have control over them.

5. Have a secretary place and screen your calls. I personally don't like secretaries who place calls for people, but it does convey legitimate power.

Other forms of Legitimate Power

There are other forms of Legitimate Power. Positioning in the market place is a form of Legitimate Power. If you can claim that your company is the biggest—or the smallest; if you claim that it's the oldest—or the newest; you have Legitimate Power. You can claim to be the most global company or you can claim to specialize. You can tell people that you're brand new so you're trying harder or that you've been in the business for 40 years. It really doesn't matter how you position yourself—any kind of positioning gives you Legitimate Power.

Respect for the law is a form of Legitimate Power. Some people obey the law only because of fear of punishment, but most of us also respect the law and follow it because of that respect. There is almost no chance of us getting into trouble if we drive without a driver's license in our possession, but most of the time we take pains to see that we have it in our pockets. It's very hard to enforce seat belt laws but I started wearing mine when California passed a seat-belt law, simply because I take pride in showing respect for the law. Do you zoom through red lights in the middle of the night if there's nobody around? Probably not, because we see the benefit of everyone obeying traffic laws without question.

Tradition is a form of Legitimate Power. (Until the turn of the century tradition and law were thought to be the only main influences on people's behavior.) If you can establish in the other person's mind that you have been doing something for a long time, you can convince her or him that it's valid without giving any other reason for doing it.

An established procedure is another form of Legitimate Power. "We have always done it this way," has power. That's why price tags have Legitimate Power. Because they say, "Here's the way this works. We put a price tag on the merchandise. You pick what you want and bring it to the cash register. We charge you what is on the price tag." Simply because of this established procedure, few people question price tags in this country. Conversely the procedure on a car lot has been established differently. "You look at the price sticker and then you make us an offer," is the established procedure, and even people who hate to haggle will follow procedure. Power Negotiators know to use "standard contracts" when getting the other person to do what we want them to do. "This is our standard contract. This is the one that everybody signs," is simply conveying the power of procedure that is a form of Legitimate Power.

So the first element of personal power is Legitimate Power, which goes to anybody who has a title, or has positioned himself in the marketplace, or who has projected that an established way of doing things exists.

Legitimate power as an intimidation factor

On the other hand when you negotiate with other people, don't be intimidated by a title. We all tend to be more intimidated by someone who's a vice president of a bank or the president of a corporation than we would by someone who didn't have a title.

For example, let's say that you're looking for a particular make and model of car. One day, in the parking lot at a golf course, you find just the car for which you've been looking and it has a "for sale" sign in the window. As you're peering into the driver's side window, trying to get a look at the mileage, the owner walks up. He tells you that he is selling it for $10,000. That seems a little overpriced, but you promise to think about it and get back to him. He scribbles his name and phone number on a scrap of paper and tells you to give him a call at the office if you're interested.

You decide that you would love to have the car, if you can get him down to $6,000 or $7,000. So you call him up and say, "I want to make an offer on your car. When can we get together and talk about it?"

"I'm really busy this week," he responds. "But my office is downtown. If you'd like to meet me here, I can give you a few minutes." So you locate his office building and the lobby directory guides you to the 24th floor, where a secretary ushers you into a penthouse suite through doors bearing large, gold-engraved signs that say President.

Inside the large office the walls are covered with plaques and diplomas, all extolling the great achievements and accomplishments of the man behind the desk—the same man that you met in the golf course parking lot. He stands up when you enter, shakes your hand, then returns to his conversation, motioning you to a chair facing the desk. He's talking about selling some shares of stock on the Swiss Exchange, and it sounds like a multi-million-dollar deal. Finally, he hangs up the phone, smiles and says, "Now how about that car? You're not going to ask me to come down on my price, are you?"

Now how do you feel about presenting your $6,000 offer? You're likely so intimidated that you will want to either excuse yourself politely, saying that you've decided not to buy the car at all, or say, "You'd let me have it for $9,000, wouldn't you?" At that point you probably wish you were buying the car from a factory worker.

What does the seller's position have to do with the value you place on the car? Absolutely nothing. If the car is worth $6,000 or $7,000 to you, it is worth the same whether you are buying it from a person who puts caps on toothpaste tubes or the President of the United States.

In fact, if you will analyze the situation more, you have assumed that this corporation president would be unwilling to take a low offer because he's not under any pressure to sell his car, when instead he may be much more willing to accept less money than he's asking for, because he doesn't need the money or doesn't want to spend a great deal of time getting rid of his car. On the other hand, that blue-collar worker may be under financial pressure and need every penny of his asking price. Don't let a title intimidate you so you're blind to the other factors that should take precedence in your consideration of what price to offer.

Some titles don't mean anything

A good reason not to let titles intimidate you is that some of them are quite meaningless.

I remember when I first came to this country in 1962, I came with only $400 in cash so I had to get a job quickly. I went to work for the Bank of America, which was willing to put me on the teller line as a trainee. It didn't make sense to me because I hadn't even learned the money yet. Do you know how confusing American money is to foreigners? We have coins that don't have the numbers on them. A dime doesn't say ten and a nickel doesn't say five. The slots on a telephone don't say dime and nickel, they say 5 and 10. The bills are all the same color and size. It was very confusing for me, but I needed a job and I wasn't going to question their judgment. So there I was on the teller line, saying to myself, "a nickel is bigger than a dime even though it's worth only half as much," when a lady approached me to get a check cashed. I said: "I'm sorry, but that check is above my limit. Would you mind taking it over to the platform to get it okayed by an officer?"

She said: "Don't you know who I am? My uncle is a vice-president of Bank of America."

I was aware that Bank of America was, at the time, the largest bank in the world and that it had 500 or 600 branches, so this information immediately intimidated me. I took the standard Nuremberg defense and explained that I was just doing what my superiors had told me to do. Off she went in a real huff. I turned to the teller beside me and told her: "I think I just got myself into a lot of trouble. I've just upset the niece of the vice-president of Bank of America."

The other teller laughed and said: "Don't you realize how many vice-presidents Bank of America has?" She pulled out the directory of vice-presidents that was like a telephone book. It listed hundreds of vice presidents. So titles are sometimes meaningless.

My daughter Julia graduated from the University of Southern California with a business-finance degree and went to work for Dean Witter, the New York stockbrokers, in their huge Beverly Hills office. One day she was talking about becoming a vice-president at Dean Witter. I told her, "Julia, you have to set realistic goals in life. That's a huge corporation and it may take you years and years to become a vice-president."

She replied, "Oh no, I think I'll be a vice-president by the end of the year."

I asked her, "How many vice-presidents does Dean Witter have?"

She told me, "I don't know, but it must be thousands. We have 35 in this one office."

There's a company that understands that titles influence people.

In his book *All You Can Do Is All You Can Do*, A. L. Williams brags that at his company he appointed 100 vice-presidents a month. If he just made it a policy to go out and shake hands with every new vice-president that alone would be a full-time job. So don't be intimidated if the person to whom you are selling has a fancy title because it may not mean a thing.

It's like the two people arguing that General Motors has so many vice-presidents they even have a vice-president in charge of head rests. To settle the argument, they finally called General Motors and said to the operator: "May we speak to your vice-president in charge of head rests?"

The operator asked: "Certainly sir, is that passenger side or driver's side?"

So don't be influenced by titles, but understand that titles do influence people.

Chapter 52

Reward Power

The second element of personal power is Reward Power. Power Negotiators know that if you can convince the other parties that making the deal with you would reward them, you have given yourself the power to influence them.

Unfortunately many people who are trying to sell their product or service never develop the self-confidence to project to the other side that they would be rewarding the buyer. These people think that the buyer is rewarding them by placing the order with them.

Remember the old Sergeant Bilko television series? The supply sergeant on the army base had more power than the colonel who was really running the base because he had a greater ability to reward the men.

The person who has the power at a taxi-cab company is not the owner, but the dispatcher, because the dispatcher has a greater ability to reward the drivers.

If your company has grown to the point where you've delegated the task of selecting which worker goes to a job and which doesn't, you may have delegated away much of your personal power. Some presidents will unknowingly relinquish power to their personnel director when they give the personnel director the right to make promotional moves and give increases in pay, and this Reward Power gives the personnel director control.

Remember Robin Givens? She was Mike Tyson's wife for about eight months. When she went to California to hire a divorce attorney I'm sure she wasn't thinking that she would be rewarding Marvin Mitchelson by giving him the case. No. She was thinking, "If I could get Marvin Mitchelson that would be really something because he's the best in the business. You can't do any better than that."

If you're selling a product or service you must believe that you're the best in the business. Then you must know how to convince your customers of that. They can't do any better than you. If you're willing to put your personal reputation and expertise on the line to solve those buyers' problems and the reputation and expertise of your company, they are not rewarding you—you are rewarding them. Of course you can't push that too far because it quickly becomes arrogance, but don't roll over the other way, thinking that your customers would be rewarding you by giving you an order. I've heard rumors that some salespeople will actually beg a buyer to give them just a small part of the company's business. Can you believe that? Doesn't it sound like a dog begging for table scraps? When you truly believe that you are rewarding the buyer, not the other way around, you will feel confident in demanding all of their business.

Take a moment now and jot down three reasons why someone with whom you negotiate would be rewarded by cutting a deal with you. If you're in sales think of the reasons why she would be rewarded by picking you over one of your competitors. If you're applying for a job or a promotion think of three ways in which picking you would reward that company.

1. _____

2. _____

3. _____

I wonder if one of the reasons you wrote was *"They get you."* That should be the number one reason that they pick you and not your competitor—not because of the quality of the product or service that you sell, but because they get you. To be successful at projecting reward power you must add value to the product or service—they must see value in buying it from you. You probably have some legitimate competition in your industry, companies that can deliver a very similar product at a very competitive price. The difference has to be you. Your knowledge of your product and service. Your knowledge of their problems and opportunities. Your ability to be creative in solving their problems and seizing their opportunities.

I wonder how many competitors you have for what you do? Two, three, or perhaps half a dozen? Guess how many competitors I have as a professional speaker? There are 3,500 members of my association, the National Speakers Association. Whenever I book a speaking engagement there are 3,499 other speakers with whom I had to compete for the privilege of being in front of that audience. Meeting planners say to me, "Roger, with all that competition, how can you charge as much as you do?" I tell them, "Because I'm good!" That may sound very arrogant and egotistical to you, but you need to have that much confidence in what you do. You need to have that much confidence that you do what you do better than anyone else. The number one reason they should pick you is that they get you, and the only way they get you is to pick you.

Reward power as an intimidation factor

Power Negotiators understand that anytime you perceive someone as able to reward you, you have given them the power to intimidate you. If you think that buyer is rewarding you by giving you an order, then you've given him the power to intimidate you. This is why you feel more intimidated when you're making a big sale than you do when you're making a small one. The potential reward is greater, so you feel intimidated. Of course, that's entirely subjective, isn't it? When you're first getting started you may feel that sense of reward over a $1,000 sale. Later on it will take a $100,000 sale to get you excited.

When the other side starts using Reward Power on you, recognize it and don't let it intimidate you. Some people are absolute masters at using Reward Power. When they're asking you for a concession, they just happen to mention that they have a big project coming on line next week, for which you might be in the running, or they'll talk about their yacht down at the harbor, or their ski cabin up on the mountain. They don't even have to come out and tell you that if you did business together you'd get to use them, it's just an implied Reward Power. Don't let it irritate you, but recognize it for what it is and don't let it throw you off base in the negotiations.

Once you recognize Reward Power and understand what they're trying to do to you, their ability to control you with it goes away, and you become a lot more self-confident as a negotiator.

Chapter 53

Coercive Power

The opposite side of Reward Power is Coercive Power. Any time you perceive someone as able to punish you, they have power over you. You know how awful you feel when the state trooper pulls you over to the side of the road and he's standing there and can write you, or not write you, a ticket. The penalty may not be very great, but the level of intimidation is very great indeed.

Incidentally, in the real estate industry in California they have a joke about this. California has more than 300,000 licensed real estate agents. If you think you have competition in your industry—try California real estate. The joke is that a Highway Patrol officer pulls you over to the side of the road and says: "Okay buddy, let me see your real estate license."

You say: "Officer, don't you mean my driver's license?"

He says: "No, not everybody in California has a driver's license."

It's hard for us to think about using coercive power on other people, but it's always present in any negotiation. If you're asking a clerk at the store to take an item back and give you a refund, both Reward Power and Coercive Power will influence that clerk's decision. If he gives you the refund graciously you will reward him by thanking him and it will be a pleasant experience. If he refuses to give you the refund, you might get angry and it will be an unpleasant experience.

Let's look at how Power Negotiators make Reward and Coercive Power work together as a powerful influencing force.

Parents use Reward and Coercive Power with their children. "If you go to bed now, I'll read you a story. If you don't eat your carrots, you can't watch television."

Salespeople stress benefits to their customers to persuade them to buy and try gently to imply the dangers of not investing. "Making this investment will do wonders for your bottom line. Do it now before the competition gets the jump on you."

Managers use the carrot and stick approach to motivate their employees. "Do a good job on this one and it'll really make you look good. Joe, watch my lips. Don't mess up on this one."

Politicians use it to maintain the balance of world peace. "Maintain a democratic government, and we'll give you favored-nation status. Mess with us, and we've got ten thousand nuclear warheads ready to take off on 15 seconds notice."

In any persuasion situation, the elements of reward and punishment are always present. Let's say that your car is in the shop. They're telling you it won't be ready until tomorrow, but you must have it tonight. You let them know specifically how you feel.

What's going on in the repair shop manager's mind as he listens to you? If he goes along with your request, you'll reward him with your gratitude and a pleasant, warm environment. If he doesn't, he's apprehensive that things will turn nasty. Power Negotiators understand these two elements and know how to skillfully to apply both of them.

People who don't understand Power Negotiation use one, but not the other. They threaten Coercive Power, but don't understand it can be much more powerful when coupled with Reward Power. You've seen people make this mistake, I'm sure. When the car isn't ready, poor negotiators get angry and try to force the other person to give in against their wishes. "If my car isn't ready by five o'clock, I'm going to sue you for everything you've got. I'll own this place." Applying fear tactics is an effective persuader, but it's often done so crudely that it backfires. Then, if the other side does cave in, they often compound the error by gloating over their victory.

Power Negotiators know the subtle application of both Reward and Coercive Power is much more effective. They imply that things will get unpleasant if they don't get what they want. When the other side looks as though they're going to give in, however, they quickly switch to reward power by showing their gratitude. "That's great, I really appreciate it. You're very nice."

Take a moment now and jot down three reasons why someone with whom you negotiate would be punished by not consummating a deal with you. If you're in sales think of the reasons why she would be punished by picking one of your competitors over you. If you're applying for a job or a promotion think of three ways in which picking anyone else would punish the company.

1. _____

2. _____

3. _____

I wonder if one of the reasons you wrote was: *"They don't get you."* That should be the number one reason that they avoid choosing your competitor—not because of the quality of the product or service that you sell, but because they don't get you if they do that. To be successful at projecting Coercive Power you must add so much value to your product or service—that they fear not buying it from you. As with Reward Power the difference has to be you. Your knowledge of your product and service. Your knowledge of their problems and opportunities. Your ability to be creative in solving their problems and seizing their opportunities.

Remember when we talked about the Bracketing Gambit in Chapter One? I told you that you should make your initial proposal so high that it brackets your real objective. Sometimes that's intimidating for you to do. You simply don't have the courage to make those way-out proposals, because you're afraid the other side will laugh at you. In my book *The 13 Secrets of Power Performance* (Prentice Hall 1994) I gave you the answer to this—you must figure out what you fear the most and do it. As with Reward Power, the answer lies in experience. Although a neophyte business person my be uptight about a $1,000 negotiation, a more experienced business person will be philosophical about losing a $100,000 negotiation. Although a new salesperson may fear losing a $1,000 sale, the experienced salesperson will not let the loss of a $100,000 sale intimidate him.

New salespeople always have trouble with Reward and Coercive Power. When they first make sales calls, they see every buyer as being able to reward them by giving them the order, or punish them by turning them down, or worse yet ridiculing them for what they have proposed. Once they've been at it for a while they recognize that selling is a numbers game just like anything else. If they're working hard at it and talking to a great number of people, there always will be a high percentage of people who will turn them down. Once they understand that it's a numbers game, their perception that people can reward or punish them goes away, and they become a lot more self-confident in what they're doing.

So any time you perceive someone as able to coerce you, they have the power to intimidate you; and one of the greatest coercive forces we know is the power to embarrass people by ridiculing them.

The fear of ridicule can stop us from accomplishing many of the things we'd like to accomplish with our lives. Many years ago, when I was learning to ski, I was skiing at Mammoth Mountain in California with friends who skied much better than I did. They said, "Roger, we're going to take you up to the cornice today."

I said, "I don't think I'm ready for the cornice yet."

They said, "Oh come on, Roger, you can make it. Let's go."

So we rode the gondola up to the top of the mountain, which is about 12,000 feet above sea level. I can still feel the tension in that tiny gondola as we drifted silently up the snow-covered face of this almost vertical cliff. It's such a daunting run that even the most experienced skiers won't talk as they approach the top. They sit there in silence, deep in their private thoughts, forcing themselves to overcome the fear of what lies ahead. Finally we slid into the terminal and stepped outside, into the icy wind. I nervously put on my skis and skied down about a hundred yards with my friends, until we were standing at the top of the cornice. A cornice is an overhang of snow, blown over the corner of the cliff by the snow. The skiers had cut a V shape through this cornice, out onto the cliff. I would have to shoot down this V shape chute, on to the face of the cliff, which is almost vertical. If I made just one slip, I'd go down the next fifteen hundred feet on my head.

I stood there, looking down through this chute, and as I saw it, I had two options. Option number one was to hike back up to the gondola and ride down, but if I did that my friends would laugh at me. Option number two, was to die! I chose to die, rather than be ridiculed. That's how strong that type of fear of punishment can be.

Recently, I skied the cornice again with my children and now they have a sign at the top that says, "When your friends say go—don't be afraid to say no."

So understand and feel comfortable using Coercive Power. Whether you approve or not, it's always present in the negotiation and your ability to use it effectively is critical to your success as a negotiator.

Chapter 54

Reverent Power

The fourth element of personal power is Reverent Power, which goes to anybody who has a consistent set of values. An obvious example of this is a religious leader like the Pope, Billy Graham, or Robert Schuller. Pat Robertson was able to make a serious run at the Presidency because he articulated one theme: You can trust me because I have a set of values and I am not going to deviate from those values. John F. Kennedy had Reverent Power. When he talked about the *mantle of power passing to a new generation, born in this century,* and when he talked about the *New Frontier* he was projecting that he believed in something—that he had a consistent set of values. His brother Robert was very good at it, too, when he ran for President. Remember his famous saying, "Some people look at things and say, 'Why?' I look at things and say, 'Why not?' "

President Clinton does not have Reverent Power. I met him at the White House once, and I can tell you that he is a very charismatic and brilliantly intelligent person who is an incredibly hard worker. His problem is that he appears to waiver on difficult issues. You never quite know whether he has the courage to stay with an issue if the going gets tough.

Lack of Reverent Power was President Carter's downfall. He was one of the nicest, most moral and ethical Presidents we've ever had. He was also one of the hardest working men who ever occupied the White House and probably among the most intelligent—he majored in nuclear physics. However, he lost his ability to influence because he appeared to vacillate on different issues. We never knew if he felt strongly enough to follow through if the going got tough.

Take, for example, his handling of the visa for the Shah of Iran. The Shah was living in his beautiful villa on Acapulco Bay. He became seriously ill and requested a visa to come to this country for medical treatment. At first Carter said no, fearing repercussions in Iran. Then he changed his mind and approved the visa so that the Shah could get cancer treatment in New York. When this created a surge of anti-American protests in Iran, Carter changed his mind again—and made the Shah move to Panama to take the pressure off the situation.

I don't think Ronald Reagan would have done that. Reagan would have made a decision, one way or the other and stuck with it.

Take, for example, Reagan's decision to deny Yasir Arafat a visa when the United Nations invited the PLO leader to address their general assembly in New York. How would you react if you got voted down 150 to two in the United Nations—and one of the two was your vote? Then the United Nations decided to move its entire assembly to Geneva to go around your decision. Wouldn't you want to take another look at it? Wouldn't you tend to think, "Maybe I went too far on that one?" No. You make a decision and you stick with it because projecting Reverent Power is the most powerful influencing factor you have going for you.

Ronald Reagan was brilliant at projecting Reverent Power. He could get away with some outrageous acts because of it. We have a law in this country that stops our government officials from ordering the assassination of another government leader. However, Reagan got away with ordering our Air Force to drop a load of 6,000 pound bombs on Muammar al-Qaddafi's tent and we loved him for it. Why? Because he was acting consistently. He told us he was that kind of person, and he lived up to his image. Conversely, the low point of Reagan's popularity was when he appeared to have been negotiating with the Iranians for the release of the hostages held in Lebanon because he'd told us he'd never do that.

The Senate spent $50 million on the IranGate Hearings and couldn't prove any Presidential wrongdoing. Yet, public opinion reacted in completely the opposite manner. We loved him for the apparent show of strength in trying to send Qaddafi into the next world as a war hero, and we maligned him for his apparent inconsistency in trying to trade arms for hostages.

How Reverent Power affected a presidency

During George Bush's first few years as President, he was all over the board on his level of consistency, and you could see his popularity ratings move in direct relationship to it. At first he was very consistent in his opposition to new taxes. "They're going to come down from Capitol Hill," he told us, "and tell me we've got to have new taxes. And I'm going to tell them, 'Watch my lips, no new taxes.' So they'll go back and talk about it and they'll come back and say, 'Mr. President, we've got to have new taxes.' And I'll say, 'Watch my lips, no new taxes.' " We loved him for it. Then he backed down on that issue, and we hated him for it—his popularity dropped from 80 percent to 45 percent almost overnight.

Along came the Persian Gulf War. How would you rate him for consistency on his handling of the war? A perfect score, right? Nobody could have been more consistent in the way they handled Saddam Hussein, and we loved him for it. His popularity soared from the forties to the nineties.

Then he faced the problem of the Kurdish refugees. One day he said, "I will not send American troops into the middle of a civil war that's been going on forever." That's great, take a stand—but stick with the stand you've taken. The very next day, he changed his mind and sent troops into Northern Iraq. His approval rating immediately dropped from the nineties to the fifties.

What clearer proof could we have? Reverent Power, the projection of a consistent set of values, influences people.

You like and admire consistent behavior in your customers. They like and admire it in you. If you're willing to take a stand for your principles, especially if it appears you're risking financial loss, it builds trust in other people, and they love you for it.

For example, you might sell computers and you have the courage to say to your customers, "Of course, you'd like to save money. And I'd favor it too, if it were the right thing for you to do—but it isn't. I know that you won't be completely happy unless you get the model with the 500 megabyte hard drive. So, I'm sorry, but I won't sell you anything less."

They love you for that. Of course, it'll raise a few eyebrows, but if you've done your homework and you're right, you'll have power with that customer. If you back down, how are they going to respect you?

Suppose your doctor told you that you needed triple by-pass heart surgery, and you said, "I think I can get by with a double by-pass." If he said, "Okay, let's try a double by-pass and see how it works out," how would you feel about him then? Would you let that person come near you with a scalpel? I don't think so.

When you project Reverent Power, the other negotiators notice it; they admire and respect the consistent set of values and it gives you a great deal of influence over them. When you're negotiating and you indicate a willingness to cut corners, or in some way pull some strings that you shouldn't be pulling, you may get a short term gain in your ability to make that sale.

However, you get a long term loss in your ability to influence that buyer over a long period of time.

Be careful that you're not setting up standards and then breaking your own standards. Don't tell that buyer that you would never cut prices and then go ahead and do it. That's worse than not setting up the standards in the first place. That's what got Gary Hart into trouble during the 1988 Presidential campaign. I don't know how you feel about the Gary Hart business, but I think that he maybe could have gotten away with spending the weekend with Donna Rice—if he'd simply said: "Oh sure. I do that once in a while. I think it's kind of fun." I think he may have gotten away with it, but don't be saying to the *Miami Herald:* "Oh, I would never do anything like that," and then go do it. Because they're going to get you every time.

Reverent Power is the most powerful influencing factor of all. Being able to project successfully that you have a consistent set of standards and that you'll never deviate from them, has an awesome affect on people. Here's why it's more powerful than the obvious influencing factors of reward and coercion. Although those two may have an immediate and dramatic effect on people, you cannot sustain them. They eventually tend to backfire on you.

The parent who's always persuading his child by offering her rewards quickly finds out the child learns to expect those rewards and will rebel if she doesn't get them.

You can pay a corporate executive $20 million a year, and in the early stages it will be a tremendous motivating factor for him. He will do anything to assure the continuation of that reward. However, year by year the value of that reward starts to diminish.

You can motivate people with coercive power—by threatening to fire them for example. However, it always backfires if you keep it up too long. When you keep on threatening, they'll either find a way to get out from under the pressure, or they'll learn to live with it.

Yet, Reverent Power just grows and grows. The longer you project that you have a consistent set of standards from which you'll never deviate, the more people learn to trust you. From that trust grows a tremendous ability to influence people in a negotiation.

Reverent Power as an intimidating factor

When people use Reverent Power on you it can be daunting because we admire that characteristic so much. When they say to you, "Yes, but we just don't do business that way. Our founder, God rest his soul, said when he first started this business 28 years ago, 'Let's just establish a fair list price for our products and never deviate from that.' " When we hear such high-flown words, we hate to go against it because we admire people who have principles and don't like to oppose them.

When someone is using Reverent Power on you in that way, you have two alternatives:

1. Establish that although they're telling you that they have never made an exception to the rule, there have indeed been exceptions. The power of precedent is a remarkable thing. If you can establish that there has been an exception somewhere down the line, it negates Reverent Power entirely. President Clinton smoked one joint of marijuana 25 years earlier and lost all credibility in the war on drugs—and he didn't even inhale. If you are in a Holiday Inn in Florida, asking for a special concession, if you can establish that the Holiday Inn in Seattle once made that concession for you, it gives you great power in dealing with that desk clerk in Florida.

2. Establish that although it may have been a good rule in the past, it's no longer the smart thing to do. I know of one Fortune 500 company that for years got away with saying, "Our founder established a policy when he first started this company that we would never deviate from list prices. We should have a fair price and everyone should pay the same." The company was able to maintain that for decades, but finally their competition started discounting and they had to follow them. Just because it has been their policy for years, it doesn't mean that it should be their policy today.

Chapter 55

Charismatic Power

The fifth element of personal power is Charismatic Power. It's probably the hardest one to analyze and explain. What is charisma? We've all heard of charismatic religions, of course. In that sense, charisma means a gift from God of a special talent, such as the ability to heal or to prophesize. In popular usage, charisma means this: A special quality that gives a person the ability to capture the imagination of another person, inspiring support and devotion.

German sociologist Max Weber was the first person to bring the term into modern day usage and present it as a learnable persuasion skill. He called it a form of authority. Until the turn of the century, we thought of authority as either law or tradition. Max Weber introduced charisma as the third form of authority. That simply with their personalities, people could influence another person.

In my book *Secrets of Power Persuasion* (Prentice Hall 1992) I spend two entire chapters explaining how to develop personal charisma, but for now let's just recognize its power and its limitations.

I'm sure you've had the experience of meeting a celebrity who has an overwhelmingly charismatic personality. When I met President Clinton I was uncomfortable because I'm at the opposite end of the political spectrum, and I'm sure he could sense that. I didn't want to say anything that would constitute an endorsement, so I said, "Good luck, Mr. President, don't let them get you down." Guess what he did. He looked at me and said, "If you'll stay with me, I'll be there." I said, "I'll be there, Mr. President." Within 15 seconds he'd gotten a commitment of support from me strictly based on the power of his personality.

Salespeople tend to overemphasize Charismatic Power. Many an old-time salesperson has told me, "The only reason my people do business with me is because they like me." Well, not nowadays. Don't fall into the Willie Loman trap. Even 40 years ago, when Arthur Miller wrote *Death of a Salesman* and had Willie Loman saying: "The most important thing is to be liked," he was making fun of it. Sure that buyer is more likely to give you an order if he or she likes you, but don't think it gives you much control. Buyers are much too sophisticated for that today. It's a long way from control of the negotiations.

Charismatic Power as an intimidating factor

Some people are very astute about using Charismatic Power on you. Without realizing it you can find yourself making concessions to them simply because you like them so much. Whenever you find yourself drawn to the other person, you should stop yourself and think, "Would I be making this concession if I couldn't stand this person?"

Chapter 56

Expertise Power

The sixth element of personal power is Expertise Power. When you project to people that you have more expertise than they do in a particular area, you develop power over them.

Just think of the people to whom you defer because of Expertise Power: your doctor, your auto-mechanic, and your plumber. I even defer to the maid who cleans my home when she tells me that I need to buy a particular type of cleaner for a special kind of surface.

I think that Expertise Power is becoming increasingly more important as the world in which we live becomes more complex. I think it started with video recorders. The moment we conceded that we couldn't figure out how to program our VCRs, we conceded that from that point on there were going to be a great many things for which we'd have to call in an expert. Perhaps it started before that. I remember standing in front of a new car that my father had bought back in the mid 1950s. "Where's the hole for the hand crank?" I asked him.

"Doesn't have one," he told me.

"That doesn't make any sense. How will you get it started when the battery won't start it?" I was used to a car that I'd have to hand crank for 15 minutes on a cold morning when my mother wanted to go into town for supplies.

"I'm not sure about that either," my father told me. "They say that if the battery won't start it, you've got a serious problem that you should get fixed."

"That still doesn't make sense," I repeated. However, I got used to that, and I resigned myself to VCRs. And I suppose that there's going to be a load more compromising before I get to my horizon. With technology leap-frog-ging over itself year by year, month by month and soon week by week, the expert is going to be king and every one of us should realize that if we don't keep on frantically being more expert in our field, the avalanche of new tech-nology will run over us.

Expertise Power as an intimidating factor

Don't let people intimidate you with Expertise Power. Remember when you first started in your business and you studied the technical side of what you do, but you weren't confident about it yet? Then you ran into someone who appeared to know more than you. Remember how intimidating that was? Don't let them do it to you. When they question your expertise, don't be afraid to say, "That's not my area of expertise, but our experts are the finest in the business. You can have complete confidence in them."

Attorneys and doctors really play this one up, don't they? They develop a whole new language that you can't understand to project to you that they have expertise that you don't have.

There's not a reason in the world why doctors couldn't write prescriptions in English, but if they did it would take away a little of that mystique, a little of that Expertise Power.

Attorneys are the same way. They develop a whole new language that we can't understand so that they project expertise power. Did you hear about the attorney who died and went to heaven? That's not the punch line. St. Peter said to him: "Boy, are we thrilled to have you here. We've never had a 125-year-old attorney before."

And the attorney said: "I'm not 125, I'm 39."

St. Peter said: "There must be some confusion—according to the hours that you've billed ..."

Chapter 57

Situation Power

The seventh element of personal power is Situation Power. This is one we're all familiar with. This is the person down at the post office who is normally powerless in any other area of her life, but in this particular situation she can accept or reject your package; she has power over you and loves to use it.

It's prevalent in large organizations or government agencies where the people don't have much latitude in the way they perform their jobs. When they do get some latitude, when they have some power over you, they're eager to use it.

I remember speaking to a huge sales rally in Halifax, Nova Scotia. The night before I got there, this group had put on the party to end all parties. These people all got bombed out of their minds. One of them got undressed to go to bed at three o'clock in the morning and then decided he'd like to have some ice in his room. He was standing there in his dazed state, trying to figure out whether it was worthwhile getting some clothes on to go get the ice. Finally he thought, "It's three o'clock in the morning. The ice machine's just around the corner from my door. Who's going to see me? I'll slip out the way I am."

Forgetting, of course, that the door would lock behind him the minute he got into the hallway.

Soon he's outside his door with his bucket of ice and nothing else, mentally debating his options. He finally decided he didn't have too many options, so he set his bucket of ice down and headed down, across the lobby of the Halifax Sheraton, and up to the young woman behind the desk. He asked for another key to his room. She looked straight at him and said: "Sir, before

I can give you another key, I need to see some identification." That's Situation Power.

The key issue in negotiating is that sometimes you get to a point where people have so much Situation Power over you that you're going to lose this one, regardless of how good a negotiator you are. If you're going to have to make the concession anyway, regardless of what you do, you might as well make the concession as gracefully as you possibly can. It doesn't make any sense to get so upset about it that you lose the goodwill of the other person— and still have to make the concession.

How many times have we been into a department store to get a refund on something and the clerk says to us: "All right, we'll do it this one time. But it's not our normal policy"? What sense does that make? If you're going to have to make the concession anyway, you might as well make it as gracefully as you possibly can, so that you maintain the goodwill of the other person.

Many years ago, when I was a real estate broker, our company built four new homes at one location. In California, we typically build with poured slabs. Just as we finished pouring the slabs, the city building inspector pulled up, walked over, and casually asked, "What are you doing?"

That seemed self-evident to us, but he wasn't known for his sense of humor, so we simply replied: "We're pouring the slabs."

"Not until I've signed off on the plumbing, you're not," he said, and we could swear that he was enjoying every minute of this. What followed must have looked like a Keystone Cops routine. Everybody was running around trying to find the signed off building permit card. With growing horror we realized that he was right. Somebody had goofed, and the inspector had enough Situation Power that we were going to have to get a crew out there with shovels, digging out the concrete before it set, so that the building inspector could glance at the plumbing and sign it off.

The point is, don't let it upset you. Power Negotiators recognize Situation Power for what it is and move into an area where they do have some control.

Chapter 58

Information Power

The final element of personal power is Information Power. Sharing information forms a bond. Any time that you share information with someone you get closer to that person. This is why, in the old days before members of Congress passed laws to restrain themselves, they were big on the lecture circuit. An association that might be penalized to a great extent by congressional legislation could hire a representative or senator to be the speaker at it's annual convention. The association could afford to pay that person a large honorarium. There wouldn't have to be any quid pro quo involved—just the fact that the lawmaker had mingled with the membership would cause him or her to bond with this industry. Pharmaceutical salespeople, who have a terrible time getting physicians to meet with them, know that they should always show up with some new piece of information, perhaps the results of a new study, because sharing information with the physician bonds them to the physician.

Information Power as an intimidation factor

Withholding information tends to intimidate. Large companies are skillful about doing this. They'll develop information at the executive level that they won't share with the workers. It's not because it's that secretive. It's not because it would do any harm. It's because these large corporations know that a level of secrecy at the executive level gives them control over the workers.

The human race has a tremendous natural desire to know what's going on. We can't stand a mystery. You can put a cow in a field, and it will stay in that field all its life and never wonder what's on the other side of that hill. Human beings will spend a billion and a half dollars to throw a Hubble telescope up in space because we have to know what's going on out there.

Withheld information can be very intimidating. Let's imagine that you've made an extensive presentation to a buying committee and the members say to you, "We need to talk about this for a moment. Would you mind waiting outside in the lobby? We'll call you when we're ready for you." Is it any wonder that you feel uncomfortable sitting outside in the lobby? We hate it when people withhold information from us.

The moment we realize they may just be doing this to us as a negotiating Gambit—that they may be in there talking about football scores for all we know, so that when we walk back into the negotiations our level of self-confidence has gone down and their level of power has gone up they can no longer intimidate us with that Gambit.

Chapter 59

Combinations of Power

Now I've taught you the eight elements that give you power over the other person. To recap they are:

- Legitimate Power
- Reward and Coercive Power
- Reverent Power
- Charismatic Power
- Expertise Power
- Situation Power
- Information Power

Take the time to rate yourself in each of those elements—not as you see yourself, or maybe not even as you really are, but as you think other people see you. How do people with whom you negotiate perceive you in each of these eight areas? Give yourself a score from 1 to 10 in each area with one being very weak and ten being very strong. The potential maximum score is 80. If your score comes out in the 60s, that's a very good number for a Power Negotiator. You have Power, but you still have empathy for the other side.

If your score is higher than 70, I'd be concerned that you're too intimidating when you're dealing with people.

Less than 60 and you have some weak spots. Examine those elements for which you gave yourself a low rating, and see what you can do to get yourself closer to a 10.

As you review this list, remember that these eight power elements are also the ways that the other side can intimidate you into thinking that you don't have any power. So the next time you're negotiating and you feel that you've lost control—that they're beginning to intimidate you—identify which of those elements is getting to you. Identifying it will help you handle it.

Now let's look at special combinations of these eight powers. First, let's look at Reverent Power, Charismatic Power, and Expertise Power. Power Negotiators know that these three are critical if you are to control the negotiations.

Do you know somebody who seems to have a much easier time persuading people to go along with his suggestions than you do? Perhaps you've sat in on a negotiation with your boss and he made it look so easy. He sat down with the other person and chatted with her for 15 or 20 minutes. He didn't appear to be talking about anything of consequence, but at the end of that time the other person said to him, "What do we have to do here? Do we need to go with the top of the line or can we get by with the standard? You tell us, you're the expert."

Here's how he got that much power over the other side: He did a good job of projecting Reverent Power, Charismatic Power, and Expertise Power.

Reverent Power: "I won't do anything that is not in your best interest, regardless of the gain to me." That builds trust, doesn't it? Charismatic Power: He has a likable personality. And Expertise Power: Your manager projected to the other side, without it becoming overbearing, that he knew more about it than she did. When you put those three together, you're very close to controlling the negotiations. You're very close to the point at which the other side will defer the decision. "Well," she'll say, "what do you think we should do?" And she has surrendered control of the negotiation to your side.

Another combination of the eight components of personal power is of particular importance to Power Negotiators. The effects of these four critical elements together are mind-boggling. When these four come together in one person, what happens is incredible. The four are:

- Legitimate Power, the power of the title
- Reward Power, the ability to reward people
- Reverent Power, the consistent set of values: I'm not going to deviate from this regardless of what happens
- Charismatic Power, the personality: the pizzazz with which to put it across

When these four come together in one person, the effect is phenomenal whether it is used for good or evil. This is what gave Adolf Hitler control of Germany in the 1930s.

He kept stressing the title—Fuhrer! Fuhrer! Fuhrer!

He kept stressing Reward Power.

He kept saying to the German people: If we do this, if we invade Czechoslovakia and Poland, this is what we'll get. The dictatorial Reverent Power—we'll never deviate from this. It is fascinating to me that Hitler, who completed his autography *Mein Kampf (My Struggle)* in 1926, wrote in it every detail of what would follow, including the expansion of Germany through Czechoslovakia and Poland into the Ukraine. Although more than five million copies had been circulated in Germany before the start of World War II, it was never translated into any other language. Hitler tightly controlled circulation of his book to within the borders of Germany, but it is hard for me to believe that some copies were not smuggled out of the country and translated. Perhaps the people who translated it simply could not believe the enormity of what he planned to do, or dismissed it as the ravings of a madman, but had we taken it seriously, we would have known every detail of his plans because he never deviated from his original intent.

Hitler also had hypnotic Charismatic Power. He could hold tens of thousands of people mesmerized with his oratory.

This was also the way that David Koresh got control over the Branch Davidians in Waco, Texas, and had so much control over them that they wanted him to tell them not only where to live, what to think, and what to say, but also when to die—the ultimate abuse of power.

David Koresh told his people that he was God. That's a pretty good title—you can't do much better than that!

He kept stressing Reward Power: If you stay with me, you're going to heaven. If you go with them, you're going to jail.

Reverent Power: We don't care what the rest of the world thinks, this is what we believe.

Charismatic Power: He had the hypnotic personality that is the trademark of all cult leaders.

On the good side is when you get a John F. Kennedy. Every president has the power of the title. Every president is able to reward, but not every president is able to project the consistent set of values. This was Jimmy Carter's undoing and Bill Clinton's albatross, because they appeared to vacillate. It was also Richard Nixon's undoing at the end.

Not every president is able to project Charismatic Power. This was Gerald Ford's problem. He had the other three elements in abundance, but he didn't have the personality with which to put it across. Throughout his career, Richard Nixon, even though he was brilliant, was dogged by the fact that few people liked him. I think that it was George Bush's downfall also, particularly since he followed Ronald Reagan, who was so charismatic. Remember that picture of Bush during the debate at Williamsburg? As Clinton leaned into the audience to answer a question, Bush was standing there looking at his watch, looking totally bored with the entire process.

John F. Kennedy and Ronald Reagan both had these four powers in great abundance, which made them the most popular presidents in modern history. You can have that kind of power if you concentrate on developing those four elements of personal power. When you do, I promise you that you'll see a remarkable transformation in your ability to influence people.

Chapter 60

The Power Of Crazy

I want to tell you about one more form of personal power and that is the power of crazy: If you can convince the other parties that you're crazy, you can have power over them. I don't think that you'll want to use it very often, but you should know about it.

Just after communist Vietnam opened its borders to foreigners again, I spent a week in Saigon and Hanoi. In Hanoi, I hired a guide to show me around. She had lived through the war, and I was eager to get her impressions. When I asked her who she thought was the best American president, I realized that she was a government employee (as everyone is under communism). She thought about it for a while and then said, "I don't know who the best president is, but I know the worst—Richard Nixon. He wants to drop nuclear bombs on us. He's crazy. He is the worst president of all." I'm confident that even Richard Nixon had absolutely no intention of dropping a nuclear bomb on Hanoi. It was a strategy that he and Henry Kissinger cooked up. They felt that if they could convince the North Vietnamese government that they were crazy, that they could force North Vietnam to the negotiating table, which they did remarkably effectively.

More recently the power of crazy really came into play when Saddam Hussein invaded Kuwait. George Bush had a huge challenge on his hands, which was to convince Saddam Hussein that he, George Bush, might be more crazy than Saddam Hussein. How do you do that? The first thing you do is throw your golf bag over your shoulder and go to Kennebunkport, Maine, for a golfing vacation—during the worst crisis this country had been in since the end of the Vietnam War. Then you send your Secretary of State, James

Baker, to Montana on a fishing vacation. Then you hide the Vice-President. Do you know what Dan Quayle was doing while this was all going on? The papers said that he was in Arizona on vacation, but I don't think that even Dan Quayle is crazy enough to vacation in Arizona in August. Pictures of Saddam Hussein at that time showed his eyes bugging out with fear. Here was a man who had suddenly realized that he was faced with a man who might just be crazier than he was!

In business, the power of crazy translates into the person who is so inconsistent in the way that he reacts that you never know how he's going to treat you. One day you can walk into his office and he'll throw his arms around you. The next time you walk into his office, he might throw you out. If you can convince someone that you're crazy, you can have power over them.

Chapter 61

Other Forms Of Power

Apart from the nine forms of power that I taught you in the previous chapters, other things can give you power:

The power of risk sharing

You can have power over the other parties if you convey that their risk is being shared by others. This is the power of a syndicated investment—the more people you can get to invest, the easier it is to get others to sign up.

If I asked you to bet me $5,000 to my $20,000 on the flip of a coin, you ought to be eager to take the bet. I'm offering you four-to-one odds on a two-to-one chance. (Professional gamblers will tell you that it doesn't matter what you bet on, as long as the odds are better than they should be.) However, the risk of losing $5,000 on the flip of a coin may be too great for you, and you may turn me down. Consider this: If you could get 100 people who were all willing to risk $50, would you then go ahead? Chances are you would because even though the return ratio is the same, you perceive that others are sharing the risk.

The same principle applies in investment syndication. If I asked you to invest $100,000 in a real estate syndication, you would be reluctant to risk that much. Even if I asked you to invest $5,000, you might consider the risk too great. However, if I told you that I have 19 other investors ready to put up $5,000 and you would be the twentieth, you would be far more likely to go along with my proposal. If I suggested that you invest $100,000 in 20 different syndications, you would be far more likely to do that than invest the entire $100,000 in one syndication because you would feel that you are lowering your risk.

What can we learn from this? Anytime that you can demonstrate that the risk you are asking the other side to take is being shared, you develop the power to influence that side.

The power of confusion

There is power in confusion. This may not sound right to you because you have always understood that a confused mind will say No. That is true—it is important to be sure that the person you're dealing with understands what he or she is getting into. However, it is also true that a confused mind can be more easily led.

You're negotiating with someone, and you tell her, "There are two possible options for you and they are very simple to understand. Let me explain them to you, and you'll be able to make a choice." That approach gives you little ability to influence her because she can readily perceive the benefits of each option and make her own choice.

However, if you said, "There are many ways to go here, and this can be very confusing. There are 25 different options open to you. Unless you're very familiar with them all, you'll have a tough time knowing which is best for you. Fortunately I'm very familiar with the options, and I have successfully guided many people who are in exactly the same position as you." The more confused I can get her, the more chance I have that she will ask me for guidance, provided I can get her to do one thing and that is trust me. A confused mind can be more easily led, but only if the person to be led trusts the leader.

Remember when the courts deregulated the long distance telephone industry back in 1984? AT&T ran a series of television ads using a trusted actor who said, in effect, "Pretty soon it's going to get so confusing that many people won't even know how to make a long distance call. Fortunately good old AT&T, the company you've been able to trust for so many years, will still be around to help you." Understandably, Sprint and MCI cried "foul," and AT&T had to pull the ads. It was a blatant attempt to control people by making the situation more confusing than it had to be.

As you can see, there is great power in confusion. The best defense that you have is just to keep your wits about you and not let the other person confuse the issue so that you surrender to their ideas. When he starts sailing off on tangents, say, "I don't see how all of these details are germane to my choices. Instead of confusing the situation, let's just stick to the key issues, fair enough?"

The power of competition

You can gain influence in negotiations if you advertise that you have many options and don't need to make a deal here and now. If you point out that there is competition for your product or services, chances are that the buyer will raise her offer. Especially if you tell her that you don't need to sell—certainly not for less than you are asking. For example, you could say to the prospective buyer, "I wish that I could give you more time to make a decision, but I need to know right now because I have two other bids already, and it's not fair for me to keep the other buyers waiting."

If you are buying, any seller finds it sobering to learn that you have many other choices and at lower prices. If you are responding to a classified ad for a boat or a car, for example, you might say "I have two others to look at this evening, at 7 o'clock and at eight. They're not asking as much as you are, but I'd like to consider yours anyway. Could I come by and see yours at six?"

In any negotiation, the side with the most options has the most power. The more you can service the perception that you have options, the more power you will have as a negotiator.

Section Seven

Negotiating Drives

Not often does someone other than a professional negotiator think about what is driving the other negotiator because we all tend to assume that what drives the other person is the same thing that drives us. Sociologists call this "socio-centrism," meaning that we tend to feel that the other person wants what we would want if we were him. Power Negotiators know that what we would want, if we were him, may have nothing to do with what he wants. Power Negotiators know that the better we can understand what is driving the other side—what he really wants to accomplish—the better we can fulfill his needs without taking away from our position. Poor negotiators get into trouble because they fear that they will be vulnerable to the other side's tricks if they let the other side know too much about them. Instead of wanting to find out what is driving the other side and revealing her drives to the other side, the poor negotiator lets her fears stop her from being that open.

In this section we'll take a look at the different things that drive the other side when someone is negotiating with you. Recognizing and understanding these drives is the secret to win-win negotiating.

Chapter 62

The Competitive Drive

The Competitive Drive is the drive that neophyte negotiators know best, and it's why they see negotiating as being so challenging. If you assume that the other side is out to beat you by any means within the rules of the game, of course you will fear meeting someone who might be a better negotiator than you or someone who is more ruthless than you.

The competitive drive certainly exists at most car dealerships. The car dealer attracts customers by offering "the lowest prices in town," but pays its salespeople based on the amount of profit they can build into the sale. It's a gladiatorial approach to negotiating: The customer wants to buy for the lowest price even if the dealer loses money and the salesperson loses his commission, and the salesperson wants to drive the price up because that's the only way he can make any money. Sound the trumpets, let the spectacle begin, and may the best person win.

Competitive drive negotiators believe that you should find out all you can about the other side, but let the other side know nothing about you. Knowledge is power, but competitive drive negotiators believe that because of this the more you find out and the less you reveal, the better off you'll be.

When gathering information, the competitive drive negotiator distrusts anything the other side's negotiators might tell him because it may be a trick. He gathers information covertly by approaching the other side's employees or associates. Because he assumes that the other side is doing the same to him, he works assiduously to prevent the leaking of information from his side.

What's causing this approach is the assumption that there has to be a winner and there has to be a loser. What's missing is the possibility that both sides could win because they are not out for exactly the same thing, and that by knowing more about the other side, each side can concede issues that are important to the other side, but may not be significant to their side.

Chapter 63

The Solutional Drive

The Solutional Drive is the best negotiating situation for you to be in. This is when the other side is eager to find a solution and is willing to calmly discuss with you the best way to do that. It means that nobody's going to threaten the other side, and both sides will negotiate in good faith to find a win-win solution.

Solutional Drive negotiators tend to be wide open to creative solutions because they feel that there must be a better solution out there somewhere that hasn't occurred to them yet. It takes an open mind to be creative. Just look at some of the variables that buyers and sellers could propose in as simple a transaction as buying a house:

- The cost of financing to the buyer could be adjusted by letting the buyer assume an underlying loan. Or the seller could carry back all the financing and remain liable for the underlying loan (called wrapping the underlying).

- The buyer could accommodate the sellers by giving them more time to move out or find another home. The sellers could even lease back the house from the buyer for an extended term.

- The price could include all or some of the furnishings.

- The sellers could retain a life estate in the house that would enable them to stay in the house until they died. This is a great idea for elderly people who need cash, but don't want to move.

- The broker's fee could be eliminated or the broker could be asked to take her fee in the form of a note, rather than in cash.
- The buyer could move in, but delay the closing to help the sellers with their income taxes.

The great thing about negotiating with someone who is in the Solutional Drive is that they have cast nothing in stone. They are not restricted by company policy or tradition—they feel that everything is negotiable because everything was at one time negotiated. Short of breaking the law or their personal principles, they will listen to any suggestion you care to propose because they do not see you as competing with them.

It sounds like the perfect solution, doesn't it? Both sides cooperating to find the perfect and fair solution. There is one caveat. The other side could be feigning when they appear to be in the Solutional Drive. Once you have put your cards on the table and told them exactly what you are prepared to do, they may revert to Competitive Drive negotiating. So if it seems too good to be true, be wary.

Chapter 64

The Personal Drive

You may encounter situations in which the main drive of the other negotiators is not to win for winning's sake or to find the perfect solution. Their main drive may be for their personal profit or aggrandizement.

A case that quickly comes to mind is an attorney who is working on a fee basis rather than a contingency basis. It would be in that attorney's best interest not to find a solution too quickly. When you run into this, you should see what you can do to satisfy that personal need for more fees. It may be in your best interest to threaten to take your solution over the attorney's head to his client. He won't appreciate that, of course, but if he feels that his client would accept the compromise if you went over his head, you may force him to accept your solution.

Another example may be a young corporate negotiator who wants to look good to her company. The last thing she wants to do is go back empty-handed, so your best strategy might be to establish that she has a time deadline and stall the negotiations until the last moment. You might be able to reach a terrific settlement in the limousine on the way to the airport if she'd rather agree to anything than go home empty-handed.

A further example is a union negotiator who wants to look good to his members. In that case, it may be in both your best interests to make an outrageous initial demand. Then he can go back to his members and say, "I wasn't able to get you everything you wanted, but just listen to their opening negotiating position. I was able to get them all the way down from that for you." If you had made a more modest opening negotiating position, it might have been difficult for him to sell it to his members because they don't feel that their union fought hard enough for them.

Chapter 65

The Organizational Drive

You may find yourself in a situation in which the other negotiator seems to have a fine Solutional Drive. She really wants to find the best solution, but the problem is that it has to be a solution that she can sell to her organization.

This happens a great deal in Congress where the senator or representative is eager for a sensible compromise, but knows that he would get pilloried by the voters in his state or district. In close votes you'll see this all the time. On both sides of the House, the politicians who have the support of their voters will commit quickly. Those who will be in trouble back home may want to support their party, but are reluctant to toe the line. So the party leadership counts noses to see how many votes they need to win. Then the party lets the members who would be most hurt by voting for the bill vote no. The ones who would be least hurt are led, like lambs to slaughter, it always seems to me, and made to vote for the bill.

When you're negotiating with someone who must please an organization, that person may be reluctant to lay out her problem for you because it would seem too much like collusion. So you need to be thinking, "Who could be giving her heartburn over this one?" Is it her stockholders, her legal department, or perhaps government regulations, that she would have to circumvent to implement the best solution? If you understand her problem, you may be able to do things to make the solution more palatable to her organization. For example, you might take a more radical position in public than you do at the negotiating table. In this way your compromise gives the appearance of making major concessions.

A company hired me once to help when the assembly workers' union went on strike. The union negotiators felt that the solution they had negotiated was reasonable, but they couldn't sell it to their members, who were out for blood. We developed a solution in which the local newspaper interviewed the president of the company. During the interview he expressed sincere regrets that he was caught between a rock and a hard place. The union couldn't sell the plan to its members, and the president couldn't sell anything better to his board of directors and stockholders. It appeared that the strike would soon force him to move production from that factory to the company's assembly plant in Mexico. The next day the workers' spouses opened the newspaper to read headlines that said, "Plant to close—jobs going south." By that afternoon the spouses had put enough pressure on the workers that they clamored to accept the deal that they had previously turned down.

If you're dealing with someone who has to sell the plan to his organization, you should always be looking for ways to make it easier for him to do that.

Chapter 66

The Attitudinal Drive

The Attitudinal Drive negotiator believes that if both sides trust each other and like each other, they can resolve their differences. Attitudinal Drive negotiators would never try to resolve a problem by telephone or through an intermediary. They want to be face-to-face with the other person so that they can get a feel for who that person is, believing that, "If we know each other well enough, we can find a solution."

Former President Jimmy Carter is very much an attitudinal negotiator. He initiated contact with the North Koreans when they were refusing to back down on their nuclear weapons program. He met with Haitian General Cedras until the brink of war and pleaded with President Clinton for just a few more minutes to reason with the General. When he finally reached a settlement, he actually invited that blood-thirsty dictator to come to his church in Plains, Georgia, to teach a Sunday school class. The problem with that kind of negotiating is that it can easily lead to appeasement of the other side. Attitudinal Drive negotiators are so eager to find good in the other side that they can readily be deceived. The classic example was when Prime Minister Neville Chamberlain of England made a last-ditch effort to avoid war with Adolf Hitler. He returned to England triumphantly proclaiming that he had averted war by giving away only part of Czechoslovakia. Hitler had already figured out that Chamberlain was a chump, and it didn't take the rest of the world long to agree with Hilter's assessment.

Certainly it helps that both negotiators know and like each other because it's hard to create a win-win solution unless both sides trust each other.

However, Power Negotiators know that something is far more important than having the other side like and trust you: You must create a solution that is in both sides' best interests. Then it is mutually beneficial for both sides to support the agreement and see that it gets implemented.

Section Eight

Analyzing Negotiating Styles

To become a Power Negotiator, it's critical to understand that you have a particular personality style, the people with whom you are negotiating have their own personality styles, and you have problems when the two don't match. This will be crucial to your success as a negotiator. In this section I'll teach you how to identify your personality style, the personality style of the other negotiator, and then how to adapt your negotiating style to his or hers.

This will also be very helpful to you in your interpersonal relationships. I conduct Power Negotiating seminars all over the country. It's always nice when people come up to me afterward, shake my hand, and say: "I've listened to your tapes for years, and you have made me a fortune." What thrills me even more is to know that I've touched people's lives. A lady in Dallas came up to me and said, "What you taught us about personality styles is the most important thing that I've ever learned in any seminar. I've been married for several years, and it's never been quite right between us. No big problems, but it's never been quite as good as it could have been. Now I can see why—we're opposite personality styles. Now I can see the things I do that irritate him. Now I know what to do about it, and, you know what, it's going to be okay." At another seminar a man asked, "Where were you eight years ago, when I went through my divorce?"

This will be important to you in many areas of your life, not just negotiating. I first got involved in analyzing personality styles when I went to a success rally at Anaheim Stadium many years ago. At a success rally, if you haven't been to one, a seminar promoter rents a big stadium and sells tickets to the event. The audience will be 5,000 to 10,000 people, and the promoter brings in top speakers from all over the country. Each speaker has about 45 minutes. The event may start at 9 o'clock in the morning and continue until late at night.

On the way home I was fascinated because my friends couldn't agree on who they thought was the best speaker. One person said, "I liked that down-to-Earth guy. Even though he wasn't a dynamic speaker, I got a lot of good information, and that's why I go to a seminar. I don't care about the way they get it across."

Another person said, "I liked the motivational speaker, the guy who jumped up on the table and had all those props on the stage. He really got me turned on, and I thought it was fantastic."

Another friend said, "I don't know why speakers have to yell at you like that. Why can't they just talk to you. I liked so and so because he seemed like such a nice person, and he's someone I'd really like to get to know."

My engineer friend said, "I didn't care for the whole thing at all because I thought it was just a bunch of hoopla. They gave each speaker only 45 minutes, and how much information can you get in 45 minutes? They didn't give the educational qualifications of the speakers when they introduced them, and I thought it was all kind of phony."

It occurred to me that if a speaker can talk to an audience and get totally different responses from the audience, then it follows that when we're negotiating with people, we can use the same approach with different people and get totally different responses.

I started to study personality styles and finally it all came together for me. The system I'm going to teach you is based on a method of classifying people that the ancient Greeks worked out centuries ago, so it is time-tested and proven. If you have been trained in sales, however, it may contradict much of the training that you have received, especially if you've been taught a canned response to any objection the buyer might raise. Power Negotiators know that you have to adapt what you're doing to the personality styles of the different people with whom you negotiate.

In the next four chapters you'll meet the four personality styles. For each of the four styles, I'll take you through four stages:

1. I will help you to identify your personality style. To do this, I want you to imagine that you've just spent three hours attending a seminar. What is your reaction to being there? I will tell you how the personality style that we're covering would react to the seminar. If you would find yourself reacting in the same way, you will know that you are probably that same personality style.

2. Then I'll describe the characteristics of that personality style.

3. Then I'll teach you how to identify the personality style of the other negotiator.

4. I'll teach you how the personality style translates into a particular negotiating style.

Then in Chapter 71 I'll teach you how to deal with the different personality styles, including some do's and don'ts, how to manage them, and how to sell to them.

Read the next four chapters to identify your personality style. You may see yourself in one and maybe in one other, but if you start seeing yourself in three or four of these, you have some work to do!

Chapter 67

The Pragmatic Personality Who Becomes a Street Fighter Negotiator

The first personality style is the Pragmatic. He will go to a seminar for one reason and one reason only, and that's because he wants to learn. Pragmatics are very much bottom-line kind of people. They won't evaluate the seminar based on whether they liked the speaker or not, or whether they had a good time or not. They'll evaluate it strictly based on the amount of useful information with which they leave the room.

They leave the seminar and say: "You know, that was a pretty good seminar. I picked up some interesting information there, but did it really have to take three hours? I bet if the speaker had taken all the stories and the jokes out, she could have given us the same amount of information in half the time. And, when I think about it, the meeting planner could have photo-copied the highlights and mailed them to us so we need not have gone to the seminar at all."

Pragmatics are very time-management conscious people. They're the people who subscribe to condensed book services, such as Executive Book Summaries. My book *The Confident Decision Maker* (William Morrow 1992) is 300 pages long and took me 9 months of hard work to write. Executive Book Summaries bought the condensation rights and condensed it down to only 8 pages. That doesn't bother me as much as the knowledge that the Pragmatic will get his highlighter and go through that, just to get the essence of the whole thing.

If you see yourself in that description, you might just be a Pragmatic.

The characteristics of a Pragmatic

Let's take a look at some of the characteristics of the Pragmatic, to see if this sounds like you. You're a very business-like person. You're not the kind of person who'll come into the office at three o'clock in the afternoon and say: "Hey gang, I know it's only three o'clock, but let's close this place up and go get a beer." You've probably surrounded yourself with time-management gadgets. Anything that makes you more efficient, you have.

You were probably the first person in town to have a voice-mail system. Remember when they first came out and everybody was saying: "Isn't it awful? You can never talk to a person any more—they expect us to talk to machines." You had one, and it didn't occur to you there was anything cold about it. You hate the thought of wasting time, and going on vacation is a waste of time to you. Your wife knows how difficult it is to get you to go in the first place, and she certainly knows better than to drag you off to a place like Cozumel or Cabo San Lucas, where there's nothing to do but sit around the swimming pool, because Pragmatics can't take much of that. By the first afternoon you're getting restless and by the evening you'll have organized a bridge tournament or a volleyball championship or anything else you can think of that will keep you active.

You don't like spectator sports for the same reason. The thought of going to the stadium and watching somebody else do something for two or three hours is not for you. You like participatory sports. You hunt, fish, fly a plane, or play basketball—anything where you can be active and involved.

Let's say your stockbroker calls you on a Friday with an investment proposal, then calls you back Wednesday and says: "Well, what do you think?"

You'll probably say: "What do I think about what?"

He'll say: "Don't you recall? We talked about that mutual fund on Friday."

"Oh yes," you'll say. "My goodness, so much has happened since last Friday. It completely slipped my mind."

How to identify the Pragmatic

The Pragmatic is very time-management conscious. He doesn't waste time with small talk. Start off the conversation by asking him about the football game that weekend and he'll very quickly get irritated and move on to business.

He doesn't take long vacations because he sees them as a waste of time. He'll use time-saving gadgets such as voice mail, E-mail, and a miniature tape recorder for taking notes.

Pragmatics probably own all the telephone prospecting machines in the country. You know the ones I mean? The machines that call you up and try to sell you insurance over the telephone.

The Pragmatic businessperson will typically have his or her calls screened. The secretary will want to know who's calling and why you're calling before putting the call through. The business environment will be formal. She'll have a secretary to place calls and confirm appointments for her who will usher you into her office rather than coming out to meet you.

Pragmatics like fast-paced participation sports such as skiing, scuba diving, flying; he may like golf, but hates how long it takes and, typically, won't take the time to do it.

He's tidy, he has an organized desk, and he always dresses formally.

The Pragmatic turns into a Street Fighter negotiator

The Pragmatic in a negotiation situation turns into a Street Fighter. A Street Fighter is a person whose sole objective in the negotiation is to win. They're negotiating to win and winning means to them that somebody else has got to lose and what's wrong with that? "That's the way the world is. Don't waste my time with all this wishy-washy win-win nonsense. Why on Earth would I be concerned about their needs in the negotiations, that's what they're here for. I expect them to fight as hard for what they want as I'm going to fight for what I want."

You would think that the Street Fighter would be the toughest personality style with which to negotiate but it's not, because Street Fighters have a flaw that makes them vulnerable. They see negotiating as a game to be won or lost, so for them there has to be a way to score the game. They become obsessed with a particular issue, and as long as you can give in on that one issue, they will give away everything else to win on the one issue by which they are scoring the game. I knew a real estate broker who thought it was an act of extreme disloyalty for any sales agent to want to leave him and go to work for a different company. He would hold an exit interview with anyone who tried to leave and fight to get them to stay. Because he was a Street Fighter personality, he would see it as a one issue negotiation—could he get them to stay? He was usually successful at getting them to stay, but at terrible cost. Sometimes they would get a higher commission split, a private office, and a company-supplied car. Even so, he felt that he had won because he had talked them out of leaving.

Identify the issue by which the Street Fighter is judging whether she won or lost, and you can control her. Perhaps you are trying to buy her business and she is determined to get a million dollars for it. If you took her a $950,000 cash offer she would turn it down because it doesn't meet her criteria for winning the negotiation. However, if you took her a million-dollar offer that asked her to carry back $200,000 of interest-free financing due and payable in ten years (considering the time value of money, that's a worse offer than the $950,000 cash offer) she will accept it because she feels that she got what she wanted. So to put this together, all you'd have to do is find a $200,000 note that you can buy for $150,000 and include it in the offer. By doing that everyone gets what they want.

The other thing about the Street Fighters is that, for them to feel that they are winning, they have to feel that the other negotiator is losing. Don't talk win-win to them. You must bleed all over them, and tell them how much they are hurting you. A classic example was Frank Lorenzo when he owned Eastern Airlines. The airline was in trouble when he got an offer from Peter Ueberroth to buy it. It would have been a win for everybody. Lorenzo would have received a fair price for his airline, Ueberroth would have been able to turn the airline around instead of putting his investors in Hawaiian Air that turned out to be a disaster, the unions were getting a piece of the action, and the buy-out would have saved the airline. However, Frank Lorenzo is a Street Fighter negotiator. How could he be winning if nobody else was losing? He turned down the offer and lost his airline.

If you're dealing with Street Fighter negotiators, don't panic because they're vulnerable. Identify the issue by which they're judging whether they're winning. Find a way to give them that, and they'll give away everything else.

Chapter 68

The Extrovert Personality Who Becomes a Den Mother Negotiator

The next personality style is the Extrovert. Extroverts go to a seminar because they want to have a good time. They're saying: "Okay, you're a professional speaker, you get me excited. I want to feel good when I leave here. I hope you're not going to throw a bunch of charts and graphs and projections up there because I really bog down in all that detail work. I love the humor and write all the jokes down so that I can try them out when I get back to the office. Remember that when I leave here today, I want to feel good."

If you see yourself in that personality style, you might just be an Extrovert.

The characteristics of an Extrovert

If you're an Extrovert, you love spectator sports. The thrill of being at that stadium with all those cheering people is about as good as life gets. You're a very emotional person and you're a very fast decision maker. If a friend calls you up and says: "Let's fly up to Chicago for the game this weekend," without thinking you'll say, "Yes, let's go, it'll be great."

You love to do fun things impulsively, and you love to make business decisions on the spot. You don't need time to think things through. Sure, that's caused you some problems in the past, but also you've been able to snatch some good opportunities out from under the noses of more cautious business people.

Real estate people know to save their curb appeal property for you. Curb appeal is what the property looks like when you first pull up out front. If it looks like Tara from *Gone with the Wind* with the tall columns up the front, you want it the moment you see it. You're emotional and you're a fast decision maker. When you fall in love with something, you want it, and you want it right now.

How to identify the Extrovert

The Extrovert is friendly and open. He'll place his own telephone calls, doesn't necessarily want his incoming calls screened, and likes to meet you in the lobby of his company to give you a personal tour. He greets everybody warmly as he walks around the building. He loves the excitement of spectator sports such as baseball or football. He'll probably have pictures of his family in the office—something a Pragmatic might think is too informal.

He'll spend time talking about his vacation or his hunting trip, but if somebody comes into the office for a business decision, he'll make the decision quickly.

She's a warm and friendly person, but she's not afraid to say "no" to you. So she's personable, but at the same time she's assertive. You'll find that her desk is probably cluttered; and she has poor follow-up. She's not a highly organized person, but she's likable and fun to be with.

The Extrovert turns into a Den Mother negotiator

The Extrovert tends to turn into a Den Mother as a negotiator. A Den Mother is someone who gets so excited about things that he tends to lose perspective. This is the person in your office who is organizing a softball team and is so excited and enthusiastic about it that it doesn't occur to him that there's anybody in the entire world who doesn't want to play softball on Tuesday evenings.

Den Mothers are the people most likely to have the whole negotiations fall down around them and not realize there was a problem. You'll see them come back into their office and kick the desk. "They went with the other company. How can they do this to me? I was out drinking with them until midnight the other night." They let their enthusiasm blind them to the reality of the situation.

Chapter 69

The Amiable Personality Who Becomes a Pacifier Negotiator

Amiable personalities will go to a seminar primarily because they want to be around people who have similar interests. The ambiance and the feeling they get from being there are the critical things to them. They tend to look around the seminar room to be sure that the other people are having a good time also, because that's important to them. Often they'll ask the speaker a question, not because they're confused, but because they think someone else in the room is confused, and they're doing it to be helpful. They say to the speaker, "Don't yell at me. I hope you're not one of those high-powered motivational speakers that races up and down the aisle, jumps up on the table, and gets us all to stand up and chant things because I can't stand that. I want to feel that during the intermission I could come up to you and talk to you and you'd be warm and friendly."

If you see yourself in that, you might just be an Amiable.

The characteristics of an Amiable

If you're an Amiable, you're emotional in your reactions to people and things. Because you like to feel comfortable before you'll make a move, you're a slow decision maker. You like to set up barriers because you hate high pressure. You probably have an unlisted home phone number, and you hate the thought of going to buy a new automobile because you know the car salesperson is going to grind you to death with high pressure tactics. Perhaps in 1947, you accidentally tore off a mattress tag—you know, the ones that say *Do Not Remove Under Penalty of Federal Law.* You've been convinced ever since that the F.B.I. is going to find out about it and have your house surrounded with bull horns: "Come on, we know you're in there, come on out."

How to identify the Amiable

The Amiable tends to set up barriers. He probably has an unlisted home phone number and may have a *No Peddlers* sign on his front door. He has probably lived in his neighborhood for a long time because he develops relationships with things, as well as with people.

She probably drives an older car because she hates high pressure salespeople. She hates the thought of going to that car lot and getting ground to death. You won't often find an Amiable in management other than in a large corporation where the very format of the organization protects her from having to make assertive decisions.

He seems to have very little sense of time management. Call him to ask for an appointment, and he'll tell you to drop by any time. He tends to be disorganized because he can't say "no" to people. When asked to be on a committee, he has a tough time refusing, so he tends to take on more work than he can handle.

Her environment is warm and comfortable. She forms relationships with the furniture in her office, with her home and with her car, and she doesn't like to change them.

The Amiable turns into a Pacifier negotiator

The Amiable turns into a Pacifier as a negotiator. His objective in the negotiations is not so much to win, as to see that everybody is happy. It's fascinating to see the opposite personality style, the Street Fighter, negotiating with the Pacifier. Because the Street Fighter will grind away on the Pacifier until she's convinced that there's not another penny left on the table, then when it's all over, the Pacifier will turn to the Street Fighter and say, "Now are you sure this is fair? I wouldn't want to take advantage of you."

Chapter 70

The Analytical Personality Who Becomes an Executive Negotiator

The fourth style is the Analytical. Unlike a Pragmatic who'll get bored in a three hour talk, the Analytical can sit through a 10-day symposium on *The Effect of High Density Building Encroachment into the Normal Habitat of Desert Rats, and the Subsequent Effect on the Ecological Food Chain* and come away at the end of the 10 days feeling: "They just scraped the surface of the topic, didn't they? Didn't get into any real depth there at all."

If you see yourself in that, you might just be an Analytical.

The characteristics of an Analytical

If you're an Analytical, you're almost a breed apart. People used to be able to spot you from the slide rule in your pocket, but now it's much more involved. You have a fancy wristwatch that does all kinds of calculations for you. It tells you the time of day in every capital city in the world and so on. You'd feel naked without your calculator and carry a backup calculator in case the first one fails. Perhaps you smoke a pipe because you're a very thoughtful person and don't like to shoot from the hip with an answer. So you can poke at your pipe while you think of exactly the right response.

I remember training a large group of architects once. To test their comfort level with ambiguity, I asked them a series of questions that could be answered with a number. I told them that if they didn't know the answer they could give a range, and they could make the range as broad as they wished. One question I asked them was, "How many license plates can you derive from a combination of six letters and six numbers?"

To me a good answer would have been "Between 15 and 20 million." A superbly accurate answer would have been "Between 17 and 18 million." Their response to the question fascinated me. They wanted to know if they could use the letter "I" and the number "1." They wanted to know if they could use the letter "O" and the number "0." I said, "What does it matter? Just give me a range." They wouldn't do that and insisted that I tell them if they could use similar-looking numbers and letters.

I noticed that the president of the company was almost falling off his chair because he was laughing so much. Later he told me, "Roger, you don't understand. Architects are trained to be precise. They can't live with ambiguity. They have to know if that building is going to stand up or fall down."

I told them that they could use similar-looking letters and numbers. Only then did they all whip out their calculators and start furiously punching in numbers to give me the answer: exactly 17,576,000.

So if you're an Analytical and someone asks you what day of the week it is, you might tell them: "Well, it's Wednesday. Except on the Island of Tonga, where it's already Thursday morning." If they show you a watch, you can tell them how to make it—and frequently do. So you're really into detail. You're a very slow decision maker, and you're unemotional in the way you approach people.

Other people find that you're the hardest person to get a decision from when they're negotiating with you, because you can never get enough information.

Real estate agents who typically tend to be the opposite, Extrovert, type of personality, tell me how Analyticals drive them up the wall. They'll show an Analytical a property on Friday and then call her up on Wednesday and say: "Well what do you think?"

The analytical will respond: "Well, I'm very close to making a decision. I've been working on it every night this week, but there are a couple more pieces of information I do need before I can make a decision. Number one, I know you told me the house was 1,908 square feet, but did you measure that with a cloth tape or a metal tape? And the other thing I need to know is, how many B.T.U. does it take to heat the swimming pool to 76.5 degrees on August 16th, when there's a volcanic dust storm blowing up from Mexico. If I had that kind of information, then I'd be in a position where I could, possibly, make a decision."

How to identify the Analytical

The Analytical will most likely be an accountant, engineer, or architect. Of all the personality styles, this is the one that you can most readily spot from what he or she does for a living.

She probably has gadget mania and is surrounded by computers, calculators, phone dialers, and so on. She was the first person in her state to have a fax machine. She's a very curious person. Show her a book, and she'll want to know when and how it was printed. She soaks up information—she just can't get enough.

He's fascinated by analysis and has charts and graphs for everything.

It's interesting to see an Analytical in a management situation. He feels he can manage everything just by generating massive amounts of information. I knew a man once who ran a huge organization with charts and graphs and projections coming out of his ears. He felt that as long as people knew where they were and what their performance had been, then, in some mysterious way, they had the tools they needed to get where they wanted to go. Of course it's good to analyze where you've been and where you are right now, but that's not an adequate substitute for the people-skills that move an organization ahead.

An Analytical is very precise about punctuality, so you'll never hear him saying: "I'll be there around lunch time." He'll say: "I'll be there at twelve-fifteen." He's very precise about figures. For example, he won't tell you that something cost just over a hundred dollars, he'll tell you it cost $104.16.

The Analytical turns into an Executive negotiator

The Analytical tends to turn into an Executive-style negotiator. Because the Analytical probably trained to be an engineer, an accountant, or an architect, throughout her life, everything's been okay as long as it's been buttoned up, nailed down, and in its place.

Analyticals don't like the push and the shove of negotiating. They like everything to be rigid and in place and their favorite expression is, "it's the principle of the thing."

The opposite personality style, the Extrovert, will say: "Hey look. We're talking about only 500 bucks here, so for heavens sakes, let's split the difference and get it started."

The Analytical will reply, "Well I understand we're talking about $500; actually, because you're proposing that we split it, we're talking about only $250 aren't we? But at this point, it's the principle of the thing that I'm concerned about."

So if you're an Analytical, be careful that you're not too rigid in the way you negotiate.

Chapter 71

How to Deal With the Four Different Styles

It's important to know what personality style you are, and it's important to understand the personality style of the person with whom you negotiate. However, it's even more important to know how to adapt your negotiating style to that of the other person.

PERSONALITY STYLES

The Analytical		The Pragmatic
	Low	
	Level	
Low Assertive	-ness Level High	
	Emotional	
The Amiable	High	The Extrovert

NEGOTIATING STYLES

The Executive		The Street Fighter
The Pacifier		The Den Mother

Take a look at these charts. The left hand chart shows the personality styles. The right hand chart translates those into negotiating styles. Now place yourself on the chart. You previously decided which one of those four you were.

Recognize that you will have the most difficulty with the personality style that is on the opposite corner to you on the chart. If you are a Pragmatic, you love other Pragmatics. They are down-to-Earth, no-nonsense people, and when you ask them a question, you'll get an answer. When you want a decision, you'll get it, and they'll live with it. It's when you have to deal with the Amiable, the opposite personality style, that you run into difficulty. That's because you're thinking quickly and unemotionally, but he's thinking slowly and emotionally. You'll make a proposal to an Amiable, and there's not a reason in the world why he shouldn't go along with it. It's clear to you that you can do the job better than the person with whom he has been dealing in the past and it should be just as clear to him. So, he ought to dump that other person and go with you, but he holds back. What he's holding back about is, "I don't feel comfortable with you yet. I want to do business with people with whom I feel comfortable. Don't tell me how much you know," they're thinking, "until you tell me how much you care."

Conversely, if you're an Amiable (bottom left), you'll have the most difficulty with Pragmatics (top right). They seem like such hard-headed people to you. They're all business, and they appear to have no feeling. So you don't feel comfortable dealing with them.

If you're an Extrovert (bottom right), you love other Extroverts because they're such fun people. At the drop of a hat they'll go off and do exciting things. It's when you have to deal with the Analytical (top left) that you run into difficulties. To you, Analyticals always seem to need too much information. They're too much into the details, and they're far too cautious in the way they do things. You should remember that accuracy is next to Godliness to an Analytical.

When an Analytical says to you, "When will you have the job finished?", he wants to hear you say: "On January 16th by 3:15 in the afternoon." She doesn't want to hear: "Oh, about the middle of January or so." She wants to hear it out to the minute.

When she says: "What's the thickness of the paint you'll use," she doesn't want to hear: "Oh, about medium, I guess." She wants to hear it down to a thousandth of an inch.

Conversely, if you're an Analytical, it seems to you that Extroverts are too flippant. They're too easy going, and they go off on different tangents without really knowing all the things that they ought to know about the situation.

Recognize that when you negotiate, you always have to deal with these personality styles. Identifying your own personality style and understanding how you're relating to the other person will be very critical to your success in negotiations.

How to identify a particular personality style

With a little practice and experience, you won't have much trouble identifying personality styles. Within 15 or 30 seconds you'll be able to place someone you meet on this chart. Let me give you some help in doing that.

First, you should place them either on the left or the right of the chart. Is this an assertive person? If he's assertive it means he's either a Pragmatic (top right) or an Extrovert (bottom right). You tell this by the firmness of the handshake, the kind of responses he gives to your questions and that he volunteered his name quickly when he met you.

Or is he the less assertive person on the left hand side of the chart? If he is, he'd have to be an Analytical (top left) or an Amiable (bottom left).

Having established that, work on placing them on the top or bottom of the chart. Are they emotional or not? Evaluate the way they say things and the warmth with which they respond to people. This is will enable you to judge whether they're unemotional on the top of the chart, meaning they're Analyticals or Pragmatics, or whether they're the emotional type of person on the bottom of the chart, the Amiable or the Extrovert.

Now you can very quickly place someone in one corner or the other of the chart. You'll find that some people have very pronounced characteristics, so you will place them way out in the far corners of the chart. Others have less pronounced characteristics and would be closer to the center.

Do's and don'ts for dealing with the personality styles

Now let's talk about some do's and don'ts for dealing with these people.

With the Pragmatic, don't waste time with small talk. You're there to negotiate, not chitchat, and her eyes will glaze over if you try rapport-building by talking about the basketball game last night. Don't overload the Pragmatic with information. She'll make a decision with the least amount of information necessary. If you try to sway her with an overly enthusiastic presentation, you'll come across as phony. Expect a fast decision based strictly on facts.

When you're dealing with an Extrovert, paint an enthusiastic picture of the benefits. Get him excited. Talk about his interests, probably football and baseball. Get to him by telling him stories of triumph and disaster. Expect a fast decision based on his level of excitement about the project.

When you're dealing with an Amiable, go slowly. Wait until he trusts you. Demonstrate that you really care about people. Be careful, because the slightest little thing will offend this person. Don't try to high-pressure him. The one thing in the world he doesn't like is being forced into making a decision. You just have to accept that when you're negotiating with an Amiable he'll need time to think things through, and you're going to have to wait until he feels comfortable with you.

With the Analytical, be accurate. When asked for figures, give them to the penny. Be prepared to give every little detail of the operation. Try to build rapport by talking about her interests. Her interests are probably engineering, accounting, analysis, and computer technology.

How to manage the personality styles

If you manage a large group of people, I'm sure you've realized by now that you have all of these personality styles working for you. It's important that you understand your own personality style and how your employees are relating to you because of their personality style.

Sometimes in my Power Negotiating seminars I'll work with a group of executives who all know each other well. I'll have each of the people analyze their own personality styles, the way that we have here. Then I'll go around the group and ask the other people who know them if that self-analysis was accurate. Are they really what they say they are? Sometimes we find there's quite a difference between what people think they are and the way other people perceive them to be.

If they all report to the same manager, I then take another tack. Providing I have cleared it with their manager first, I say to them: "Okay, tell me about the personality style of your leader." It's fun to do that because sometimes I get very specific answers. Sometimes the entire group will laugh and say: "Oh, he's a Pragmatic, he's so business-like. He'll never go for a beer with us after work and never shows up at the company picnics," and so on.

Other times they'll say: "Aw, he's an Extrovert. The most fun person we've ever worked for. He's always doing exciting things."

Other times they'll say: "Amiable, no question about it. Oh, just the nicest, warmest, sweetest person in the entire world. Probably not as business-like as he should be, but we just love him."

Sometimes they'll laugh and say: "Oh, he's Analytical. He's got two computers in his office and he's got a wall full of charts."

So sometimes the employees all agree on the personality style of their manager; but on other occasions I get different answers as I go around the room. Some people will say their boss is Analytical, some more Amiable, some see him as an Extrovert, and some as a Pragmatic.

What's happening is that Analyticals are saying that their boss is Analytical. Amiables are saying that their boss is Amiable. Extroverts are saying that he's Extrovert, and Pragmatics think he's a Pragmatic. It means that their manager has adapted his style of dealing with people to conform to each employee's individual personality style. How smart!

The manager who knows how to adapt to her employees' personality styles knows that when the Analytical accountant comes into her office with a proposal, she should say: "You know Joe, I don't want to jump into this. I really think we ought to get all the information we possibly can. Could you take a couple of weeks and really prepare an in-detail report for me so we can really work this through thoroughly?"

Whereas when the Extrovert comes into her office with the same proposal, she might say: "Joe, this is fantastic. I love it. This will set this whole organization on its ear. Let's go for it, and let's start right now."

When the Amiable comes into her office, she'll say: "You know, we've really got to consider the impact of this on the people. The people who work with us are so nice, and they've been so loyal to us over the years, I don't want to do a thing that would offend even one of them."

To the Pragmatic who is making the same proposal, she might say: "This isn't a religion, this is a business. I need to get the bottom line on this thing. How's this going to affect profits?"

It's good business to be smart enough to adapt the way you react to the personality style of the different employees with whom you deal.

How to sell to the different personality styles

Now let's look at how understanding personality styles can help you make a sale. How can you use this to persuade that potential customer to pick you? This method of analyzing personality styles probably contradicts many of the things that sales trainers have taught you. Here are my four inaccurate generalities of selling:

First inaccurate generality: Always be enthusiastic

The one rule that all sales trainers seem to teach is: "Be enthusiastic. How can you expect the customer to be enthusiastic about buying from you, if you're not?" Well, enthusiasm is wonderful with Extroverts, because they feed off that kind of excitement. It's also great with Amiables because they get a warm feeling from the enthusiasm. They're thinking, "I can sense how good he feels about it, so it must be a good idea."

However, enthusiasm turns off the Pragmatic. "Oh, don't give me that phony sales pitch," she's thinking. "Just give me the facts I need to make a decision."

And there's no way you can tell me that enthusiasm will bowl over an Analytical. He's not going to make a decision until he feels that he has enough information.

Second inaccurate generality: Dominate the other person

A famous sales trainer used to teach that the only way a salesperson ever learns to close is to close too hard and too soon. I've even heard of ABC seminars, which stands for "Always Be Closing," as if prospecting, qualifying, and building desire don't mean a thing.

Closing too hard and fast is not a problem for the assertive personality styles, the Pragmatic and the Extrovert. They know that salespeople work on commission and expect them to ask for the sale. Furthermore they will get suspicious if the salesperson doesn't push them to buy. However, putting pressure on Amiables really turns them off and you cannot persuade Analyticals until they have all the facts.

Third inaccurate generality: Ask lots of questions

Another thing that sales trainers teach salespeople is to dominate the conversation. They teach that when the buyer asks you a question, you should answer with a question. "Can you get the job done in 90 days for me?"

"Would you like it done in 90 days?"

"Can you give me 60 days to pay?"

"Would you like 60 days to pay?" And so on.

This is great with Analyticals because they love questions. They'll sit there all day asking and answering questions.

It's also great with Amiables because it's a sign that you care about them.

But when a Pragmatic asks you a question, he wants an answer. He doesn't want to play verbal Ping-Pong with you.

It's the same with the Extrovert. True, he'll make a fast decision and always be swayed by emotion, but he's assertive and doesn't want to beat around the bush.

Fourth inaccurate generality:
People always buy with emotion

Another thing that sales trainers teach you is that people buy with emotion, not logic. The only reason they would need any logic at all is to justify the emotional decision they have just made.

That's certainly true with the Extrovert personality. Donald Trump spent millions on pink Italian marble for the lobby of the Trump Tower because he felt that it was the right thing to do.

It's true with the Amiable because the relationship is important to her.

But Pragmatics don't spend money with emotion, they spend because it's going to generate the return they want. I remember staying at a brand new hotel in Freemantle, Australia, for the America's Cup races. A smart Australian investor had built the hotel and then sold it to Japanese investors just before the race. A clever thing to do, because when the Australians lost the cup back to Dennis Conner, Freemantle lost most of its ability to attract tourists. The location of the hotel was great, right on the beach. The lobby was magnificent, one of the finest that I've seen in any hotel anywhere. However, the rooms were a disgrace. Even though it was brand new, it was obvious that they'd been furnished and fixtured very cheaply. I'm sure that the Pragmatic developer's line of thinking had been: "These Japanese investors are not going to inspect every room before they buy. They'll invest based on the lobby and the location. Why spend money on something they'll never see?"

Certainly Analyticals don't make a buying decision with emotion either. They'll make a buying decision because all the numbers are in line.

Chapter 72

Negotiating Styles

Now let's take a look at these different personality styles and see how their style of negotiating is different from what I want you to become, which is a Win-Win Power Negotiator.

Let's take a look at each element of the negotiations.

The negotiating goals of the four types

First let's look at goals in the negotiations.

- The Pragmatic/Street Fighter's goal is clear. Her goal is victory—she plans to win in the negotiations.
- The Extrovert/Den Mother's goal is to influence the other people. He has so much fun changing other peoples' minds that he loves to take a position against the other side, just to see if he can turn their thinking around.
- The Amiable/Pacifier's goal is agreement. He feels that if he can get everybody to agree on something everything else will fall into place.
- The Analytical/Executive's goal is to have order in the negotiations. To get the negotiation on a formal format so that the procedures they establish produce a solution.

The goal of the Win-Win Power Negotiator, which is what I want you to become, is a wise outcome for all parties involved.

The negotiating relationships of the four types

Let's take a look at the relationships that exist in the negotiation process when you have these different personality styles involved.

- The Street Fighter has a tendency to frighten people. She's sitting there on the edge of hostility, and she's implying: "If you don't go along with what I want, it's going to get very uncomfortable here and you're not going to like it."
- The Den Mother personality tries to do it all by inspiring the other person. By getting them so excited that she'll be able to sway them over.
- The Pacifier wants to develop relationships. "If we like each other well enough, we'll all agree," is his philosophy.
- The Executive really ignores the relationships and negotiates strictly based on facts.

The Win-Win Power Negotiator learns how to separate people from the problem—by bringing the people back from their emotional relationships with each other and concentrating on the resolution of the issue.

The negotiating styles of the four types

Now let's look at the negotiating style of each of the four personality styles.

- The style of the Street Fighter is very hard and domineering.
- The style of the Den Mother is excitable.
- The style of the Pacifier is soft, maybe too soft. He may too easily give in on things.
- The Executive remains detached from the personalities.

The Win-Win Power Negotiator learns how to be soft on the people, but hard on the problem. She's easy going, friendly, likable, and courteous with all the people involved in the negotiations, but she keeps concentrating and hammering away on the problem.

The negotiating faults of the four types

Each of the four personality styles has it's own particular fault as a negotiator.

- The Street Fighter, the dominant personality, tends to dig into a particular position. Determined to get what she wants from the negotiation, she won't budge even when it would be better to yield.

- The Den Mother tends to ignore the others and is not sensitive enough to what's really going on in the negotiations.
- The Pacifier's fault is that he's too easily swayed.
- The Executive's fault is that she's inflexible.

The Win-Win Power Negotiator has no faults.

	STREET FIGHTER	DEN MOTHER	PACIFIER	EXECUTIVE	POWER NEGOTIATOR
GOAL	VICTORY	INFLUENCE	AGREEMENT	ORDER	WISE OUTCOME
RELA-TIONSHIP	THREATENS	ENTHUSES	DEVELOPS	IGNORES	SEPARATE PEOPLE FROM THE PROBLEM
STYLE	HARD	EXCITABLE	SOFT	DETACHED	SOFT ON PEOPLE HARD ON PROBLEM
WEAKNESS	DIGS IN	IGNORES OTHERS	EASILY SWAYED	INFLEXIBLE	
METHOD	DEMANDS LOSSES	EXCITES	ACCEPTS LOSSES	RIGIDITY	CREATES OPTIONS
DEMANDS	POSITION	ENTHUSIASM	AGREEMENT	SYSTEMS	SOLUTIONS

Power Negotiators work to get people off of positions
so that they can concentrate on issues.

The negotiating methods of the four types

Their method of negotiating differs greatly too.

- The Street Fighter demands losses from the other people. He doesn't feel that he can win unless other people lose.

- The Den Mother wants to inspire people, to get them turned on to a particular idea. She feels that if they're excited about it enough, then they'll go for it.

- The Pacifier tends to accept losses. His theory is that if they make concessions, the other side will want to reciprocate.

- The Executive is too rigid in her style of negotiating.

The Win-Win Power Negotiator learns how to create options in the negotiations where nobody loses.

A key issue in the negotiating process is that the Win-Win Power Negotiator works to get people off the positions that they have taken, largely because of their personality styles, so that they can concentrate on interests.

This is a key point because positions can be 180 degrees apart, whereas interests can be identical.

Look at the changing relationship between the United States and Russia. For forty years the Russians had adopted a position that "there's no sense arguing with the capitalists, they're not going to change until they dominate the world. Why negotiate with them?" Similarly, we Americans had taken the position that the Russians were so inflexible that it was a waste of time to talk to them. We'd known that ever since Khrushchev pounded his shoe on the table at the United Nations that they wouldn't stop until they dominated the world with their philosophy.

Those were positions that both sides had taken. For 40 years we concentrated on positions. Positions can be 180 degrees apart even when interests are identical. Without question we both have a mutual interest in world peace. We both have an interest in reducing our military expenditures. We both have an interest in becoming trading partners.

So a Power Negotiator learns to get people off positions that they have taken, so that they can concentrate on their mutual interests.

The key to being able to do this is to become familiar with the different personality styles of the people with whom you negotiate and learn how they approach things differently. Then, even though they may have taken a radically different position from yours, work on getting them off that position and concentrating on your mutual interests.

Chapter 73

Win-Win Power Negotiating

Finally, let's talk more about win-win negotiating. Instead of trying to dominate the other person and trick him into doing things he wouldn't normally do, I believe that you should work with the other person to work out your problems and develop a solution with which both of you can win.

Your reaction to that may be: "Roger, you obviously don't know much about my industry. I live in a dog-eat-dog world. The people with whom I negotiate don't take any prisoners. They eat their young. There's no such thing as win-win in my industry. When I'm selling I'm obviously trying to get the highest price I possibly can, and the buyer is obviously trying to get the lowest possible price. When I'm buying the reverse is true. How on Earth can we both win?"

So, let's start out with the most important issue: What do we mean when we say win-win? Does it really mean that both sides win? Or does it mean that both sides lose equally so that it's fair? What if each side thinks that they won and the other side lost—would that be win-win?

Before you dismiss that possibility, think about it more. What if you're selling something and leave the negotiation thinking, "I won. I would have dropped the price even more if the other person had been a better negotiator"? However the other person is thinking that she won and that she would have paid more if you had been a better negotiator. So both of you think that you won and the other person lost. Is that win-win? Yes, I believe it is, as long as it's a permanent feeling. As long as neither of you wakes up tomorrow morning thinking: "Son of a gun, now I know what he did to me. Wait until I see him again."

That's why I stress doing the things that service the perception that the other side won, such as:

- Don't jump at the first offer.
- Ask for more than you expect to get.
- Flinch at the other side's proposals.
- Avoid confrontation.
- Play Reluctant Buyer or Reluctant Seller.
- Use the Vise gambit: You'll have to do better than that.
- Use Higher Authority and Good Guy/Bad Guy to make them think you're on their side.
- Never offer to split the difference.
- Set aside impasse issues.
- Always ask for a trade-off and never make a concession without a reciprocal concession.
- Taper down your concessions.
- Position the other side for easy acceptance.

Besides constantly servicing the perceptions that the other side won, observe these four fundamental rules:

Rule one of win-win negotiating: Don't narrow the negotiation down to just one issue

The first thing to learn is this: Don't narrow the negotiation down to just one issue. If, for example, you resolve all the other issues and the only thing left to negotiate is price, somebody does have to win and somebody does have to lose. As long as you keep more than one issue on the table, you can always work trade-offs so that the other person doesn't mind conceding on price because you are able to offer something in return.

Sometimes buyers try to treat your product as a commodity by saying, "We buy this stuff by the ton. As long as it meets our specifications we don't mind who made it or where it comes from." They are trying to treat this as a one issue negotiation to persuade you that the only way you can make a meaningful concession is to lower your price. When that's the case you should do everything possible to put other issues, such as delivery, terms, packaging, and guarantees onto the table so that you can use these items for trade-offs and get away from the perception that this is a one-issue negotiation.

At a seminar, a commercial real estate sales person came up to me. He was excited because he'd almost completed negotiating a contract for a very large commercial building. "We've been working on it now for over a year," he said. "And we've almost got it resolved. In fact, we've resolved everything except price, and we're only $72,000 apart." I Flinched because I knew now that he'd narrowed it down to one issue, then there had to be a winner and there had to be a loser. However close they may be, they were probably heading for trouble.

In a one issue negotiation you should add other elements so that you can trade them off later and appear to be making concessions. In August 1985, FBI agents arrested Gennady Zakharov, a physicist who was a member of the Soviet delegation to the United Nations. The FBI had caught him red-handed (pardon the pun) as he paid cash for classified documents on a New York City subway platform. A week later the KGB arrested Nicholas Daniloff, the Moscow correspondent for the *U.S. News and World Report*. Nine months earlier they had set Daniloff up for just such an opportunity by having a KGB agent dressed as a priest ask him to deliver a letter to the U.S. embassy.

Now the Soviets were demanding the release of Zakharov in exchange for the release of newly-arrested Daniloff whom they had branded as a spy. Outraged by the blatancy of their move, Reagan refused and the incident began to threaten the up-coming arms control summit. Everybody knew that the fate of Zakharov and Daniloff was insignificant when compared to the potential for world peace at the summit, but by now both sides had dug into their positions and were blind to their mutual interests. It was a one issue negotiation: Would we trade Zakharov for Daniloff or wouldn't we? President Reagan was adamant that he wouldn't be a patsy for the KGB.

To the rescue came Armand Hammer, the chairperson of Occidental Petroleum, who had been doing business in Russia since the revolution. He knew that the way to break the deadlock was to introduce another issue into the negotiations so that the Russians could offer a more palatable trade-off. He suggested to the Russians that they also agree to release dissident Yuri Orlov and his wife, Irina Valitova. This broke the deadlock because Reagan, who had dug into his position of not trading a Russian spy for an American journalist, could find the new trade acceptable because it didn't violate his previously stated position.

So if you find yourself deadlocked with a one-issue negotiation, you should try adding other issues into the mix. Fortunately there are usually many more elements than just the one main issue that are important in negotiations.

The art of win-win negotiating is to piece together those elements—like putting together a jigsaw puzzle—so that both people can win. Rule one is, don't narrow the negotiations down to just one issue. While we may resolve impasses by finding a common ground on small issues to keep the negotiation moving as I taught you in Chapter 10, you should never narrow it down to one issue.

Rule two of win-win negotiating: People are not out for the same thing

Rule number two that makes you a win-win negotiator is the understanding that people are not out for the same thing. We all have an overriding tendency to assume that other people want what we want, and because of this we believe that what's important to us will be important to them. But that's not true.

The biggest trap into which neophyte negotiators fall is assuming that price is the dominant issue in a negotiation. Many elements other than price are important to the other person.

- You must convince her of the quality of your product or service.
- He needs to know that you will deliver on time.
- She wants to know that you will give adequate management supervision to their account.
- How flexible are you on payment terms?
- Does your company have the financial strength to be a partner of theirs?
- Do you have the support of a well trained and motivated work force?

These all come into play, along with half-a-dozen other factors. When you have satisfied the other person that you can meet all those requirements, then, and only then, does price become a deciding factor.

So, the second key to win-win negotiating is this: Don't assume that they want what you want. Because if you do, you further make the assumption that anything you do in the negotiations to help them get what they want helps them and hurts you.

Win-win negotiating can come about only when you understand that people don't want the same things in the negotiation. So Power Negotiating becomes not just a matter of getting what you want, but also being concerned about the other person getting what he or she wants. One of the most powerful thoughts you can have when you're negotiating with someone is not "What can I get from them?" but "What can I give them that won't take away from my position?" Because when you give them what they want, people will give you what you want in a negotiation.

Rule three of win-win negotiating: Don't try to get the last dollar off the table

The third key to win-win negotiating is this: Don't be too greedy. Don't try to get the last dollar off the table. You may feel that you triumphed, but does that help you if the other person felt that you vanquished him? That last dollar left on the table is a very expensive dollar to pick up. A man who attended my seminar in Tucson told me that he was able to buy the company that he owned because the other potential buyer made that mistake. The other person had negotiated hard and pushed the seller to the brink of frustration. As a final Nibble, the buyer said, "You are going to put new tires on that pickup truck before you transfer the title, aren't you?" That was the straw that broke the proverbial camel's back. The owner reacted angrily, refused to sell his company to him, and instead sold it to the man at my seminar.

So don't try to get it all, but leave something on the table so that the other person feels that she won also.

Rule four of win-win negotiating: Put something back on the table

The fourth key to win-win negotiating is this: Put something back on the table when the negotiation is over. I don't mean by telling them that you'll give them a discount over and above what they negotiated. I mean do something more than you promised to do. Give them a little extra service. Care about them a little more than you have to. Then you'll find that the little extra for which they didn't have to negotiate means more to them than everything for which they did have to negotiate.

Now let me recap what I've taught you about win-win negotiating:

- People have different personality styles, and because of this they negotiate differently. You must understand your personality style, and, if it's different from the other person, you must adapt your style of negotiating to theirs.

- The different styles mean that in a negotiation different people have different goals, relationships, styles, faults, and also different methods of getting what they want.

- Winning is a perception, and by constantly servicing the perception that the other person is winning you can convince him that he has won without having to make any concessions to him.

- Don't narrow the negotiation down to just one issue.

- Don't assume that helping the other person get what she wants takes away from your position. You're not out for the same thing. Poor negotiators try to force the other person to get off the positions that she's taken. Power negotiators know that even when positions are 180 degrees apart, the interests of both sides can be identical, so they work to get people off their positions and concentrating on their interests.

- Don't be greedy. Don't try to get the last dollar off the table.

- Put something back on the table. Do more than they bargained for.

Postscript

So now you are ready to graduate as a Power Negotiator. The skills you have learned will give you the power to command any business situation so that you can smoothly get the best deal for yourself and your company. Far more importantly, these skills will give you the power to manage conflict in your life. From now on there should never be a time when you lose control of a situation because of anger or frustration. From now on you will be in control of your life. From now on you may let yourself get angry or upset, but only as a specific negotiating technique—you will never be out of control. Even when it's only a simple matter such as getting your son to clean his room, or persuading your daughter to go to bed on time, you will be in control.

From now on you will understand that any time you see conflict, it is because one or more of the participants does not understand Power Negotiating. Whether it's an argument with a spouse, a boss firing an employee, a worker going on strike, a crime being committed or an ugly international incident, Power Negotiators know that it happened because the participants did not know how to get what they wanted without resorting to conflict.

I look forward to the day when all conflicts are avoided because people know how to get what they want with good negotiating skills. I invite you to share this vision with me by pledging now to remove conflict from your life, and the lives of those around you, by always practicing good negotiating skills. The example that you set will help lead us into a bright new future where violence, crime, and wars become anachronisms.

Speeches and Seminars by Roger Dawson

If you hire speakers for your company or influence the selection of speakers at your association, you should learn more about Roger Dawson's speeches and seminars. He will customize his presentation to your company or industry so that you get a unique presentation tailored to your needs. You can also make arrangements to audio- or videotape the presentation to be used as a continuous training resource.

Roger Dawson's presentations include:

Secrets of Power Negotiating

Secrets of Power Persuasion

Confident Decision Making

The 13 Secrets of Power Performance

To get more information and receive a complimentary press kit, please call, write, or fax to:

Roger Dawson Productions
PO Box 3326
La Habra, CA 90632
Phone: (800) YDAWSON (932-9766)
Fax: (818) 854-3595

Here's a listing of Roger Dawson's audio and video cassette albums available from Roger Dawson Productions, P.O. Box 3326, La Habra, CA 90632.

You can order by calling (800)YDAWSON (932-9766) or by faxing (818) 854-3595.

Audio Cassette Programs

Secrets of Power Negotiating
6 cassette audio album with workbook and 24 flash cards. $65

This is one of the largest-selling business cassette albums ever published, with sales of over $20 million. You'll learn 20 powerful negotiating gambits that are surefire winners. Then, going beyond the mere mechanics of the negotiating process, Roger Dawson helps you learn what influences people, and how to recognize and adjust to different negotiating styles, so you can get what you want regardless of the situation.

Also, you'll learn: A new way of pressuring people without confrontation • The one unconscious decision you must never make in a negotiation • The five standards by which every negotiation should be judged • Why saying *yes* too soon is always a mistake • How to gather the information you need without the other side knowing • The three stages that terrorist negotiators use to defuse crisis situations, and much, much more.

Also available with 228 page Synergistic Learning
companion program in three-ring binder. $99

Also available customized for contractors and subcontractors. $65

Secrets of Power Negotiating for Salespeople
6 cassette audio album. $65

This program, which supplements and enhances Roger Dawson's famous generic negotiating program *The Secrets of Power Negotiating*, teaches salespeople how to negotiate with buyers and get higher prices without having to give away freight and terms. It's the most in-depth program ever created for selling at higher prices than your competition and still maintaining long-term relationships with your customers. Guaranteed to dramatically improve your profit margins or your money back.

Special Offer. Invest in both *Secrets of Power Negotiating* and *Secrets of Power Negotiating for Salespeople* and save $20. Both for only $110.

Secrets of Power Persuasion
6 cassette audio album. $65

In this remarkable program, Roger Dawson shows you the strategies and tactics that will enable you to persuade people in virtually any situation. Not by using threats or phony promises, but because they perceive that it's in their best interest to do what you say.

You'll discover why credibility and, above all, consistency are the cornerstones of getting what you want • You'll learn verbal persuasion techniques that defuse resistance and demonstrate the validity of your thinking • Step by step, you'll learn to develop an overwhelming aura of personal charisma that will naturally cause people to like you, respect you, and to gladly agree with you • It's just a matter of mastering the specific, practical behavioral techniques that Roger Dawson presents in a highly entertaining manner.

Secrets of Power Performance
6 cassette audio album. $65

With this program, based on his book, you'll learn how to get the best from yourself—and those around you! Roger Dawson firmly believes that we are all capable of doing so much more than we think we're capable of. Isn't that true for you? Aren't you doing far more now than you thought you could do five years ago? With the life-changing secrets revealed in this best-selling program, you'll be able to transform your world in the next five years!

Confident Decision Making
6 cassette audio album, with 36-page workbook. $65

Decisions are the building blocks of your life. The decisions you've made have given you everything you now have. The decisions you'll make from this point on will be responsible for everything that happens to you for the rest of your life. Wouldn't it be wonderful to know that, from this point on, you'll always be making the right choice? All you have to do is listen to this landmark program.

You'll learn the following: How to quickly and accurately categorize your decision • How to expand your options with a ten-step creative thinking process • How to find the right answer with reaction tables and determination trees • How to harness the power of synergism with the principle of Huddling • How to know exactly what and how your boss, customer, or employee will decide, and dozens more powerful techniques.

The Personality of Achievers
6 cassette audio album. $65

You can learn how to go beyond your most ambitious goals with this breakthrough program. Life's high achievers know that there is no substitute for action—the positive, disciplined transformations of thoughts into deeds. This program identifies what makes people high achievers and shows you what—and how—these super-successful people think, how they act, and how they inspire others to help them succeed. It contains fascinating studies of personalities and behavior and transforms them into practical, common-sense strategies that will lead you to uncommon success.

Video Training Programs

Guide to Business Negotiations   70 minute VHS video $55
Guide to Everyday Negotiations   45 minute VHS video $55

If you're in any way responsible for training or supervising other people, these videos will liven up your staff meetings and turn your people into master negotiators. Your sales and profits will soar as you build new win-win relationships with your customers. Then use these programs to develop a training library for your employees' review, and for training new hires.

Special Prices for Career Press Readers

Mention this book when you place your order and receive a 20 percent discount. All major credit cards accepted.

Index